Japan's High Technology Industries

Japan's High Technology Industries

Lessons and Limitations of Industrial Policy

Edited by
Hugh Patrick

with the assistance of
Larry Meissner

University of Washington Press
Seattle and London

University of Tokyo Press

*This book is sponsored by
the Committee on Japanese Economic Studies
and is published with the assistance of a grant
from the Japan Foundation.*

Published in Japan and Asia by University of Tokyo Press
ISBN 4-13-047037-X   UTP 47375

Library of Congress Cataloging in Publication Data

Japan's high technology industries.

    "Sponsored by the Committee on Japanese Economic Studies" — T.p. verso.
Includes bibliographies and index.
    Contents: Japanese high technology industrial policy in comparative
context / Hugh Patrick — Regime characteristics of Japanese industrial
policy / Daniel I. Okimoto — Industrial policy and factor markets : biotechnology
in Japan and the United States / Gary Saxonhouse — [etc.]
    1. High technology industries — Government policy — Japan. 2. High
technology industries — Government policy — United States. I. Patrick, Hugh T.
II. Meissner, Larry. III. Committee on Japanese Economic Studies (U.S.)
HC465.H53J37 1986 338.4'76213817'0952 85-40973
ISBN 0-295-96342-5

Foreword

The crucial and in many respects beneficial United States–Japan economic relationship has concurrently engendered a range of contentious issues, leading to the recent atmosphere of roiling debate and mounting tension. Few questions are as centrally important as those involving the methods and organization by which Japanese companies, and the nation, engage in their competitive drive.

The Japanese approach to its high technology industries—the focus of ongoing debate and potential conflict between our two countries—is an area of particular interest and concern. For too long, the American response to the Japanese challenge has been based on outdated and stereotypical perceptions of the Japanese reality.

The United States–Japan Foundation therefore eagerly supported the research of this group of internationally respected specialists which has resulted in this book. Particularly at this time, this statement of facts and informed interpretation has an immediate relevance to our relationship with Japan that should be helpful to public and private decision makers and observers alike.

RICHARD W. PETREE, PRESIDENT
United States–Japan Foundation

Contents

Introduction

High technology industries, industrial policy, and the Japanese economy are individually important topics of scholarly interest and public policy consideration in the United States. Japanese industrial policies toward high technology industries—the fusion of these three topics—has produced a new, qualitatively different subject of deep concern, both intellectually and in terms of U.S. public policy debate and formulation, which has at times resulted in more heat than light. This book aims to provide a careful, objective analysis and evaluation of Japanese high technology industrial policy and assess its relevance for the United States.

Is Japanese high technology industrial policy a model for the United States to emulate? Is it an "unfair" application of government policy by the Japanese? "Fairness" is a murky concept in international economics and even in the politics of the international system. Even if Japan is not deemed to be behaving unfairly, does its industrial policy behavior require a special American response if the United States is to restore competitiveness in its own and world markets? Is Japanese industrial policy in its actual practice in fact very effective? And if it was effective earlier, will it continue to be in the new circumstances of the 1980s? What are the Japanese government's industrial policies toward high tech industries, what resources are involved, and how successful will the policies be? What can America learn from the Japanese experience? Many views abound, as do American stereotypes of the Japanese system of industrial policy and its effectiveness.

American policy interest in Japanese industrial policy for high technology industries heats up and cools down, depending on the current status of both the domestic industrial policy debate and the economic relationship between the United States and Japan. However, the underlying economic and public policy issues are long term and profound in nature. They strike at the heart of concerns in all advanced industrial democracies as to the proper role of government in the marketplace: how and whether the political economy of government involvement results in more, or in less, efficient allocation of resources over time, and the extent to which government policy can fine-tune the supply side of the economy by sector-specific industrial policies, to note two of the central issues underlying the industrial policy debate.

To understand the nature of Japanese high technology policy in the new circumstances of the 1980s and beyond, and to assess its relevance for both the Japanese and American economies, in 1983 several specialists on the Japanese economy decided to organize a research project, under the auspices of the Committee on Japanese Economic Studies, on these topics. I agreed to be project organizer. We recognized that the issues are many and complex, and that it would be naïve to expect to produce a simple, straightforward, and yet *accurate* treatise on the contemporary Japanese application of industrial policy of high technology industries.

We decided, I believe correctly and successfully, that the richness of a complex mixture of perspectives, skills, and knowledge of outstanding specialists in various aspects of industrial policy was requisite to sort out intelligently the many issues involved. We knew we should include case studies of specific high technology industries, of certain policy instruments especially important in the high technology arena, and of government policy formulation and implementation in practice. The general framework should encompass both immediate and long-range studies, and these studies should be explicitly comparative, particularly between Japan and the United States. And all this had to provide an adequate context for all the specifics so necessary to make the analysis authentic and comprehensive. The problem was how to implement this vision of the integration of multiple dimensions and points of view.

To say that we deliberately planned a multidimensional matrix to incorporate effectively these multiple contexts and requirements would be to stretch a point. Our first objective was to assemble a research team of quality scholars (1) who knew a great deal about various elements of the complex story to be told about Japanese high technology industrial policy, (2) who had detailed, specific knowledge and could place it in a broader perspective, and (3) each of whom was very much his own person regardless of discipline of specialization or nationality. The team was to include economists, political scientists, specialists on Japan, comparativists, Japanese, Americans, scholars actively involved in policy debate and advice in each country. And we did create such a team—with great success, I believe, as this volume attests.

In fact this book does embody a multidimensional structure. It provides concrete case studies: Okimoto on the information industry, Saxonhouse on biotechnology, and Imai on the full range of high technology industries. At the same time these chapters deliberately address a broader, and each quite different, set of issues. Okimoto (chapter 2) examines the systemic (or regime) characteristics of the way the Japanese government, mainly through its bureaucratic arm, the Ministry of International Trade and Industry (MITI), formulates, implements, and administers high technology industrial policy; and describes in some detail the full panoply of industrial policy instruments, which he classifies as technology push, supply-side (cost reduction), and demand pull, and their specific application to the information industry. Saxonhouse (chapter 3) examines relevant Japanese factor market imperfections in some detail, arguing persuasively that in Japan industrial policy is a needed, though only partial, offset to market imperfections; and he provides further comparative evidence on policy instruments. Imai (chapter 4), drawing on his experience as chairman of MITI's New Media Advisory Committee, provides insights into the still fluid nature of this information communications concept, and provides alternative general, long-run policy scenarios reflective of cutting-edge thinking about these matters in Japan. In a different type of case study, Yamamura (chapter 5) carefully describes and evaluates the Japanese and American approaches to a particularly important high technology policy instrument, the joint research project involving the cooperation of large, competitor firms in the same industry, which Japan has applied especially in the information industry.

Concurrently the other chapters place these materials in a broader context, while delving down to and relying on concrete sector-specific data and data on specific policy issues to illustrate and buttress their arguments. The underlying concern of each chapter is how to think critically about high technology industrial policy, from the particular vantage point of that chapter. Patrick's introductory overview (chapter 1) provides the setting by discussing the concept and definition of high technology industrial policy, and by tracing the evolution of Japanese industrial policies and policy instruments since the 1950s; he argues that Japan has undergone a sea change since the 1970s in the basic conditions in which industrial policy promoting high technology industries takes place. Murakami (chapter 6) takes this perception of recent discontinuity and writes it large. He provocatively argues that Japan is just beginning, with the rest of the advanced industrial world, a third century-long technological epoch (or "paradigm" in his terminology). The specific features of this new, unfolding era are unclear and uncertain; accordingly so too is the role of government and of industrial policy. Eads and Nelson (chapter 7) bring the volume to a fitting end in their explicitly American and Japanese comparative overview of the specific policies that make up industrial policy, and propose general lessons for the United States from the Japanese experience.

Before turning to certain of these substantive themes in modest detail, let me make several additional general points.

First, there was no attempt to impose a particular model of Japanese industrial policy in general, or in high technology industries in particular, on the participants. At the same time, it is fair to say that no one advocates the position that Japanese economic growth has been state led and that industrial policy has been the integral component, with private business a willing follower of government bureaucratic leadership. On the other hand, no one argues that although Japan has had an industrial policy, it has been an incoherent and ineffective one. These alternative schools of thought are briefly described by Patrick in chapter 1. (Alternative interpretation of Japanese industrial policy, and the scholars identified with the various schools, are discussed in somewhat more detail in Lincoln 1984 and Zysman and Tyson 1984.)

Within these extremes, our views range considerably on some issues and more narrowly and subtly on others. Much depends on the period considered, since all agreed (as is discussed below) that industrial policy and its effectiveness were substantially different in the past decade than in the high growth era from the mid-1950s to the early 1970s. Thus, Murakami characterizes industrial policy in the high growth era as having been quite successful, while Patrick and Saxonhouse view it as having made some positive but on the whole quite modest contributions to that rapid growth. Reflecting their respective disciplines, the economists tend to begin their analysis first in terms of the operations of markets in Japan's private enterprise system and then to evaluate the role of government policy in light of market failures or imperfections, while political scientists quite naturally begin with the role of the state (bureaucracy) in setting and implementing policy.

There has been no attempt to impose or negotiate a consensus or set of interpretations. This Introduction accordingly is my interpretation of the project as a whole and of the chapters that make up this volume. And there are differences in interpretation or judgment. Thus Eads and Nelson propose permitting joint generic research projects among American competing firms under carefully specified terms; Okimoto concurs, citing American cases of joint research under military contracts. Yamamura takes a more cautious, indeed cautionary, approach to this important policy issue. On the other hand, differences may be more apparent than real; for example, Eads and Nelson stress Japan's highly favorable tax policy for investment and innovation in high technology industries. Saxonhouse argues it is smaller in terms of actual and tax expenditure (deductions, exemptions, and credits) than in the United States or Europe, a position supported by Okimoto's quantitative comparisons. My interpretation is that such benefits are rather substantial in all advanced industrial countries.

Second, our central objective has been to describe and analyze, to diagnose objectively in terms of the realities of Japanese high technology industrial policy in practice—not to prescribe policies for either nation. Of course a certain dollop of prescription by some of the authors is inevitable and indeed desirable. Not all the prescriptions are the same— in part because the specific pathologies are different, in part because diagnoses even among specialists can and do vary. Much prescription is implicit in the analysis of each chapter, and each author addresses the issue explicitly. Some of this discussion is taken up in my summary of "lessons" for the United States below.

Third, there was general agreement on the contours of the concepts and definitions of industrial policy and of high technology industries. Issues of definition are explicitly addressed by Patrick and Imai. Industrial policy involves direct or indirect government intervention in the marketplace, typically by a range of policy instruments, in order to achieve a different allocation of resources to specifically defined priority industries at any point in time than would occur through the normal operations of the marketplace. High technology industries rely substantially more than average on the application of new science-based technologies to products or production processes. They are characterized by a high ratio of R&D expenditures to sales; a high ratio of scientists, engineers, or computer programmers in their work forces; and a high share of new products in total sales.

We have defined technology concretely in terms of specific industries, notably microelectronics, biotechnology, new materials, and new sources of energy. Imai evaluates Japanese industrial policy in all these areas. Most of our case study material derives from the first two—microelectronics, "the heart of current high technology" to use Yamamura's phrase, or what Imai and Okimoto both term the information industry, namely semiconductors, computers, and telecommunications; and biotechnology, including pharmaceuticals, touted by some as *the* high technology industry of the future. These are the most important sectors, quantitatively and in terms of recent, current, and projected Japanese high technology industrial policy. Specific chapters (by Okimoto and Saxonhouse, respectively) are devoted to these two industries, but these industry materials are used throughout, especially by Imai, Yamamura, and Eads and Nelson.

Japanese policy clearly is to promote these high technology industries, to create and maintain their international competitiveness; in many respects so too is American policy, as is discussed below. As becomes clear in these chapters, the essential, indeed key, ingredient is the promotion of industry-specific R&D, directly and indirectly. Also of importance are ample capital availability and requisite labor skills, as well as assured markets. Japanese high technology policy is quite different from its industrial policy toward structurally depressed or declining industries, where the political power of major industries in trouble dictates an ameliorative policy of structural adjustment. There is, nonetheless, the common Japanese rationale that the purpose is to smooth and accelerate the process of efficient resource allocation in terms of Japan's evolving, long-run comparative advantage. Both are in contrast to Japan's industrial policy toward agriculture, which is defensive, reflective of agrarian political power, and gives high weight to goals of income distribution relative to economic efficiency. These broader issues of Japanese industrial and sectoral policy are noted but not considered in any depth in this volume.

Several themes run through all these chapters and give the volume its broader coherence, even while each chapter stands on its own. I comment briefly on six overarching themes.

1. Any appraisal of Japan's high technology industrial policy, and its industrial policy in general, must identify the period under consideration. The Japanese economy, and its economic policy, underwent a sea change in the 1970s. In Murakami's provocative framework, Japan, together with the United States and Western Europe, is just entering a new technological epoch, for which a new intellectual, institutional, and policy paradigm will be required. From another perspective, by the mid-1970s or so Japan had caught up to the United States in civilian (though not military) technology. For Japan, as a follower economy in the 1950s and 1960s, what were new (high) technologies and new industries already existed in the United States. Industrial policy had a clear model to follow; it was relatively easy to catch up by picking "winner" industries. Only since the 1970s has Japan developed high technology industries, in the dual sense of firms more or less at the technological frontiers in industries that are *globally* defined as high technology industries. Accordingly, industrial policy toward high technology industries is a relatively recent concept in Japanese policy making. With no clear model to follow, it is more difficult for policy makers to identify the winner industries, and especially the winner technologies, of the future. The new policy focus has to be preeminently to encourage business-based R&D, an inherently risky unknown.

The Japanese economy has gone through other major transformations over the past decade, in addition to "catching up with the West." The average annual economic growth rate has slowed from 9–10 percent to 4–5 percent. The central government has been running very large budget deficits. As the economy has grown to immense size, its enterprises have become increasingly strong and less desirous of government help; rather they press for deregulation. Japan has achieved international status as a large economy, a major player in the international economic system; no longer can it be accorded the "small country" privilege of its behavior and performance being ignored by others. Japan has liberalized its imports substantially, under great foreign pressure; it no longer can readily use overt trade or investment barriers—earlier such important policy instruments—to protect its high technology industries from foreign competition. A number of barriers, public and private, remain but are under erosion from continuous external attack.

Whatever judgment each author may have of the degree of success of Japanese industrial policy in the 1950s and 1960s, all would agree that it is now less pervasive, less strong, and less effective, though not nonexistent or emasculated. The danger, ironically, is that Americans may mistakenly "learn lessons" and promote industrial policies based on Japan's past—policies applied in an era of extraordinarily successful economic growth by a follower catching up quickly, policies likely to be irrelevant for the future of nations and industries at the technological frontier. Indeed, our purpose is to describe and analyze Japan's current policies and policy instruments for its high technology industries. They are substantially different from those of the past. It is a new game in a new domestic and international environment.

2. These chapters are in principle explicitly comparative, mainly between Japan and the United States. This shows up especially in the chapters by Eads and Nelson, Saxonhouse, and Yamamura. In addition, Eads and Nelson bring to bear European high technology industrial policy experience in very expensive research projects, and Okimoto stresses that the European Community provides far more government research subsidies than Japan, though he is not optimistic about the results. Murakami frames his long-term analysis in terms that are relevant for developing nations as well, yet argues that Japan is such a special case in the history of industrialization that it can be regarded as unique. I think none of the rest of us agree with this "uniqueness" position.

Eads and Nelson argue persuasively that in practice the American and Japanese cases of government support of (the same) high technology industries are less different than the stereotypes imply. Both governments provide substantial public support of generic R&D. Both have provided specific domestic demand stimuli in the early stages of development of high technology industries. In the United States, military procurement has been particularly important. Deprived of that demand source, the Japanese government and its agencies have nonetheless provided preferred access to markets, such as telecommunications equipment by NTT (Nippon Telegraph and Telephone), pharmaceuticals for the national health system, and, until recently, have restricted imports and foreign direct investment.

Yet there are important differences. American public goals have been directed preeminently toward military security, Japanese toward private industrial development. U.S. government support of R&D is concentrated heavily in basic science and graduate-level scientific and engineering education, unlike Japan. As Saxonhouse aptly stresses, these areas produce significant public goods which are quite readily available to Japanese and other foreigners as well as to Americans. Although the Japanese educational system produces better trained high school graduates and more B.S.-level engineers, especially electrical engineers, than the United States (as emphasized by Eads and Nelson, and Patrick), Saxonhouse stresses that the United States produces far more M.S. and Ph.D. graduates in engineering and the sciences.

Another example of differential degrees of generating public goods is the past regulatory treatment of the two national telecommunications systems, AT&T and NTT. The compulsory licensing to all applicants of AT&T patents is contrasted by Okimoto with the limitation of NTT research results initially to a small "family" of Japanese large, closely associated private firms. This difference in national treatment of the public aspect of R&D affects the specific ways in which high technology industries develop, and their relative competitiveness, in the United States and Japan. The process of telecommunications deregulation, now under way in both countries, is in principle designed to increase competitiveness. The implications for R&D and its dissemination are not yet clear.

3. Differences in American and Japanese capital and labor markets for their respective high technology firms affect both high technology industrial structure and performance. Japanese capital market structure and imperfections are addressed in all the case-study chapters—Okimoto, Saxonhouse, Imai, Yamamura. The Japanese financial system is similar to that in continental Europe. Large firms in Japan in the past have relied on bank loans as a major source of funds in the absence of the well-developed bond, stock, and other financial markets that characterize the American system. Large firms maintain close ties with a lead bank and cross-hold shares with a group of affiliated firms (epitomized in the *keiretsu*). Imai generalizes that Japan relies somewhat more on organization and somewhat less on markets as the principle for resource allocation, compared with the United States. Phrased differently, the Japanese industrial system uses long-term implicit contracts based on personal knowledge and trust relatively more than impersonal, clearly defined spot markets. These arrangements provide large firms a financial advantage of high debt-equity ratios and the ability to fund projects at a relatively low cost of capital. Both Okimoto and Yamamura argue that this provides a mechanism for greater government ability to signal and implement its policies. In contrast, small firms are at a disadvantage. In high technology industries in particular the lack of a Japanese venture capital market contrasts with the highly developed American system in which innovative, small, high technology firms have ready access to finance. Saxonhouse further argues cogently that Japan has required industrial policy precisely to compensate, at least partly, for its capital market failures.

He extends that argument in contrasting the markets for scientific and engineering personnel in the United States and Japan. The Japanese labor market system of entry-level hiring and permanent employment, coupled with lack of small venture capital start-up opportunities, constitutes a serious barrier to the flow of information from firm to firm. So too does the relatively more limited formal and informal interchanges of occupation-related professional conferences. On the other hand, Imai sees the intensive informal networking among different firms as an important vehicle for information exchange and a basis for establishing reciprocal, sequential, implicit deals based on mutual trust. Certainly all would agree that the government-sponsored joint research project among major firms is an important mode of interfirm R&D communication in Japan.

4. As all the chapters make clear, the government's role varies substantially—over time, by industry, in its application of policy instruments, in putting together a package of incentives to encourage firms to innovate and invest. While many approaches are used, the key to success in high technology industries at the frontiers of knowledge is a substantial commitment of corporate resources to R&D. The rationale for government incentives to promote more R&D activity than would take place through the signals of private markets is well known. Certain R&D projects are so large scale, the uncertainties of success so high, the gestation period so long, the difficulties even of calculating probabilities of success so great, that private enterprises invest less in R&D than is socially optimal. Moreover, some R&D generates externalities the benefits of which the producers are unable to capture. MITI officials and other Japanese policy makers, intellectually more skeptical of the dynamic efficiency of private markets than many Americans, have been quick to latch onto such rationales to justify their policies.

In general, the intellectual environments for government-encouraged, commercially oriented R&D differ. As Okimoto notes, MITI officials are not content to sit back and let the market take its meandering course, especially where high technology industries are involved. While never explicitly stated, a strong strategic element seems implicit in this thinking (just as it is explicit in American thinking), consistent with Japan's comprehensive security concept of national defense. This, however, extends beyond the central themes of this volume.

The political-economic process by which high technology policy is actually made and implemented is considered in greatest detail by Okimoto. He carefully describes the specific characteristics of Japan's political economy that make it remarkably well suited for selective state intervention and the administration of industrial policy. In his view, MITI accordingly has been able to do a reasonably competent job, more so than the United States or Europe has. He stresses three distinctive and crucial features. The continuation in power for some thirty years of a probusiness government founded on the Liberal Democratic Party has resulted in a relatively low level of politicization of Japan's strong, elite bureaucracy, insulating it to a considerable degree from political interest groups. MITI, and in somewhat different context, NTT, have used nonlegalist, informal, and generally market-conforming policies. And the government bureaucracy and large firms have developed a synergistic, positive working relationship, based on substantial formal and informal networking. One might add that in high technology the industrial policy instruments involve carrots, not sticks. A full range of methods are marshaled to promote R&D: tax incentives, subsidies, low interest loans, government procurement, joint research, administrative guidance. Yet all the high technology industry case studies make clear that the financial and fiscal incentives at least are quite modest, in absolute amount and relative to their counterparts in the United States.

In a somewhat different perspective, Imai evaluates the effectiveness of Japanese government industrial policy over a wide range of high technology industries. He concurs with Okimoto that MITI has been most successful in the information industry, and concurs with Saxonhouse that it has not been successful in biotechnology. He finds that industrial policies have not done well in computer software, new materials, chemicals, or new energy sources. He sees the new regionally based technopolis policy, modeled after Silicon Valley and the North Carolina Research Triangle, as a mechanism for the transfer of existing technologies rather than the basis for new technological breakthroughs. Japan needs a new, different policy mechanism for high technology. He illustrates the vaguely specified, seemingly inchoate policy process in its early formative stages in his description of current policy thinking (in which he has been intimately involved) in that recent MITI catchphrase, the "new media industry."

5. What does the future hold for Japanese high technology industrial policy? That has not been a central question of this project: our purpose has been to describe, analyze, and evaluate past and current policies. Nonetheless, thoughts about the future are expressed, some quite explicitly. I think we all would agree that the Japanese government will continue active pursuit of a high technology industrial policy, but is not at all likely to devote a large share of government resources to it. Moreover, success will be more problematical because the uncertainties and risks are greater. With the increasing liberalization of capital and labor markets, as well as increasing deregulation in other sectors, and with technological and commercial change occurring faster than the government can keep up with, the balance is likely to be tilted increasingly toward the marketplace. Okimoto ends his chapter by saying: "Perhaps the best measure of success with respect to Japanese industrial policy will be the extent to which it renders itself progressively unnecessary."

That, however, is an evaluation, not a prediction or projection. I think Japanese high technology industrial policy will become narrower in one dimension and broader in another. That is, as markets work increasingly well, the government will focus its sector-specific policies and resources increasingly on organizing and coordinating large-scale, long-term, high-risk joint generic research projects with large firms. At the same time, once the present budgetary crunch is resolved and as thinking on educational reform comes to consensus, the government will develop a strategy and devote substantial resources to the creation of a comprehensive, first-class basic science research and training apparatus. That will not occur quickly, but it will occur. The slogan of a "knowledge-intensive society" may even evolve into "a society of basic and applied science for the world" in another decade or so.

Both Imai and Murakami call for a new type of industrial policy for Japan. Given the Murakami model of long-term technological change and his view that we are embarking on a new epoch, he states that "continuation of the old industrial policy is a serious strategic error." What is needed in Japan and in the West are new policies that engage in creative destruction of the now counterproductive political-economic institutions and structures of the past, including especially the existing government-industry linkage. Failure to adjust will harm not only each major country individually but all of them collectively because of increasing economic and technological interdependencies. How this challenge of the future can be, or will be, met will be the grist for studies that lie ahead.

Finally, what are the "lessons" for the United States? Let me stress that this is *not* the bottom line. While this book provides much information, analysis, and especially insight, its central purpose is not to draw policy conclusions or make prescriptive recommendations for the United States. The study stands on its own: it informs us about Japan, and it informs us about America. And it does so in ways that are directly policy relevant.

That said, some of us—appropriately the American participants in the project—felt it natural and desirable to address the issue of relevant lessons for the United States, and each has done so. Indeed, that is a major objective of the Eads and Nelson contribution, and some conclusions are drawn at the end of Patrick as well.

The first lesson from the Japanese experience in high technology industrial policy is that there is no simple or single blueprint that has been or can be applied in Japan, much less the United States. Moreover, we urge American policy makers to exercise caution on at least three points: (1) Be sure the story is correct; do not be mislead by stereotypes that miscast essential features of Japanese high technology industrial policy. (2) Beware of thinking that the Japanese experience as a follower during the high growth era of the 1950s and 1960s is relevant now, for either the United States or Japan. (3) Be sure any transplants—of policies, instruments, institutions—are compatible with the American economic, political, institutional, and cultural environment. Moreover, be alert for negative as well as positive lessons from Japan's experience. There is no need to emulate Japan's mistakes.

The second lesson is "Get the basics right," to use the Eads and Nelson phrase; or, as Patrick more prosaically puts it, have the correct macro-industrial policy. There are several essential components. One is sufficient government R&D incentives to overcome private underinvestment in R&D as determined in the marketplace alone, which is a consequence of benefits external to the company as well as the "public goods" nature of much knowledge. A second is the development of an adequate educational infrastructure at all levels, particularly in mass secondary school learning and college-level scientific and engineering education. Third is the right macroeconomic environment to encourage investment and productivity growth; to set a competitive international value of the dollar by trade criteria through an appropriate fiscal-monetary mixture; and to establish a sectorally more neutral tax system. One of Saxonhouse's findings is that effective tax rates on capital by sector vary far more widely in the United States than in Japan, the obvious result of special-interest tinkering with the tax code.

The third lesson is, as Eads and Nelson propose, moving government R&D efforts downstream from basic research to generic technology development, while avoiding the stage of being involved in the commercialization process.

Fourth, Eads and Nelson propose allowing more joint R&D among competing large firms than the United States has historically permitted under its antitrust laws and in terms of the social, political, and economic environment in which those laws are administered. It is not that the authors believe any less in antitrust legislation and implementation; rather, they see the social benefit of joint research outweighing the possible anticompetitive costs, especially in light of new definitions of markets that transcend national boundaries. Most of the other authors in this volume concur with this judgment. Yamamura, however, is more cautious, concerned about the actual trade-offs between costs and benefits and fearful that reductions in competition will prevail in the long run as the consequence of such a policy change.

This Introduction has delved only selectively, and then not at full depth, into issues considered in these chapters. Each of the essays is rich in insights, provision of evidence, and argumentation. And each is very different from the others. Yet they blend together unusually well; the whole is considerably greater than the sum of the parts. I encourage the reader to examine the following chapters deeply and carefully. The rewards will be substantial.

The Committee on Japanese Economic Studies, which among its other activities organizes research projects on the contemporary Japanese economy of relevance for the understanding of United States–Japan economic relations and hence as an input to policy formulation, has been the sponsor of this project. As director of this project, I am indebted to my colleagues on the Committee and to all others who have participated.

Our thanks go especially to the United States–Japan Foundation, which provided the Committee on Japanese Economic Studies a grant in support of this project. Moreover, the Foundation made their good offices (in both senses) available for a three-day intensive seminar in March 1984 in which preliminary versions of these papers were presented. Ronald Aqua graciously hosted the meetings on behalf of the Foundation. Those discussions were forthright, exciting, and most useful in the extensive revisions the chapters subsequently underwent. In addition to the contributors to this volume, whose names and affiliations are listed at the back of the book, the seminar included the following participants: Donna Doane, Assistant Professor, Department of Economics, Cortland State University; Peter J. Katzenstein, Professor, Department of Government, Cornell University; Larry Meissner, portfolio manager and editor; Henry Rosovsky, Lewis P. and Linda L. Geyser University Professor of Economics, Harvard University, and a member of the Committee on Japanese Economic Studies; Kazuo Sato, Professor, Department of Economics, Rutgers University, Editor of *Japanese Economic Studies*, and a member of the Committee on Japanese Economic Studies; and Shoko Tanaka, Ph.D. candidate, Department of Government, Cornell University.

I thank also Martha Lane, Jackson School of International Studies, University of Washington, and Irita Grierson, Department of Economics, University of Michigan, who helped in the administration of this project, including the seminar meeting. My deep thanks go to Robert Uriu, who contributed valiantly in the final editorial process. And my deepest thanks go to my colleague and friend, Larry Meissner, for his devoted efforts in working with me on the extensive and intensive editorial process with all the authors.

Hugh Patrick

REFERENCES

Lincoln, Edward J. 1984. *Japan's Industrial Policies*. Washington, D.C.: Japan Economic Institute of America.

Zysman, John, and Laura Tyson. 1984. "U.S. and Japanese Trade and Industrial Policies." Paper prepared for the United States–Japan Advisory Commission.

Japan's High Technology Industries

Chapter 1

Japanese High Technology Industrial Policy in Comparative Context

Hugh Patrick

The United States in the mid-1980s is engaging in an important, perhaps crucial, national debate on the goals, nature, and effectiveness of governmental economic policy and its appropriate role in the American economy and society. As one significant element of this debate, much is being made of industrial policy. What the term "industrial policy" means depends on the user; it ranges from being a euphemism for centralized government planning and intervention to a buzzword referring to the more coherent application of policy tools already in use in the United States. Interest in industrial policy, however defined, has been heightened by perceptions of deep-seated difficulties in the American economy not treatable by traditional policy measures, by perceptions of Japanese industrial success and its competitive challenge to certain important American industries, and by perceptions of the success of Japanese industrial policy.

At the same time, debate is under way on U.S. trade policy, ranging from very narrow specific issues to the appropriate nature of the international economic system and the respective roles of the United States and Japan in it. The application of industrial policy by foreign nations, notably Japan, is perceived to provide competitive advantage to selected targeted industries, to the disadvantage of their American counterparts.

Thus, perceptions of Japanese industrial policy have entered the American debate on economic policy in two major ways: as a possible model to emulate in developing a United States industrial policy; and as a shaper of Japanese industrial structure and comparative advantage, especially vis-à-vis major American industries. It is not surprising that the main focus of American attention has been to understand how Japan over time has successfully developed a number of major and now highly competitive industries (steel, motor vehicles, shipbuilding, consumer electronics) and

3

to see an emerging competitive challenge in so-called high tech industries—currently semiconductors, computers, robotics, telecommunication systems, optical fibers, new materials, solar batteries, industrial application of biotechnology, and the like. Less American attention has been given to Japanese policies for declining industries, and only limited attention to Japanese policies for defense industries.

This chapter is divided into four parts. In the first section I briefly discuss and define the nature and scope of the concept of industrial policy in general and high tech industrial policy in particular. This is important because the term "industrial policy" has been defined and used in quite different ways within the United States, and in Japan as well.

The main purpose of this chapter is to provide a general assessment of Japanese industrial policy—its successes and its failures—because that is an obvious requisite for those attempting to derive possible lessons and implications for U.S. policy. Simplistic and misleading myths and stereotypes abound regarding the Japanese economy and Japanese industrial policy, and we should beware of what may be incorrect "lessons." All too often perceptions of the Japanese economy are outdated, conditioned excessively by the earlier high growth era—from the mid-1950s to the early 1970s—when Japanese industrial policy was in its heyday. Japanese industrial policy is discussed and evaluated in the second and third sections.

In the final section I consider the relevance of the Japanese industrial policy experience for the United States, in its debates on both industrial policy and trade policy.

The Concepts of Industrial Policy and High Tech Industries

Every nation pursues policies that significantly affect both the aggregate productive capacity of the economy and its particular industrial structure. Some policies have these goals explicitly, others have indirect and at times unanticipated effects on the economic structure. Some policies are macro, others micro.

The term "macro industrial policy" has been used to describe policies, especially incentives to save, to invest, and to engage in R&D, that increase the productive capacity of the economy in the longer run while leaving it to the marketplace to allocate resources among specific industries. Macro industrial policy accordingly is focused on the supply side of the economy, in distinction from aggregate demand management which typically uses fiscal and monetary policy instruments. Macro industrial policies have long characterized Japanese economic policy in practice, though seldom described as such. A broad definition of macro industrial policy includes any macroeconomic policies to increase the quantity and especially the quality of the factors of production—labor, capital, and natural resources—and the general level of technology. This definition incorporates educational policy as an important element. It is noteworthy that Japan has an elementary and secondary school educational system that produces a substantially higher average level of literacy and of competence in natural sciences and mathematics than in the United States. It also has a college system, predominantly private and of heterogeneous quality, that produces more engineers and especially electrical engineering college graduates than the United States, though fewer at the graduate level.

Industrial policy more typically is defined in micro terms: identification of certain specific industries deemed to have sufficient national importance to merit and receive differentially favorable policy treatment in order that those industries have access to resources in degrees or timing different from what would occur through the normal operations of the marketplace. A range of policy instruments can be used: direct subsidy payments, tax benefits, government-supported financing, protection from imports or promotion of exports, direct government purchases, funding of relevant R&D, special regulatory provisions, and so forth. The central point is the *differential* advantages government policy provides selected—targeted, if you will—industries to their benefit and to the relative disadvantage of all other industries. Those propounding industrial policy as so defined assert that the marketplace is not operating optimally owing to market imperfections or outright market failure, so that specific government intervention is warranted.

This definition of industrial policy, without reference to its basic objectives, to the policy environment, and to the utilization of specific policy instruments, is quite general. By this definition, the United States in fact pursues an industrial policy in the priority it gives to defense and aerospace industries, for example; and the continental West European nations do so through regional development programs that in practice are keyed to certain basic industries such as steel. That is, simply referring to the "national importance" of an industry while focusing on the resource reallocative results of government policy does not quite catch what the debate is mainly about, since the definition does not include the goals that give an industry national importance. (Unfortunately the goals are also often obscure in debate, or patently self-serving.)

The U.S. International Trade Commission (USITC) provides a precise but narrower definition in its recent study of Japanese industrial targeting. Equating industrial policy with "targeting," the report says: "International targeting is coordinated government actions that direct productive resources to give domestic producers in selected industries a competitive advantage" (USITC 1983, p. 20). This definition has two important elements. It visualizes policy implementation in terms of a coherent package of specific policy instruments. And it makes the objective of industrial policy explicit: to increase the competitive advantage of selected industries in relation to the rest of the world, that is, in a global market context. The industries selected provide tradable goods. There is an important normative implication some derive from this definition: it is natural and acceptable for a government to direct productive resources to military industries to achieve national security goals, but it is not acceptable or fair for a government to interfere directly to create competitive advantage for selected civilian industries.

The national security dimension creates two conceptual problems. First, civilian-oriented and military-oriented high tech industries are highly intertwined, so it is at times difficult to separate long-run competitive marketplace and national security interests. Second, the definition and determination of national security, and the routes to its achievement, are not unilinear or simple. Prevention of military attack is a central objective, but not the only one. Japanese thinkers and policy makers have stressed the importance of comprehensive security, which includes economic as well as military aspects. Its most important component is guaranteed access to whatever is essential for maintenance of the national economy. The obvious essentials are industrial raw materials, exemplified by oil, and foodstuffs. Less obvious but in the long run probably equally important for any major advanced industrial nation is access to technological innovation and its fruits. A country must also be able to pay for imports essential for national security: it has to produce goods demanded in world markets and it has to have access to those markets. To the extent this broader definition of national security is used (or invoked) it is easier to argue that many high tech industries are strategic in a national security sense.

One can also argue that high tech industries are strategic in an economic sense for large, modern, high income nations seeking to expand economic power and well-being. In an excellent, comprehensive, comparative study, Nelson (1984) lays out this argument well. High tech industries are the leading industries in a Schumpeterian sense. Two rationales can be provided for government industrial policy in support of these industries: the product cycle implies eventual loss of specific competitive advantage, while R&D to gain advantage is not fully appropriable by those engaging in it; interindustry externalities accrue to users of high tech products, and domestic users benefit earlier and more rapidly than foreign users.

High tech industrial policy focuses on the industries of the future, the winners, those for which comparative advantage lies ahead. However, there is another important element of industrial policy, namely to "rationalize" or support major industries in cyclical or other temporary difficulty, or facing structural problems of declining competitiveness and comparative advantage in major product segments ("helping the losers adjust to adversity,'' as it is sometimes crassly described). Any general evaluation of Japanese industrial policy must consider programs for industries in difficulty as well as those for important industries of the future.

What is meant by high tech industry? In some respects the definition is analogous to that of heavy industry: it is not very precise but everyone has some intuitive understanding, frequently in terms of specific industry examples. There is a broad consensus that certain industries are high tech: semiconductors, computers, telecommunications, and biotechnology. Beyond these, and even as regards subindustries of these four, there is less agreement. In general "high tech industry" is a category that aggregates a number of specific industries with common characteristics— much like such categories as heavy industry, basic industry, or consumer durables. Similarly, one can conceptualize high tech industrial policy as being at an intermediate level between macroeconomic policy and (micro) industrial policy for specific, targeted industries.

The essential feature of a high tech industry is its great reliance on the application of new science-based technologies to products or production processes. Yet sophisticated technological innovation takes place in most industries; the "green revolution" in agriculture and the new fibers in textiles are examples in sectors generally deemed decidedly low tech. Thus, innovation per se, and even involvement with science, is not a sufficient condition. The intensity of scientific and technology effort and the speed of innovation are important features of a high tech industry, involving the production of significant new knowledge from a strong science base; in other words, being at the global scientific and technological frontiers. Rather than a dichotomy between high technology and low technology industries, it is better to think of industries as spread over a continuum between these two extremes. The position of any given industry may shift along the spectrum as new scientific knowledge (often exogenously) emerges, or a given line of scientific inquiry and technological application significantly slows down. More important probably, completely new industries emerge at the high technology end of the spectrum as a consequence of science-based innovation and new demands for the products (Doane 1984).

Quantitative indicators provide a useful, pragmatic approach to the problem of definition. A high tech industry is characterized by a high ratio of scientists, engineers, or computer programmers in its work force; a high ratio of R&D expenditures to its sales; and a high proportion of new products in its total sales. It is likely to have high actual and projected rates of growth of output and demand for its products. Capital intensity of production is not a particularly good indicator.

While new consumer products may be the consequence of high technology industrial development, implicit in much of the discussion of high tech industrial policy is the perceived strategic nature of the industry—not only in military terms but as a basic capital or intermediate product which has diffused more widely throughout the economy. Thus video cassette recorders and other consumer electronics, rather than being considered high tech industries, are often seen as the consequence of other high technology industries such as semiconductors. Personal computers are considered high technology because of their productive usage, not the consumption pleasures they provide. The perceived linkages and externalities of almost an infrastructural nature are one reason why success in high tech industries is perceived as vital to the economic growth, well-being, and especially preeminence of a nation.

That an industry is high tech does not mean preferential treatment through industrial policy is required or necessary. The economic case for government support is the standard one of market imperfections or failure: high returns on average R&D activity combined with only partial appropriability by the doer; external benefits; high risk due to ignorance and uncertainty, often compounded by long lead times or the huge scale of required expenditures relative to firm size. However, the fact that much private R&D has occurred and does occur without specific incentives does suggest many high tech industry activities would take place without special preferential treatment (industrial policy), and hence that such government programs create economic rents rather than incentives for additional activity. On the other hand, timing in the dynamics of high technology industrial development can be very important. In rapidly developing high technology industries, being first or very close to first may provide significant learning and cost advantages over potential competitors. But there are also cases in which the initial innovation has not succeeded in solving sufficiently the scientific, technological, production, or even marketing problems, and has lost out to closely pursuing followers.

Given the characteristics common to high tech industries and which distinguish them from other industries—in degree rather than kind—government policies to provide special benefit to high tech industries can derive either downward from macro policies or upward from specific industry policies, as is in the case in Japan. In the United States, preferential treatment is intentionally provided high tech industries through macro policies that provide favorable tax treatment of R&D, rapid depreciation, and public training of engineers and scientists. These policies are premised on high tech industries spending relatively more on R&D than other industries, buying or selling relatively more capital equipment, and employing relatively more holders of degrees in science and engineering.

The Japanese experience in industrial policy illustrates many of the conceptual and definitional issues of industrial policy. It is to that experience we now turn.

Japanese Industrial Policy

A careful, detailed examination of Japanese industrial policy over the postwar period shows that it has often been ad hoc in nature, not always carefully thought out or focused, usually quite flexible in response to changing analyses and circumstances, and on occasion subject to considerable political pressures. In other words, like much of history it was complex and messy, rather than simple and clear-cut. Nonetheless, by virtue of hindsight we can abstract and generalize from the detailed realities of the historical record in order to present general patterns and characteristics, without thereby claiming more for Japanese industrial policy than is warranted.

With these caveats in mind, Japanese industrial policy can be characterized as follows. Its goal has been to enhance economic growth by anticipating dynamically efficient allocation of resources by the criterion of world as well as domestic prices; to this end it has selected certain key industries as essential for preferential treatment; and it has provided such treatment through a comprehensive, coordinated set of policy instruments. Japan has conducted its industrial policy in a generally conducive and supportive domestic policy environment: there has been a consensus on what was being done, and general economic policies and conditions were conducive to success.

It is important to keep in mind that the goals, policy instruments, and policy environment have changed dramatically during the postwar period. The postwar Japanese economy has gone through three phases: a decade of postwar reconstruction following the devastation of World War II; almost two decades, from the mid-1950s to 1973, of superfast GNP growth (about 10 percent annual average); and the most recent decade of 4 percent growth in a domestic and world environment of oil crises and stagflation. Industrial policy has evolved from one period to the next in response to these changing circumstances.

Well into the second phase, Japan was a low-income, developing country, and pursued trade and industrial policies like those of many other follower countries. Industrial policy played an important role from the beginning, initially with a strong domestic market orientation; reconstruction was felt to require special government help for the fertilizer, electric power, coal, steel, and transport industries. To some extent this built upon government thinking and programs initiated in the 1930s and even earlier. As the Japanese high growth era progressed, industrial policy, and the intellectual rationalizations of it, reached their heyday. New industries—chemicals, petrochemicals, and other intermediate goods—were added to the list for preferential support. These, like the other industries earlier, were regarded as high tech industries for Japan but were already well established in the United States.

Between 1955 and 1973 the Japanese GNP increased almost six times in real terms. By the early 1970s Japan had become the world's third largest industrial economy (following the United States and the USSR), with per capita incomes comparable to Western Europe. This profound surge of growth transformed the industrial structure and changed substantially the needs and conditions of industrial policy. Still, there were very few sectors in which Japan was pushing out the frontiers of knowledge. It was very successful at learning and applying the best proven technologies, but with only incremental improvements. Even so, MITI was beginning to generate visions of "knowledge-intensive" (high tech) industries.

Japanese industrial policy as an ideal type came into its own in the high growth era. It is useful to characterize it first in these ideal-type terms, next to indicate the changes that have taken place in industrial policy in the past decade, and then in the next section to provide an appraisal of the effectiveness and ineffectiveness of Japanese industrial policy in both its historical and present contexts.

Japanese Industrial Policy as an Ideal Type

Ideal types are a useful device for deriving general theoretical principles and patterns, even though they have been only imperfectly achieved in reality. The following depiction, by being formulated in idealized (one might say antiseptic) terms, provides a basis both to evaluate changes in Japanese actual high tech industrial policies and practices over the past decade and to appraise their relevance for possible American industrial policy. A cautionary note is important: to describe the ideal type means neither that it was the way industrial policy operated in practice nor that it had particularly effective results. Indeed, as is considered in the next section, I am skeptical of the claims put forth as to the great effectiveness of Japanese industrial policy.

Japanese industrial policy has been pragmatic and economic in its orientation. The basic goal has been to create the productive capacity for rapid growth by accelerating the transfer to resources to the major industries of the future, while smoothing the process of decline of uncompetitive industries: "picking winners and phasing out losers." In principle "winners" should meet the following criteria: (1) industries of significant size in which Japan would have future comparative advantage as the relative supplies and costs of its factors of production changed with domestic growth and evolving international economic conditions, and as learning curve economies were achieved (infant industry cases); (2) industries for which domestic and world demand would have high income elasticity; and

(3) industries in which Japan would become internationally price competitive. However, as is discussed below, only in the past decade has the general level of technology, human and physical capital, and economic production provided an adequate base for Japanese industry to move into high technology industries in any broad-based way.

The emphasis of Japanese industrial policy has been on economic growth and economically efficient resource allocation. Economic efficiency has come to be defined in terms of world markets, not (protected) domestic markets, and in terms of competitive prices, high quality, and other non-price attributes. In contrast, a major goal of American industrial policy has been to maintain the industrial basis for military strength, in quality and quantity but not in price. The contrast in policy goals between American military prowess (and the development of comparative advantage and export sales in military hardware) and Japanese economic and commercial strength is striking. The United States has also pursued policies to help specific industries, such as textiles, steel, and automobiles—largely to "save" jobs—but mainly by restriction of imports. Agriculture is one sector in which American industrial policy has been most successful. While there may be a major distinction in principle between the Japanese emphasis on efficient resource allocation and U.S. and West European emphasis on the redistribution of income, the political economies in practice are not so different; Japanese policy makers have continuously provided support for inefficient but politically powerful farmers and small businesses on the grounds of more equal income distribution.

Japanese industrial policy has been designed, implemented, and justified by the Ministry of International Trade and Industry (MITI). MITI has been quick to argue market failure, so-called excessive competition, the need to catch up to best Western technologies and practices, and hence the need for government intervention. Its rationale (at times after the fact) for industrial policy has included the following themes: the private market mechanism inadequately allocates resources for long-run growth; MITI officials emphasize instances of market failure (external economies or diseconomies, public good effects, private underinvestment in R&D), and Japanese labor and capital market imperfections. One senior MITI official has argued that Japanese are so locked into their own company (group) and are so competitive in relation to others that they go beyond the bounds of normal economic behavior and engage in excessive competition—with each other as much as with foreigners.

MITI officials apparently believe they can better anticipate the long-run strategic needs of the economy than the marketplace, which inevitably has too short a time horizon and is unwilling to assume enough risk quickly enough. They believe they can anticipate where the market will go, thereby speeding up its operation. The goal is to reach the same place as the market solution but more rapidly and (in the case of declining industries) at less social cost. Underlying the definition of future key industries is an implicit strategic sense as to what industrial structure will be required for Japan to be a major economic power ten to twenty years in the future. This includes semiconductors, computers, telecommunications, nuclear energy, and other high tech industries. Since the late 1970s, MITI has placed greater emphasis on the other aspect of industrial policy—assisting in the structural adjustment process of major uncompetitive, declining industries such as aluminum, petrochemicals, and textiles. The MITI rationale is pragmatic: in scaling down an industry it is more efficient to close the least efficient plants and achieve economies through (government-encouraged) merger rather than bankruptcy.

The Japanese implementation of industrial policy has several important elements. First, once an industry has been selected for support, MITI has put together (in negotiations with the Ministry of Finance) a comprehensive package of support: accelerated depreciation allowances, special R&D funding (often through the industry association) and tax benefits, loans through the Japan Development Bank or other government financial institutions, and so forth. Second, the policy measures try to anticipate and to use the marketplace rather than replacing it, by providing various incentives to business to allocate resources as desired. Such an integrated package of policies, based on market incentives to encourage business behavior in desired directions, contrasts with the more piecemeal American approach of reliance on a single method to aid specific industries without building in incentives to alter business behavior, as exemplified by de facto restrictions on imports of textiles, automobiles, or steel.

Third, MITI policy in principle has encouraged the combination of a competitive environment and effective economies of plant scale in any chosen industry. Indeed, this was the real success of Japanese industrial policy in the high growth era of the 1950s and 1960s: rapid, efficient industrialization involving entry of new firms, which promoted competition in the domestic market. Non-Japanese firms were generally not allowed in during the early stages, but there was sufficient competition to make firms efficiency oriented even as they profited from a protected market. Thus Japan, more rapidly than other nations industrializing behind import barriers, was able to achieve international competitiveness in a number of new important industries, ranging from consumer electronics to steel to small cars to certain types of semiconductors and computers. To be sure this was not neoclassical ideal-type perfect competition. Rather, it involved firms competing in dynamic oligopoly market structures. Consumers paid relatively high prices, especially in the early stages of an industry; but MITI-encouraged pressures to increase efficiency and productivity and to reduce costs so as to become internationally competitive (typically with the threat of eventual loss of protection) eventually brought domestic prices down as well. However, there were important exceptions to this generally positive picture, notably petroleum refining, where optimum scale and low-cost production were not achieved.

Just how micro has Japanese industrial policy been? Let us consider three levels: an individual firm; an industry, narrowly or more broadly defined; and a productive sector, such as manufacturing, construction, agriculture, or services. Japanese industrial policy has been at the industry level, usually rather broadly defined. MITI has not chosen individual firms as national champions; it has not particularly favored one large firm over another; while it will help an industry in trouble, it usually will not help an individual firm in trouble of its own making. However, its policies have usually benefited large firms relative to small. This seems to have been particularly the case with high tech industries in which only a few large firms have been able to participate in government-sponsored R&D projects, or those of the government-owned Nippon Telegraph and Telephone (NTT) monopoly. The robotics industry is one counterexample, but none of the early entrants were very large.

At the broad sectoral level, the cumulative effect of both industrial policy and macroeconomic policy was to provide preferential access to resources to business, especially large firms, at the expense of housing, consumer credit, or social infrastructure. Agriculture, a lagging sector, also received special help. In the United States, in contrast, resources were preferentially allocated to defense, aerospace, and housing as well as agriculture (which is subsidized in all major advanced industrial nations). And within industry it may well be that the macro system of tax and other incentives have affected specific industries in the United States even more differentially than in Japan; certainly the taxation of corporate profits varies more widely by industry in the United States.

The Japanese domestic policy environment has been favorable to industrial policy and to economic policy generally. High priority is still given in Japanese government policy making to economic issues, domestic and international. But changing economic and political circumstances (as discussed below) have brought about major shifts in the relative importance of various objectives. The almost simpleminded focus in the 1950s and 1960s on economic growth and efficient resource allocation through the private sector resulted in an unbalanced growth pattern with insufficient attention to environmental problems, housing, and social infrastructure. By the early 1970s, economic policy came to embody a broader mix of goals, including price stability and social welfare (mainly transfer payments for health and old age). Even so, the emphasis has persistently been on private enterprise and the operation (and influencing) of the market mechanism, with the first claim on scarce resources going to business rather than government.

Japanese are very competitive, and there are many areas and problems of conflict in Japan as in other societies. Japanese society is built on individual participation in groups—the family, the school class, the work place—and societal norms stress the importance of harmony through cooperation and at least formal consensus. This mutes and makes more subtle the normal conflicts of interest and adversarial relationships of life. Accordingly, labor-management relations and government-business relations are considerably more cooperative and mutually beneficial than in the adversarial, suspicious, more individualistic American society and its institutions; in Japan these relationships are seen as positive-sum, not zero-sum, games. Of course in a rapidly growing economy, distributional issues were less salient and cooperation easier; it made more sense to focus on increasing the size of the pie than on how to slice it up. And business in Japan has benefited substantially from the continuance in power of the probusiness, conservative Liberal Democratic Party (LDP) ever since 1955. It has also benefited from an easier antitrust environment within which, with MITI approval, targeted industries could form temporary antirecession cartels and high tech firms could participate in joint R&D projects (Yamamura, this volume). I consider the implications of different institutional arrangements in Japan and the United States in the final section.

Changes in Japanese Industrial Policy in the Past Decade

Over the past decade Japanese industrial policy has changed significantly as Japan has achieved affluence ("caught up with the West"), business has become strong and independent, growth has slowed greatly, the price of energy has risen dramatically, and Japan has adopted a free trade policy in principle and greatly liberalized most of its imports. These have affected substantially the goals, policy instruments, and policy environment for industrial policy.

Two major trends are discernible in the recent evolution of Japanese industrial policy. Industrial policy has become less important in overall government economic policy, in terms both of the objectives and the instruments of industrial policy. And industrial policy has developed a tripartite focus: high tech industries, the winners of the future; major, structurally depressed, industries in trouble; and energy and, to some degree, other natural resources.

First affluence, then much-slowed growth, have greatly altered the general policy environment for industrial policy. In the early 1970s the public debate on unbalanced growth resulted in increased priority for social infrastructure, pollution and other environmental control, social welfare (especially retirement and health benefits), and housing. Thus the share of general government expenditures in GNP rose by more than ten percentage points, to 33 percent by 1980. Business came to be seen, correctly, as strong and able to grow on its own; major industries no longer needed the special benefits of industrial protection. Moreover, with strength came greater desire by big business for independence from MITI and other government bureaucrats; business leaders do not want to be beholden to or dependent on them, and are more resistant to their intrusion.

The two oil crises, much-slowed growth, and the rapid transition from a neoclassical to a Keynesian economy have probable had an even more profound effect. Until 1974, economic growth was fueled by high rates of business investment and high rates of saving; the operative constraint in other than brief cyclical downturn was supply capacity relative to burgeoning demand. Since 1974, the constraint on growth has been inadequate private and total domestic aggregate demand. Saving rates have declined somewhat but remained high; private business investment has slowed more rapidly, so that ex ante saving has been substantially greater than investment demand. Pump-priming through huge deficit-financed increases in government expenditures has covered part of the gap but not all. And the need for deficit-financing persisted in time and amount beyond the political will to engage in it; by 1983 Japanese public sector debt, which had been negligible a decade earlier, was a larger percentage of GNP than in the United States.

This made the traditional emphasis of industrial policy on winners much less important. With the economy awash in surplus saving, most in financial assets, the problem was how to encourage businessmen, indeed anyone, to invest and spend rather than how to ration credit to them. With slow growth, income redistribution became more important than economic efficiency in the political economy of government policy. Government resources went increasingly to farmers, small business, and old people.

In the past several years the main focus of government policy has been the macro problems associated with the huge central government budget deficits. The political decision has been to reduce the budget deficit even at the cost of slower growth (so much for the rapid growth policy of yesteryear); because it has been politically impossible to raise corporate or personal income tax rates, the main effort has been to hold the line on or even reduce expenditures. The narrowing of the deficit, from 6 percent to slightly under 4 percent of GNP, has been the consequence of the upward drift of tax revenues in GNP due to progressive tax rates and a leveling off of the rise in expenditures. In a related move Prime Minister Nakasone has given priority to broadly defined "administrative reform," including deregulation of industry and finance, reduced budget subsidies to agriculture, and fundamental reorganization of certain public corporations, notably the deficit-ridden Japan National Railways, which has been a major drain on the government budget. Big business has pushed hard for these reforms and other measures to hold down growth of government expenditures, correctly perceiving that otherwise tax increases would fall heavily on business, at least directly.

One of the most important changes in the policy environment is that Japan is no longer insulated from the rest of the world. Foreign governmental pressures—especially American—have intruded on the cozy domestic arrangements that have been so much a part of Japanese industrial policy. Japan is now a major economy and world trader—indeed, the challenger of American and European industrial might—first in steel and cars and now semiconductors, computers, telecommunications, and other high tech areas. Its actions, policy and otherwise, inevitably invite scrutiny and at times reactions by the United States and others. Japan has truly become an interdependent member of an interdependent world. As one of the three pillars of the liberal international economic order— together with the United States and the West European industrial democracies—Japan can no longer use trade policy as an instrument of industrial policy; it must reduce trade barriers, not raise them.

The variety and power of policy instruments to implement industrial policy have been reduced substantially. Most important, in the present world environment and given Japan's commitment to the liberal trading system in principle, MITI is no longer able to impose foreign exchange or import restrictions—tariffs, quotas, nontariff barriers—to help new potential winner industries. Import barriers for most high tech industries have now typically been reduced to minor levels. New industries and new products cannot benefit from newly imposed barriers. Japanese policy and behavior is rather closely monitored, especially by the United States, in order to press for further liberalization and to prevent new restrictions.

As Trezise (1983a) points out, as a share of GNP, government resources going to business are not large relative to the United States and Western Europe; and most of those resources do not go to the three categories targeted by industrial policy—high technology, declining industries, and energy. The largest proportion of government subsidies go to agriculture, then energy, small business, and the Japan National Railways. Government R&D expenditures are relatively low (Nelson 1984). About half go through the Ministry of Education for university science and technology support, including faculty salaries and administrative costs. About a quarter is allocated to the Science and Technology Agency for essentially high tech purposes: space, ocean, and energy projects. About an eighth of government R&D expenditures come under MITI jurisdiction; more than half of that goes for energy. MITI's funds to support manufacturing R&D were on the order of a modest $350 million in fiscal 1983 (Trezise 1983a).

The government provides selective tax benefits, but they are widely dispersed; everyone gets something. The Ministry of Finance has calculated that gross revenue losses in fiscal 1981 from all special tax measures were about 1,100 billion yen (about $5 billion). Half was for exemptions on interest on deposits for small savers, and another quarter was related to health and other social insurance. Somewhat more than $1 billion went to business in accelerated depreciation, special reserve accounts, and R&D tax credits. While the government loan program through its financial institutions is not inconsequential (though less than 10 percent of total loans), most now goes to small business. Export credits are for ships and plants—standard big-ticket items. The Japan Development Bank, always viewed as a prime instrument of industrial policy, has lost its focus and historic rationale. Energy is now the single largest category in its incremental loan portfolio, on the order of 40 percent (about $2 billion in 1981). Only some 10 percent went to high tech industries other than energy.

MITI is losing its historic role as the predominant initiator, agent, and implementer of industrial policy. Many relevant issues of high tech (and other) industrial policy no longer fall preeminently in its manufacturing sector domain. The Science and Technology Agency and the Ministry of Education are in the high tech R&D act. This is not just in terms of budget resources, as the recent interministerial conflict on the appropriate law for copyrighting or patenting computer software exemplifies. Telecommunications and NTT come under the Ministry of Posts and Telecommunications; it is initiating the new legislation on use of telecom munications lines for value-added networks (VAN) linking computers and data banks. NTT itself has been privatized, though still subject to government regulation. The Ministry of Welfare is responsible for standards and other procedures which continue to restrict imports of pharmaceuticals, medical equipment, and the like.

For all these reasons, coherence in Japanese industrial policy has attenuated. But one should not count out industrial policy or MITI's role in it, especially in the high technology arena. High tech industries have three major needs: assured markets, encouragement of R&D, and finance. Government-related procurement, including that of NTT as well as remaining public corporations, provides an immense market still substantially protected by a wide range of "buy Japanese" regulations and tax incentives. High tech R&D is encouraged through tax write-offs, government loans, subsidies, government industrial research labs (many under MITI jurisdiction), favorable antitrust provisions, and government funding for joint, cooperative, R&D projects among major corporations. Finance depends on industrial structure. Large firms moving into high tech activities can readily utilize internal funds and borrowing capacity. The major problem has been the provision of risk capital to new, small firms. Venture capital institutions are in their infancy, but that is now rapidly changing. Quite large amounts of Japanese and foreign venture capital funds apparently are becoming readily available; the problem is mainly to develop venture capital markets, and to create an environment in which creative scientists and engineers (usually in large firms) are willing to leave secure positions and become entrepreneurs. These issues are elaborated upon with substantial industry-specific detail in the companion essays in this volume by Imai, Okimoto, Saxonhouse, and Yamamura.

While MITI's activist role in an industrial policy for high tech industry and energy has to be coordinated with a number of other ministries in addition to its traditional working relationship with the Ministry of Finance, it has continued to reign supreme in industrial policy for the structurally depressed manufacturing industries hit by high energy costs (aluminum, petrochemicals, etc.), low world demand (shipbuilding), or high labor costs (textiles, simple assembly operations). Of course, Japan's largest uncompetitive industry is agriculture, over which MITI has no jurisdiction. Considerable MITI effort since the late 1970s has gone into policies for losers, as reflected in the successful efforts to have the Structurally Depressed Industries Law passed in 1979 and revised and extended in 1983. This is a new thrust, and is dictated by the twin realities of great structural uncompetitiveness and slow domestic growth. While government industrial policy earlier helped adjustment in coal mining and cotton textiles in the 1960s, labor transfer was achieved fairly smoothly because rapid growth created other job opportunities. Earlier structural adjustment programs were primarily bailouts of the owners and their financiers. Even in the present slow job-opportunity growth environment, that may well be the situation for more recent programs in structural adjustment as well.

Evaluation of Japanese Industrial Policy

In my judgment, industrial policy has been somewhat beneficial for the Japanese economy but its extent and efficacy have been overrated by many. Japan has pursued a relatively coherent industrial policy, but its effect has not always been as intended, in degree or in direction. MITI has supported a number of specific industries and has had some notable successes. It has had some important failures—even aside from the promotion of petrochemical, aluminum, and other energy-intensive industries in the 1960s which were made uncompetitive by the sharp rises in energy prices in the 1970s. And there are a number of important industries, such as automobiles and consumer electronics—indeed virtually all consumer goods—in which the government did not take any differentially supportive role but which have succeeded on their own.

The Effectiveness Debate

Among specialists on Japan's political economy there is no clear consensus regarding the effectiveness of Japanese industrial policy. Rather, there are honest differences of opinion among respected scholars. This is not the place to review that debate and its considerable literature in any detail, but its existence needs to be borne in mind. Broadly speaking, there are two schools. By considering each in its stereotypic form, the nature of the debate is illuminated, even though most specialists place themselves somewhere between these two extremes.

One school sees Japan as embodying a state-guided capitalist system in which MITI and industrial policy have played a central role. In this view, government leadership has been the key to Japan's economic success, with business a willing follower. An extreme version of this approach is encapsulated in the phrase "Japan Inc.," which is, however, a red herring; all scholars agree it is too simplistic and naïve a concept for what is a much more complex, variegated, multidimensional set of relationships among the triad of Liberal Democratic Party politicians, central government bureaucrats, and big business leaders. Essentially, the responsibility for determining the goals of economic policy and seeing to it they are achieved is attributed to the bureaucracy: politicians reign, bureaucrats rule, business follows.

Chalmers Johnson has provided the most sophisticated argument for the efficacy and centrality of Japanese industrial policy, in his outstanding book *MITI and the Japanese Miracle* (1982) and other recent writings (1984) and speeches. But his, and this school's, main point is more fundamental: Japanese capitalism has a different structure from that of Western capitalism; there is a "Japanese system" of capitalism. In it the main role of the state is developmental; in the West it is regulatory. Johnson has well stated this position in a speech before the Japan Society (1983): "There are four fundamental structural features that exist in all the East Asian capitalist developmental states, including Japan. These are: (1) stable rule by a political-bureaucratic elite that does not accede to political demands that would undermine economic growth; (2) cooperation between public and private sectors under the overall guidance of a pilot planning agency; (3) heavy and continuing investment in education for everyone, combined with policies to ensure the equitable distribution of the wealth created by high-speed growth; and (4) a government that understands the need to use and respect methods of intervention based on the price mechanism." In this perspective, industrial policy is embedded in the system, and is a key feature of it. Data on the relatively modest level of government resources going to high tech (or other) industries do not adequately affect their initiating impact in this model of state-led, private sector-implemented capitalism because of systemic features and signaling effects to private industry and finance. These themes are also developed by Borrus, Millstein, and Zysman (1983) among others.

The other school denies the validity of the state-leadership developmental model, or of an otherwise defined model specific to the Japanese economic system, or of the central and efficacious role of industrial policy in it. These themes have become intertwined in the debate, but conceptually one can disentangle them. One thus can hold that Japanese institutions and practices cumulate to define a distinctive Japanese economic system but in which industrial policy does not play a particularly central, effective, or coherent role. Alternatively, one might argue that specific institutional differences are not so fundamental that they comprise a distinctive system but that industrial policy is important and effective. Or, one can hold that while Japan has articulated and pursued an industrial policy and does indeed have certain specific institutional features, neither aspect is central to our understanding of the basic characteristics of the Japanese economy and its economic performance.

The second school sees the basic source of Japan's economic growth as being in a vigorous private sector which, taking advantage of the private market mechanism, has energetically, imaginatively, and diligently engaged in productive business investment, commercially oriented research and development, in the saving to finance those activities, and in the development of a supportive system of labor-management relations. Business entrepreneurs were and are the engine of growth. At the same time, the government is given credit for having pursued macro demand and industrial policies beneficial to private sector growth. The government helped contribute to a favorable economic environment—as did the postwar international economic system—but the major impetus to growth was from the private, market-oriented sector.

The most articulate proponent of this position is Philip Trezise, who has argued that Japan has an industrial policy but it is not particularly coherent, focused, or effective. An early statement appears in *Asia's New Giant* (Trezise 1976); recent statements include his testimony before the Joint Economic Committee (1983a) and his essay in the *Brookings Review* (1983b). Lincoln takes this position in an essay which, among other themes, is critical of the first school (1984). My own view (initially stated in Patrick and Rosovksy 1976) is that industrial policy may well have helped the growth process to some degree, but it did not play a leading or central role.

The Japanese central government bureaucracy is certainly able and powerful; but it is by no means monolithic. Japanese ministries are more entrenched and autonomous than their counterparts in the United States. Each ministry has its own, at times self-serving, definition of the national interest. The Ministry of Finance, and certainly the Ministry of Agriculture, Forestry and Fisheries, perceive the national interest quite differently from the way MITI does. MITI and the Fair Trade Commission take different positions on antitrust and industrial policy. Jurisdictional disputes and turf problems are as abundant in Japan as in other national bureaucracies. While MITI has jurisdiction regarding the domestic activities and foreign trade of most manufactures, other ministries have responsibility for certain important sectors: Ministry of Finance for all the financial institutions, Posts and Telecommunications for telecommunications, Welfare for medical equipment and pharmaceuticals, Agriculture for food processing, Transport for civil air transport, shipping, trucking, and taxis, for example. MITI's industrial policy does not and cannot cover all industrial activities.

Government policies that encourage all industries, such as import protection in the 1950s and 1960s, in effect protect none differentially. The main result is simply to give priority to business over households. This is important, because the essence of industrial policy is that it differentiates among industries by providing only certain industries specially large incentives. Recent research by Saxonhouse (1982, 1983, 1985) indicates that the differential impact among industries has probably been substantially less than was earlier believed. This supports an earlier study by Pechman and Kaizuka (1976) on specific tax concessions granted to specific industries; they make the point that such concessions were so widespread, despite being specific to each industry, that the *differential* impact was relatively modest. Japanese industrial policy may have started on a micro basis with specific priorities, and some certainly persisted; but the bandwagon effect became so widespread, especially in trade protection but also in tax concessions, that its effect was akin to macroindustrial policy of helping virtually all industry.

If industrial policy is successful, one might expect an industrial structure quite different from what would result from the operation of purely market forces. A successfully anticipatory industrial policy might in the long run result in the same industrial structure, but at any specific time one would expect supported "winner" industries to be overrepresented and "loser" industries underrepresented. Yet this has not been the case. Japanese industrial structure has been and is very similar to that of other industrial nations when adjustments are made for market size, per capita income level, natural resource endowment, and distance from world markets (Saxonhouse, 1982, 1983, 1985, and his essay in this volume). This is not to say that past Japanese industrial policy has not had substantial effects. But it does indicate that the picture is more complex and less well understood than some would suggest.

The results of MITI's policies in targeting specific industries have been mixed in practice. One can credit the combination of MITI policy, market forces, and the mixture of Japanese business leadership and follow-the-leader business behavior for having created a generally highly competitive market environment in Japan. And there have been industries targeted successfully. However, industrial policy has not been successful in a number of major industries, with consequent high costs to consumers, savers, or taxpayers. The government in the 1950s and 1960s, through the Japan Development Bank, pumped immense amounts of low-cost loans to marginally profitable ocean shipping firms, since private financial institutions refused to lend much. MITI has long targeted the commercial aircraft industry, with no commercial success. It could not prevent excessive domestic entrants into vehicle production for the domestic market, and later was unable to effect merger among competing smaller producers. The fundamental problems of the automobile industry have been masked in the 1980s by the so-called voluntary export restraints to the American market, which in practice significantly raised prices and profits on those sales for all Japanese producers. The greatest MITI failure, however, has been in the way it handled scale and entry in the petroleum refining industry. In order to reduce the large foreign share in Japanese oil refining, MITI promoted the entry—under pressure from a number of business groups each of which wanted a piece of the action—of a large number of too small Japanese refining plants and companies with inadequate capacities to upgrade facilities to optimum scale. The successive oil crises and pressures for trade liberalization since 1973 have made clear the failure and high social cost of the MITI-generated structure of Japan's petroleum refining industry. These mistaken policies and problems have carried over into some petrochemical products as well.

The ultimate test of the success of Japanese industrial policy is whether it led to a significantly more rapid GNP growth rate than would have occurred otherwise. This is at the core of the scholarly debate. Japanese industrial policy in general seems to have anticipated where the market would have taken the industrial structure anyway, though with some major exceptions as just noted. MITI's contribution was to encourage certain industries, which were already growth industries, to develop sooner than they might have otherwise. If so, such an industrial policy may have had some success in accelerating the growth rate. Several recent case studies provide data and insights on the role and effectiveness of Japanese industrial policy in specific industries, including Okimoto, Sugano, and Weinstein (1984), Dore (1983), Borrus, Millstein, and Zysman (1983), Wheeler, Janow, and Pepper (1982), Magaziner and Hout (1980), and U.S. government publications (USITC 1983; USGAO 1982a, 1982b). The problem is that we do not yet have comprehensive, definitive studies that determine conclusively the degree and nature of the effectiveness of Japanese industrial policy, especially for Japan's overall growth performance.

New Policy Needs

Industrial policy in Japan today is in a fundamentally different position from what it was ten to fifteen years ago. Its goals are less clear-cut, more diffuse; there is a new focus on high technology industries, but the ability to identify and pick "winner" products and processes has decreased sharply; and the range and strength of policy instruments have diminished sharply. There have been a number of major forces, but two in particular, at work to bring about this sharply changed environment for high technology industrial policy. First, from about the mid-1970s, depending on the industry, Japan has reached the technology frontier in most civilian goods sectors; it no longer is a follower nation. Having caught up, Japan no longer has the American model for evolving industrial structure. While very specific technologies may be identifiable, "winners" are no longer so obvious; it is considerably more difficult for MITI bureaucrats to pick them. Second, until the early 1970s, protection from imports was used as a major policy instrument to support Japanese manufacturers. Japan, as a major leader in the international economic system, can no longer use trade barriers very effectively to assist high technology industries.

Nonetheless, we should not underestimate the Japanese government's ability to implement a high technology industrial policy, and in ways consonant with present GATT (General Agreement on Tariffs and Trade) rules. The focus of Japanese government attention on high tech industries is a recent phenomenon. Most important, it is a natural consequence of the long-run process of industrialization. Only after Japan had achieved a high level of technological sophistication, capital stock, human skills— "caught up with the West," in the slogan of the 1970s—was it a natural step to move into high tech industries. And this has been predominantly a private sector phenomenon, as firms have developed new products and what are now categorized as entirely new industries. As Dore (1983) has perceptively discussed, in the latter half of the 1970s a consensus began to emerge in Japan which visualized Japan as a producer as well as consumer of technology. This was owing in part to the worldwide tendency to attach greater importance to technological innovation, in part to greater self-confidence within the business, government, and academic technology elite in Japan. The enunciated rationale for government involvement is textbook: very large scale projects, high uncertainty, long lead times, thereby high risk, and social need.

Given a different set of industries, new needs, and the new international environment, the mix of instruments for high tech industrial policy is almost necessarily different from that of one or two decades earlier. Standard protectionist trade policy instruments—tariffs or import quotas— are no longer a feasible way to help high tech industries; U.S. and other foreign governmental pressures are too strong. Those pressures are not limited to trade; equal access to Japanese markets for foreign-owned firms operating in Japan is of comparable importance, as reflected in emphasis on the rule of equal national treatment. Nonetheless, Japanese high tech firms continue to have preferential access to Japanese government procurement. This is enhanced in high tech industries by close linkages between

R&D prototype developmental activities and subsequent equipment purchases, especially in (though not limited to) NTT and telecommunications.

Other essays in this volume provide considerable information on and analysis of Japanese high tech industrial policy, ranging from specific industry studies to overall assessments. Inevitably and desirably, government support to R&D receives major attention, in part because it is the main instrument MITI uses to encourage research in the development of a wide range of fairly specific products. At issue are both the institutional arrangements, notably joint research by major companies typically under government auspices, and government funding of R&D.

Of MITI's 1983 R&D expenditure budget of 2,244 million yen ($955 million), 45 percent was for energy, 28 percent for infrastructure consolidation (including certain MITI labs and the patent system), and 18 percent for high tech projects (Dore 1983, table 2). These are relatively modest amounts of resources spread over a number of projects. Most projects, however, involve substantially larger multiyear commitments. Dore (1983) concludes, in his case study of the twelve projects of the ten-year "next generation base technologies program" begun in 1981 (and making up only 3 percent of MITI's 1983 R&D budget) that almost all the projects were selected well before the commercialization stage, by reasonable criteria, through consultation of young MITI officials with industry and to some extent academic specialists. He argues that the generation of economic rents (that is, the financing of projects private firms would do anyway) is limited because the funding is for contract research with patents going to the government; and that the receipt of contracts strengthened the position of industry researchers in their respective firms, perhaps inducing thereby a larger commitment of firm resources.

Declining Industries

While much attention has been given to Japanese industrial policy for high tech industries, easing the structural adjustment of declining industries may become as important a component of overall Japanese industrial policy as efforts to pick winners. As Japan's comparative advantage continues to evolve—owing to the continuing spread of the industrial revolution to the developing nations, to Japan's own future growth pattern, and to changing world relative prices of energy and other commodities and products—structural adjustment problems will become more severe in Japan, as they have in all advanced industrial nations. While MITI helped the adjustment process in coal mining and cotton textiles in the late 1950s and early 1960s, most of its experience in declining industry programs is very recent, indeed under way at present.

It is more difficult to persuade firms to contract than to expand—to scrap equipment, reduce capacity, rationalize, merge, change business, or go out of business. The policy mix is likely to be different too: more direct subsidies, greater reliance on low interest loans, virtually forced closing of plants and even merger of firms. The record of industrial policy to date in helping declining industries is mixed. The policy package in the early 1980s for shipbuilding was apparently effective; capacity was reduced by one-third without major bankruptcies (Uriu 1984). However, capacity adjustment and reorganization has been slower in aluminum, petrochemicals, electric furnace steel, and other depressed industries. Aluminum production has dropped precipitously, from a capacity of 1.6 million tons to production of 300,000 tons (Samuels 1983). MITI policy simply has not been able to keep up with the dictates of the marketplace, given very high Japanese electricity costs and MITI's inability to halt the surge of imports since 1979.

It is unclear whether industrial policy for declining industries has resulted in a more efficient restructuring of firms and industries, or at less social cost, than simply allowing the marketplace to work. Indeed it is unclear whether MITI policy has anticipated, or simply followed, the adjustment process forced by market conditions. However, viewing the choice as simply that of adjustment via the free market or via MITI is politically naïve. These are powerful industries, with large debts to powerful banks. It may well be that the Japanese government, for the same domestic political reasons as in the United States and all industrial democracies, has to take some kind of ameliorative action. The MITI programs of structural adjustment of declining industries may not be optimal, but they certainly are preferable to such ad hoc measures as direct government subsidies or new protectionist barriers against competitive imports.

There is a certain irony that many structurally depressed industries in Japan today are those that two decades ago were targeted as "winners" or at least as basic industries. Part is because MITI officials, like private and public policy makers everywhere, did not anticipate the energy crisis and fivefold rise in relative prices of energy in the 1970s. However, part is the consequence of earlier errors in selecting targets; it is unlikely that dynamic comparative advantage would change so rapidly as to shift an industry from winner to loser category in only two decades.

Implications for the United States

What is the relevance of Japanese industrial policy for American economic policy? There are implications for two major policy areas: U.S. trade policy and U.S. industrial policy. In each there are four policy options: to take no specific action; to seek Japanese reform; to emulate; to counteract its effects on comparable U.S. industries.

Japanese industrial targeting has come to figure prominently in the current American debate on trade policy, being labeled by some as an unfair trade practice injurious to the American industry whose Japanese counterpart is receiving special Japanese government support. U.S. trade law permits countervailing action where Japanese and other imports are either subsidized or dumped and thereby cause injury to the domestic industry, or where the amount and rate of growth of imports is so large as to be the main cause of injury to the domestic industry. U.S. multilateral and bilateral trade negotiations with Japan also aim to eliminate Japanese import restrictions that protect targeted Japanese industries from competition from the United States in the Japanese market. On the whole, the implications of Japanese targeting for export competitiveness to the American market have generated more vociferous concern, though some have voiced concern over limited access to specific Japanese markets as a consequence of industrial targeting even though the particular instruments do no fall within the normal trade policy domain.

An extreme view is that Japanese industrial targeting is per se an unfair trade practice because it confers unfair degrees of competitiveness on Japanese firms. Under existing American and GATT law only current government subsidies are regarded as an unfair practice. Japanese exports essentially are not subsidized at all, so this offers no remedy for American import-competing industries. The injury test under Section 301 of the Trade Act of 1974 is sufficiently strong that few American industries have been able to avail themselves of it.

The basic problem is what has been termed "original sin": the specific industry exporting to the United States no longer receives targeted Japanese government support, but it did earlier in its development. Thereby, industrial policy is unfair because of the future advantages it creates for export competitiveness. To counteract these effects of (Japanese) industrial policy, various legislation has been introduced before Congress—reciprocity bills, bills to strengthen Section 301, and bills to strengthen dumping and countervailing duty laws (Suomela 1983). In general the main intent and impact of these legislative proposals is, under the guise of "unfairness," to raise protectionist barriers against imports. Implicitly or explicitly the legislation is particularly aimed at imports from Japan.

Governmental support of major industries in most industrial nations has been almost inevitable. On the one hand, new high technology industries—such as aircraft, computers, and semiconductors in the United States—received their initial impetus and support from government because of their military-strategic significance. On the other hand, as is stressed by Murakami in this volume, in the long-run process of the international spread of the industrial revolution virtually every country has been a follower in most industries and accordingly has provided its industrial infants protection of one sort or another.

There are two difficulties with the original sin position. First, since almost all major industries in all countries received special government support at some stage of their development, they are all guilty of original sin. If the United States were to apply the original sin argument to Japanese industrial policy, Japan could make a similar case against American industries. This is particularly true of high tech industries, where government-funded R&D and procurement has been so important (Nelson 1984, and Eads and Nelson in this volume).

Second, application of the original sin argument by the United States against Japan opens a Pandora's box with profound implications for the functioning and even the structure of the international economic system. It would provide a rationale for West European nations to restrict many American exports, for the United States to restrict imports from many newly industrializing, developing economies—indeed for virtually every country to restrict imports from every other. Perhaps an international agreement could be negotiated through GATT to set a statute of limitations on original sin, but that seems unrealistic and unlikely.

In sum, the policy approach of trying to counteract the perceived effects of Japanese industrial policy by new trade-restrictive countervailing measures is not in American national interest. It is protectionist; and it potentially could seriously damage the international economic system.

Reform of current Japanese industrial policy may be a more sensible and viable American trade policy objective. It is unrealistic to expect Japan to eschew completely industrial policy in any of its three target areas: high technology, energy, and structurally depressed industries. Indeed, in a rather unthought-out, decentralized, nonpackaged way the United States pursues (industrial) policies to help firms in the same three areas. The reality is that all advanced industrial nations—Japan, the United States, Western Europe—pursue high tech industrial policies, through R&D support, government procurement, regulatory mechanisms, and outright subsidies. Each government tries to succor its own, even within a market context. Nonetheless, even though there are analytical arguments suggesting that Japanese and other foreign industrial policy (targeting) can harm the U.S. economy, Krugman (1984) persuasively argues that as an empirical matter none of these arguments holds up.

The aim of U.S. efforts to reform Japanese industrial policy is, and should be, to achieve free trade flows, equal market access, and equal national treatment for competitive American firms in Japan—in both high tech and declining industries. Beyond that, national policies supporting the development of high tech industries, the presumed future winners, does

not contravene the rules of the international economic system—so long
as support is not explicitly antitrade. The problem of course is that all
targeted support is implicitly biased against imports or towards exports
in the favored industry, and conversely in those industries not receiving
such special benefits. Favored industries benefit; those not favored are
hurt; the macro implications are not clear. Given the close intertwining
of military and economic strategic objectives in government high tech policies, it is unlikely that a better set of international trade rules can be devised
and adopted.

Proponents of an American industrial policy à la Japan seem to intend
more of an emulation of perceived Japanese success than a fight-fire-with-
fire approach counteracting a Japanese industrial policy which may not
be desirable but is inevitable. Such an American industrial policy involves
far more than a few selected institutional changes such as easing antitrust
enforcement provisions and providing an environment for corporate joint
research activities (Baxter 1983). As the earlier discussion of the concept
of industrial policy indicates, an American industrial policy would provide preferential support to selected civilian industries through a comprehensive set of policy instruments that would enhance their market
competitiveness. On the whole the "lessons" of Japanese industrial policy
for any such American industrial policy should be cautionary.

First, American policy makers should beware of facile generalizations
and stereotypes about the nature and effectiveness of Japanese industrial
policy, and on the whole should be skeptical of that experience. The evidence is far from complete. There were many factors that contributed to
Japan's two decades of superfast growth up to 1973 and its still-good economic performance of the past decade relative to the United States and
Western Europe. In my judgment industry-specific industrial policy has
had a moderately useful, but not the central, role in Japan's economic
success; it has made less of a policy contribution than macro industrial
policy or aggregate demand policy.

Second, it is even less clear whether Japanese-style industrial policy in
its historical or especially in its current manifestations is appropriate for
the United States. In what ways and to what extent can an industrial policy
system be incorporated into the ideology of American economic policy
and help achieve its basic goals, and fit into the existing panoply of policy
instruments, institutional arrangements, and governmental administrative
structure? The answers are not at all obvious.

Third, what I have termed macro industrial policy has made a significant contribution to Japanese growth: general tax incentives to business
to invest productively and to engage in R&D, and to households to save;
and the development of a highly effective public education system. Macro
industrial policy, like industry-specific policy, can and should rely on the

marketplace. Thus the risks, costs, and inability to appropriate fully the benefits of R&D mean government funding of R&D can be desirable, in both Japan and the United States. One important historical reason for Japanese industrial policy was the shortage of capital and an inadequate framework of financial institutions to allocate capital well. The United States has very well developed financial markets, and so has less need of industrial policy. On the other hand, in certain respects Japanese labor markets and institutions work better than their American counterparts, notably in on-the-job training and maintenance of high rates of employment. Certainly any American industrial policy should take into account manpower needs and conditions, but in a macro rather than a micro context.

Fourth, it is easier for a nation to pick potential future winner industries when it is in a follower position. It can study the industrial structure of more advanced nations to learn its potential future competitiveness. The United States, however, is at the technological frontiers; no other countries provide a model of future industrial structure. It is very unlikely that American government bureaucrats, scholars, or other experts can judge better than the market-place what the specific products and industries of the future will be. More general policies—support of basic R&D, improvement of the educational system, general incentives for investment and saving—will be more effective in enhancing sustained economic growth than special governmental support of specific new industries.

Fifth, recent Japanese and American experience suggest that once a country is at the technological frontiers, import restrictions may not be an efficient instrument of industrial policy either for high tech industries or for solving the structural problems of mature industries in trouble. Moreover, protectionism is not an appropriate policy for advanced industrial nations; it is destructive of the generally beneficial international economic system so carefully crafted and nourished since 1945. As the preceding discussion and the other essays in this volume indicate, Japan does have a high tech industrial policy, or at least a set of policy instruments used to promote the growth of high tech industries. But the resources allocated are modest and their effectiveness not yet clear. The emphasis nonetheless is on civilian-goods industries and cost competitiveness. U.S. high tech industries also have flourished and benefited from much the same set of government incentives as their Japanese counterparts, although military-strategic needs have been at the forefront, with only partial spillover to civilian production.

Sixth, perhaps the most important lessons from Japanese industrial policy are how to deal most effectively with important industries in trouble and needing structural adjustments. The reality of the political economy of any democratic industrial nation, including the United States and

Japan, is that the political and social costs of adjustment in major industries are too great to allow a government to rely solely and simply on the market mechanism. Whether consumers and taxpayers and economists like it or not, the government is likely to take some steps to help American textiles and steel and automobiles, and indeed has done so. American policy solutions have tended to be ad hoc, and import restrictive. They have not really provided incentives for management and labor to bring about the changes needed in those industries if they are to be efficient, and cost and price competitive. Japanese industrial policy for structurally depressed industries may provide a better second-best solution than the second-best solutions the United States has been using thus far. This is probably where the best case can be made for an American industrial policy: to have a coherent, efficient program of adjustment for major industries in difficulty. The postwar evidence is they will receive help anyway, mainly in the form of protection from imports, through the operation of interest group politics in the American political system.

Seventh, if the United States should decide to employ industrial policy to achieve important economic objectives, it can learn from the Japanese methods of implementation. Policy should be long-range, consistent, and promarket (competition-promoting), and mobilize a package of mutually supportive policy instruments. The criterion of effectiveness should be economic efficiency, as measured by cost and price competitiveness in world, not just United States, markets. And since the benefits of industrial policy in the first instance accrue to the owners, managers, and workers of those industries targeted for preferential treatment while the costs are borne by taxpayers or consumers, then the beneficiaries should be required to meet performance goals in order to justify the support received.

Finally, one can regard Japanese industrial policy as reflective and symbolic of a host of specific institutional differences between the Japanese and American capitalist systems. This raises broader, more speculative, and more important issues worthy of a separate study. Are the systems fundamentally different? If so, what needs to be done about it? These are both empirical and conceptual questions, which require an agreed definition not only of the essence of capitalism but on its acceptable or unacceptable institutional forms. In my view, Japanese capitalism is not fundamentally different from Western capitalism, though it is more akin to continental European than the Anglo-American cases. All capitalist economies share fundamental similarities. In comparisons of specific U.S. and Japanese institutional arrangements there is the danger that one country will be depicted as being far out on the spectrum. All nationalities tend to be xenophobic (or history-culture bound): their own institutions, despite their imperfections, are regarded as the norm—if not better than those anywhere else.

But suppose Japanese capitalism is fundamentally different. What are the policy options for the United States? One option is to adopt the Japanese system more or less in toto. Hardly anyone seriously considers that as desirable, much less feasible. A second option is to demand that Japan change its system so that it becomes just like that of the United States (the proposal of Secretary of Commerce Baldridge). This is equally infeasible—and probably equally undesirable. A third option is to exclude Japan from the international economic system by establishing special rules (local content, reciprocity, etc.) for economic transactions with Japan. This is a perverse and dangerous approach: Japan is just too large and it could result in the dangerous formation of discriminatory regional blocs. It would simply be an excuse for American protectionism. Rather, the issue is how better to integrate the Japanese economy into the world economic system.

The last option—I feel the only real option—is to have a general mechanism of adjustment that takes into account differences among economies in institutions and in industrial and other economic policies as well as in factor endowments. The world does have such a mechanism: the multilateral exchange rate system. The flexible exchange rate system makes it possible for economies to adjust to institutional as well as other changes at home or abroad. With this option working, the others are not necessary. The essential feature is not whether exchange rates are fixed or fluctuating, but whether the system is truly open, multilateral, freely operating, and based on the free flow of goods, services, and capital. In either system, or variants thereof, a country has to shape domestic macroeconomic policies—on both the supply and demand side—in light of the realities of economic interdependence as reflected in balance of payments and exchange rate relationships. In macrosystemic terms the case has yet to be made that it matters economically whether one country pursues an industrial policy or not.

REFERENCES

Baxter, William F. 1983. "Antitrust Law and the Stimulation of Technological Invention and Innovation." Presented to the Preparatory Conference on Government Organization and Operation and Role of the Government in the Economy, University of San Diego, July 19–21.
Borrus, Michael, James E. Millstein, and John Zysman. 1983. *Responses to the Japanese Challenge in High Technology: Innovation, Maturity, and the U.S.-Japanese Competition in Microelectronics*. Berkeley: Roundtable on International Economy.
Doane, Donna Lisa. 1984. "Two Essays on Technological Innovation: Innovation and Economic Stagnation, and Interfirm Cooperation for Innovation in Japan." Ph.D. dissertation, Yale University.

Dore, Ronald. 1983. *A Case Study of Technology Forecasting in Japan: The Next Generation Base Technologies Development Programme.* London: Technology Change Centre.

Johnson, Chalmers. 1982. *MITI and the Japanese Miracle: The Growth of Industrial Policy, 1925–1975.* Stanford: Stanford University Press.

Johnson, Chalmers. 1983. "American Underestimation of Japanese Industrial Policy." Speech at the Japan Society, New York, December 15, 1983, reported in its *Business Luncheon Notes.*

Johnson, Chalmers, ed. 1984. *The Industrial Policy Debate.* San Francisco: ICS Press.

Krugman, Paul R. 1984. "The U.S. Response to Foreign Industrial Targeting." *Brookings Papers on Economic Activity* 1:77–121.

Lincoln, Edward J. 1984. *Japan's Industrial Policies.* Washington: Japan Economic Institute of America.

Magaziner, Ira C., and Thomas M. Hout. 1980. *Japanese Industrial Policy.* Berkeley: Institute of International Studies, University of California.

Nelson, Richard R. 1984. "Policies in Support of High Technology Industries." ISPS Working Paper 1011, Yale University.

Okimoto, Daniel I., ed. 1982. *Japan's Economy: Coping with Change in the International Environment.* Boulder, Colo.: Westview Press.

Okimoto, Daniel I., Takuo Sugano, and Franklin B. Weinstein, eds. 1984. *Competitive Edge: The Semiconductor Industry in the U.S. and Japan.* Stanford: Stanford University Press.

Patrick, Hugh, and Henry Rosovsky. 1976. "Japan's Economic Performance: An Overview." In Hugh Patrick and Henry Rosovsky, eds., *Asia's New Giant: How the Japanese Economy Works,* pp. 1–61. Washington, D.C.: Brookings Institution.

Pechman, Joseph A., and Keimei Kaizuka. 1976. "Taxation." In Hugh Patrick and Henry Rosovsky, eds., *Asia's New Giant: How the Japanese Economy Works,* pp. 317–82. Washington, D.C.: Brookings Institution.

Samuels, Richard. 1983. "The Industrial Restructuring of the Japanese Aluminum Industry." *Pacific Affairs* 56(3):495–509.

Saxonhouse, Gary. 1982. "Evolving Comparative Advantage and Japan's Imports of Manufactures." In Kozo Yamamura, ed., *Policy and Trade Issues of the Japanese Economy,* pp. 239–69. Seattle: University of Washington Press.

Saxonhouse, Gary. 1983. "The Micro- and Macroeconomics of Foreign Sales to Japan." In William Cline, ed., *Trade Policies in the 1980s,* pp. 259–304. Cambridge: MIT Press.

Saxonhouse, Gary. 1984. "Service in the Japanese Economy." In Robert P. Inman, ed., *Managing the Service Economy: Prospects and Problems,* pp. 53–83. Cambridge: Cambridge University Press.

Suomela, John W. 1983. "Can Our Trade Laws Deal with Japanese Industrial Targeting?" Paper presented to ASSA meetings, December.

Trezise, Philip H., with the collaboration of Yukio Suzuki. 1976. "Politics, Government, and Economic Growth in Japan." In Hugh Patrick and Henry Rosovsky, eds., *Asia's New Giant: How the Japanese Economy Works,* pp. 753–811. Washington: Brookings Institution.

Trezise, Philip H. 1983a. "Industrial Policy in Japan." Prepared statement before the U.S. Congress, Joint Economic Committee, July 13. In *Industrial Policy, Economic Growth and the Competitiveness of U.S. Industry,* Vol. 1, pt. 2, pp. 71–90. Washington, D.C.: Government Printing Office.

Trezise, Philip H. 1983b. "Industrial Policy Is Not the Major Reason for Japan's Success." *Brookings Review* 1(3):13–18.

U.S. General Accounting Office. 1982a. *Industrial Policy: Japan's Flexible Approach.* Washington, D.C.: GAO/ID-82-32.

U.S. General Accounting Office. 1982b. *Industrial Policy: Case Studies in the Japanese Experience.* Washington, D.C.: GAO/ID-83-11.

United States International Trade Commission. 1983. *Foreign Industrial Targeting and Its Effects on U.S. Industries, Phase I: Japan.* USITC Publication 1437. Washington, D.C.: Government Printing Office.

Uriu, Robert M. 1984. "The Declining Industries in Japan: Adjustment and Reallocation." *Journal of International Affairs* 38:99–111.

Wheeler, Jimmy, Merit E. Janow, and Thomas Pepper. 1982. *Japanese Industrial Development Policies in the 1980s: Implications for U.S. Trade and Investment.* Croton-on-Hudson: Hudson Institute.

Yamamura, Kozo. 1967. *Economic Policy in Postwar Japan: Growth Versus Economic Democracy.* Berkeley: University of California Press.

Yamamura, Kozo. 1982. "Success That Soured: Administrative Guidance and Cartels in Japan." In Kozo Yamamura, ed., *Policy and Trade Issues of the Japanese Economy: American and Japanese Perspectives,* pp. 77–112. Seattle: University of Washington Press.

Chapter 2

Regime Characteristics of Japanese Industrial Policy

Daniel I. Okimoto

Until the late 1970s, few Japanese companies were strong enough to challenge America's commercial and technological dominance in the information industries. The computer, semiconductor, and information processing industries were born in the United States. Almost all the breakthrough technologies and revolutionary new products—the transistor, integrated circuit, microprocessor, vacuum tube computer, super-, mini-, and microcomputers, fiber optics, office automation equipment, and basic software programs—bear the label "Invented in America." Over the postwar years, researchers at Bell Laboratories, Fairchild, and Intel have advanced state-of-the-art technology while U.S. giants like IBM have set the pace for commercial developments around the world.

American supremacy is no longer uncontested. As in the case of the old-line manufacturing sectors, Japanese corporations have come from far behind—in a surprisingly short time—to catch up with American frontrunners. In such product lines as telephones, video terminals, and printers the Japanese have once again demonstrated their virtuosity in high-quality manufacturing. In such sophisticated technologies as very large scale integrated circuit (VLSI) memory chips and fiber optics, Japanese companies have succeeded in capturing large segments of world markets, primarily on the strength of low prices and high reliability. And notwithstanding stereotypes about Japanese shortcomings in truly innovative research, the Japanese seem to be making dramatic strides in such cutting-edge areas as artificial intelligence, knowledge-based expert systems, and the Fifth Generation computer (Feigenbaum and McCorduck 1983). The speed with which the Japanese have closed the gap has been so impressive as to deprive American frontrunners of the false sense of comfort that came with their long period of technological and commercial hegemony and the dubious stereotypes about Japan's inability to innovate.

Japan's rapid advance in high technology is commonly attributed to the government's capacity to "target" certain "strategic" industries with high growth potential. In the information industries specifically, MITI is often given prime credit for devising industrial policies that nurtured this sector from infancy to the threshold of maturity. Foreign competitors have criticized MITI's role as midwife because they object to the "unfair" industrial policy measures that, from their point of view, have permitted Japan's information industries to catch up so quickly. I have argued elsewhere that the role of industrial policy in the development of Japan's semiconductor industry—while unquestionably important and in some areas indispensable—tends to be overrated (Okimoto 1984a). It is the dynamism of the interplay between public and private sectors that has thrust the semiconductor industry to the forefront.

This essay looks at the range of industrial policy instruments used by MITI to promote Japan's information industries; these policy instruments are compared with what is done elsewhere in the world, especially in the United States. Industrial policy for high technology can be grouped into three broad categories: technology push, other supply-side measures, and demand pull. The main thrust of technology push is examined in terms of the organization of national research projects and NTT-related R&D. Other supply-side measures are taken up: research subsidies, taxes, and antitrust and administrative guidance. Then demand-pull policies are analyzed, and some conclusions are drawn and a few implications of Japan's shift from smokestack to high technology are explored.

Included under the category "information industries" are microelectronics, computers, information processing, and telecommunications—the largest and, to date at least, most successful sector of Japanese high technology. Because these industries differ from those of the smokestack sectors, where Japan has also achieved world renown, the substance of industrial policy has had to be carefully tailored to suit the functional needs of the information industries. (The characteristics of information industries differ in some respects from those of other high technology endeavors, such as aircraft and biotechnology. There are also differences within the information industries between telecommunications and information processing.) And as these industries have developed, the particular mix of policy instruments have had to be altered. This suggests that in order to assess the significance of what MITI has done to expedite the development of the information industries, we must first have some sense of the distinctive characteristics and functional needs of the information industries.

Functional Requisites

Although the information industries are diverse, there are certain characteristics which MITI has had to keep in mind in tailoring industrial policies that fit their particular needs and circumstances (for a fuller analysis, see Okimoto 1983). The functional requirements include:

For private corporations
   Staying abreast of swiftly changing technology
   Sustaining high rates of investments in R&D
   Innovating in order to stay competitive, bartering for other technol-
      ogy, and being quick to enter new product markets
   Moving down steep learning curves
   Expanding the volume of production and sales, thereby lowering per
      unit costs
   Recouping up-front R&D investments through rapid commercializa-
      tion of products
   Stressing process technology, product reliability, and after-service
   Exporting actively and taking a global view of markets
   Meeting climbing levels of capital intensity
   Overcoming conservative, risk-averse strategies and mobilizing to
      undertake risky and uncertain projects
   Coping with relatively brief product life cycles

For the government and industrial policy
   Coming from behind and catching up with foreign frontrunners
   Staving off the threat of being overwhelmed by such foreign Goliaths
      as IBM and AT&T
   Compensating for deficiencies in the market mechanism that lead to
      neglect of basic research
   Offsetting the high uncertainties, risks, and costs associated with R&D
   Ensuring that adequate supplies of capital are allocated to the infor-
      mation industry
   Providing optimal tax provisions and incentives
   Avoiding needlessly wasteful duplication of national R&D efforts
   Achieving research economies of scale
   Creating a climate conducive to vigorous market competition
   Facilitating the diffusion of technology
   Coming up with ways of generating greater domestic demand
   Promoting related and end-user industries
   Handling international trade and investment issues
   Taking care of all relevant legal matters (e.g., patent protection,
      antitrust)
   Providing for the education of technological manpower

In addition to such sector-specific characteristics, Japanese industrial
policy has had to take account of peculiarities in Japan's private sector
as well, such as: underdeveloped capital markets; lack of a strong venture capital market; lack of a rich tradition of innovation in new product
lines by small, independent companies comparable to the merchant semiconductor houses in the United States; an industrial system that has been

oriented to latecomer catch-up; dominance of large, diversified, vertically integrated corporations; high debt-to-equity ratios for many of these corporations; a pronounced tendency for Japanese firms to underinvest in basic R&D; second-rate university-based research; an industrial and educational system that has not been geared to concentrate on state-of-the-art innovation; and the absence of a well-developed system of military-related R&D and procurements.

The functional requisites of Japanese industrial policy can easily be extrapolated by putting together the lists of sector-specific and private sector characteristics. For MITI, promoting the information industries has involved several tasks. First, because of the crucial importance of technological innovation, particularly in light of pronounced learning curve effects, MITI has had to place special emphasis on technology-push policies (Wakasugi 1984). Cultivating innovation has been especially urgent because Japan's industrial system has been geared to latecomer catch-up, with Japanese companies lagging behind in a number of advanced areas of technology. Second, and closely related, has been the need to reduce the costs and risks of R&D investments in order to induce private corporations to allocate adequate capital for important R&D projects. Since reliance on private sector incentives alone has not been sufficient, MITI has had to find ways of compensating for market shortcomings by sponsoring basic research.

Given the underdevelopment of capital markets, and the heavy reliance of Japanese corporations on bank loans, moreover, the government has felt compelled to find ways not only of channeling funds to priority sectors but also of easing the downside risks of debt financing. Lacking the wherewithal for massive government purchases, MITI has had few viable alternatives to the adoption of an industrial policy designed to strengthen supply-side measures. Of course, MITI has exploited—with considerable ingenuity—most of the indirect ways of boosting demand, the functional equivalents of assured procurements; but in the absence of massive military demand, MITI has had to concentrate on supply-side measures, almost by default.

While, as demonstrated in the United States, there are advantages to R&D systems geared to national security, particularly in the area of generating breakthrough technologies and new product lines, Japan has not suffered much from MITI's lack of purchasing power. Indeed, concentrating on supply-side factors has probably worked out for the best. The history of industrial policy in the United States and Europe indicates that serious distortions occur when industrial policy is used as a substitute, not as a supplement for, basic market forces (see Price 1981, pp. 17–42, 84–118; Wachter and Wachter 1983, especially the chapter by Eads). Innovativeness and commercial dynamism seem to flourish where the discipline of market competition is most vigorous. From MITI's perspective, therefore, the central task of industrial policy for high technology has been to supplement and enhance market forces, thereby achieving important industrial goals and advancing national interests, without introducing political rigidities or economic inefficiencies.

A workable industrial policy for high technology thus seems to call for just the right blend of market dynamism and organizational direction, laissez-faire capitalism and state intervention, supply-side incentives and demand-side support. Although the instruments used must not destroy the vitality of the market mechanism, MITI officials believe they cannot simply sit back and let the market take its course—not when Japan lags behind other countries, or when market outcomes might not be optimal from the standpoint of Japanese national interests. Organizational direction is necessary in Japan because of the nature of the country's complex and finely meshed industrial system—a system that functions on the basis of competition and cooperation, market and hierarchy, public and private sector interpenetration, government-business interdependence, and consensus. The state is, in some senses, the integrative mechanism that keeps the whole system functioning as a comparatively cohesive whole. For Japanese industrial policy to be effective, therefore, MITI must steer the information industries in the right direction by articulating a long-term vision, identifying clearly defined and feasible goals, forging a binding consensus, and mobilizing resources to realize the vision set forth. In short, the tasks that befall MITI are demanding and difficult, and we shall see what instruments of industrial policy have been used to fulfill the functional requisites of the information industries.

Japan's Political Economy: Regime Characteristics

Whether the instruments of industrial policy can be used to meet the functional requisites of specific sectors at specific stages of their development depends decisively on the structure of a country's political economy. The institutional structure determines how effective industrial policy is in at least three respects: (1) by expanding or contracting the range of industrial policy measures realistically available, (2) by determining which specific policy instruments are selected for use from the range of possibilities, and (3) by structuring the processes by which industrial policy is implemented. Abstract goals are sorted out as they pass through the pulling and hauling of the political system; those that make it through are tempered by political realities, compromised by competing public policy objectives, and often distorted by interest group pressures.

A permeable institutional structure, lacking centralized power for orderly, interest aggregation, is apt to limit the range of industrial policy instruments available because the government will be under intense political pressure to adopt policies that cater to the narrow, short-term interests of organized interest groups. It will probably not have the latitude to select policy options considered optimal from long-term economic or national interests.

No industrial policy, regardless of how brilliantly conceived, stands much chance of succeeding if the politico-economic system within which it is administered is disorganized. The effectiveness of industrial policy hinges more on the framework of political institutions within each country than on its ideological underpinnings (Katzenstein 1985). The inventory of industrial policy instruments is fairly standard. National differences arise from the choice of specific policies, their particular mix, and manner of implementation. The variations are explained largely by institutional factors.

I have argued elsewhere that the reason industrial policy has worked better in Japan than practically anywhere else is its unique combination of effective political institutions and a resilient private sector characterized by the commingling of market and organizational elements (Okimoto, forthcoming). In the political domain, a number of institutions stand out as facilitating the administration of industrial policy. Japan has a long tradition of competent bureaucratic administration, and MITI, the agency in charge of industrial policy for most manufacturing sectors, has been one of the most influential ministries in the country (for the best and most comprehensive treatment of MITI, see Johnson 1982). MITI's effectiveness stems from a variety of factors, including the superior quality of its higher civil servants, its internal organization, its large corps of ex-officials in key private sector positions, and the unusually broad scope of its jurisdictional authority.

MITI's ability to intervene effectively in the economy through the vehicle of industrial policy has also been greatly facilitated by the state's extensive regulatory control over financial institutions. John Zysman argues that the nature of a country's financial system holds the key to its capacity to administer industrial policy (Zysman 1983, pp. 55–95). In countries with mature capital markets, such as the United States and United Kingdom, the allocation of capital through the impersonal, decentralized market limits the state's capacity to implement industrial policy. By contrast, in countries where capital markets are less developed and where banks play a more prominent role, such as Japan and France, the state is in a much better position to extend a visible and vigorous hand in the functioning of the industrial economy. Owing to their heavy reliance on bank borrowing, Japanese and French corporations tend to be more dependent on, and susceptible to, state intervention than their counterparts in capital market systems. Highly levered companies look to the state to provide not only preferential loans and R&D subsidies but also a whole range of other supportive policies, including quick and effective countercyclical measures, stable interest rates, and trade assistance. By the very nature of the financial system, therefore, the structure of government-business relations is much closer in Japan and France than in the United States and United Kingdom. The state has more levers and broader leeway to project its power.

In systems where private enterprise has less autonomy to keep the state at arm's distance, the lines of demarcation between private and public sectors and between state and society are harder to keep distinct. The situation is conducive to the state's projection of power. In Japan, MITI's capacity to administer industrial policy is greatly facilitated by the vast and amorphous network of formal and informal intermediate organizations that lie in what I call the "intermediate zone" between state and private enterprise (Okimoto, forthcoming). Falling into the former category are public corporations such as Nippon Telegraph and Telephone (NTT), quasi-governmental organizations in key functional areas of the economy (Johnson 1978, pp. 25–60); special nonprofit entities like the Information Technology Promotion Agency, the organizational umbrella for important projects in the area of information processing; and mixed public-private undertakings like the Japan Electronic Computer Corporation (JECC), which played a crucial role in assisting Japanese computer companies establish a firm foothold in the computer leasing business through favorable financing (Imai et al. 1982, pp. 131–34). Informal intermediate organizations—those not requiring special legal dispensation—include industrial associations, business federations, MITI advisory councils, Diet member caucuses, and countless study groups, linking MITI officials with leaders from industry, banking, the legislative branch, the mass media, labor, and academics—the core centers of power in Japan.

These intermediate organizations, which extend the tentacles of state throughout the private sector, perform a variety of vital functions in Japan's economy, operating as regulated natural monopolies, raising revenues, making developmental investments, building social overhead infrastructure, channeling funds for industrial targeting, redistributing income to the less efficient sectors, gathering and circulating information, organizing national projects, planning for regional development, promoting particular industries and technologies, serving as forums for informal deliberations, forging consensus, and aggregating intraindustry and interindustry interests. From the standpoint of implementing industrial policy, the functions they perform are absolutely indispensible. National research projects, for example, would be hard to organize were it not for cooperative research associations.

In addition to the cluster of intermediate organizations, and equally critical from a functional point of view, is the maze of informal personal relationships connecting MITI officials with leaders from industry, industrial associations, the Liberal Democratic Party (LDP), and colleagues from other ministries. The networks of personal relationships, which are especially dense in Japan because of the social homogeneity, educational hierarchy, and concentration of political and economic activities in Tokyo, grow out of functional and ascriptive factors. Not only do they serve as vehicles for heavy information transmission; they also provide MITI officials and industry leaders opportunities to sit down over dinner and sake to consolidate close relations and engage in painstaking rounds of *nemawashi*, informal consultations preceding formal policy decisions. For societies like Japan's which function on the basis of concensual decision making, the role of human networks (*jimmyaku*) can scarcely be overstated. By providing a means of transcending the boundaries of formal organizations, such networks make the bureaucratic state, and government-business interactions, highly adaptable to fast-changing circumstances.

None of the political institutions mentioned so far—the superior quality of higher civil servants, regulatory control over the financial system, intermediate organizations, or personal relationships—can be considered unique to Japan, even though there may be differences in degree and form. England and France also have proud traditions of bureaucratic governance, with capable officials recruited from elite educational institutions. France has a similar financial system. The United States and Germany rely on intermediate organizations and elite networks (though admittedly not quite as extensively). Thus such institutions ought to be considered necessary but not sufficient explanations of effective industrial policy. What, in the political domain, sets Japan apart?

Of the unique factors, the most important by far is the long, unbroken dominance of the Liberal Democratic Party over the Diet since 1947. Unabashedly pro-business in orientation, the LDP has been consistent in its support of economic growth. As a consequence, government policies in postwar Japan have not careened or taken sharp U-turns, as they have in the United States and most countries in Western Europe where there have been frequent turnovers in power. Japanese firms have had the luxury—experienced almost nowhere else—of operating in a highly predictable and favorable business environment. This has made a difference in the capacity of Japanese corporations to engage in strategic planning.

The LDP's long rule has also made bureaucratic-legislative-industrial interactions closer, simpler, and more effective. In something approaching a de facto division of labor, the LDP has permitted MITI extraordinary leeway to oversee the operation of Japan's industrial economy, even though the constitution invests authority unambiguously within the Diet (which the LDP controls). The LDP is willing to grant MITI such autonomy not just because of MITI's impressive postwar track record—which has contributed to the consolidation of the LDP's own base of power—

but also because the imperatives of electoral politics, in combination with the structure of bureaucratic power, have had the effect (so far) of causing the LDP to focus more of its attention on the nonmanufacturing, labor-intensive sectors, like agriculture.

Thanks to its unusual degree of freedom from political interference, MITI has been able to implement what can be considered a nonpartisan, depoliticized industrial policy of almost pristine conceptual purity, compared with that in the United States and United Kingdom. MITI and industry can forge a consensus, shaping the content of industrial policy, and once that consensus is forged, it is very difficult for the LDP to change it. The LDP's control over the Diet thus means that Japanese industrial policy is consensually arrived at, nonpoliticized, and stable, the product of close consultations between MITI and industry.

The tasks that fall to Japanese industrial policy have also been simplified by the comparative weakness of national labor unions. One reason corporatism has not emerged in postwar Japan, while it has in Western Europe, is because of organized labor's relatively weak national voice. As is well known, labor is organized into company-based, enterprise unions in Japan; national federations, loosely composed of company units, have lacked the kind of solidarity that seems to develop more readily from horizontal craft unions.

Among the major industrial states, Japanese labor unions would have to be considered politically the weakest. In terms of national power, they cannot be compared with organized labor in the United Kingdom, Italy, or West Germany. While Japanese workers have won larger increases in real income than workers in many other countries—thanks to the country's record-setting growth rates from 1952 to 1972—the capacity of organized labor to shape economic or industrial policies is limited, to say nothing of its ability to mobilize votes, tip the scales of party alignments, or have its interests and views accurately represented by a closely aligned, socialist or labor party in power. Not having to deal with labor intransigence has made it easier for MITI and industry to reach consensus; however, it is hardly surprising that the substance of Japanese industrial policy, reflecting that consensus, has had a discernible bias in favor of producer interests.

Japan's political economy is also unusual, when compared with government-business relations in the United States, in the imperfect but surprising convergence of state and industrial interests. Japan probably comes closer than any other major state to embodying Charles L. Schultze's ideal of relying on private sector incentives to achieve collective interests and national goals. Government "intervention often fails," writes Schultze, "not because it relies unnecessarily on regulation or other command-and-control devices, but because in other ways it ignores the

role of properly structured economic incentives for achieving social goals"
(Schultze 1977, p. 63). Japan is able to reconcile private and public interests
and capitalize on the dynamism of the private sector because MITI and
industry make a concerted effort to meet partway. MITI sees the promotion of business interests as benefiting the nation; private corporations
are willing to make allowances for collective interests. In consequence,
MITI and industry are able to avoid the adversarial confrontations that
strain government-business ties in the United States and subvert the
administration of industrial policy.

Beyond the regime characteristics of the ruling conservative coalition
and the relationship between the bureaucracies and majority party, Japan's
political economy differs from those in the West in that the nature of Japanese society seems to require centralized coordination on the part of the
state. Nakane Chie characterizes Japan as a "frame" society, composed
of numerous vertically organized groups competing vigorously against each
other, with only weak horizontal links holding society together: "These
characteristics of Japanese society assist the development of the state political organization. Competing clusters, in view of the difficulty of reaching agreement or consensus between clusters, have a diminished authority
in dealings with the state administration. Competition and hostile relations between the civil powers facilitate the acceptance of state power and,
in that group is organized vertically, once the state's administrative
authority is accepted, it can be transmitted without obstruction down the
vertical line of a group's internal organization." (Nakane 1970, p. 102).

Nakane understates the strength and pervasiveness of horizontal ties
in Japan, but she does not exaggerate the pivotal importance of the state's
role. To counteract the pull of centrifugal forces, political authority is
needed to provide overall coordination and horizontal cohesion. Consensus, or at least the norms of consensual procedures, offers the most
effective means of keeping intergroup rivalries from pulling society apart;
this is evident not only in Japan but in socially fragmented countries like
the Netherlands, as Arend Lijpart has pointed out (1977, pp. 25-52). Since
consensus cannot be easily reached by rivalrous private groups, some central authority—the state—must serve the critical role of coordinating consensus, mediating conflict, encouraging healthy competition but trying to
steer groups away from following hostile strategies that yield the worst
outcomes in the "prisoner's dilemma," and safeguarding collective
interests.

The state is thus a linchpin. Its power is not based on the concentration
of legal authority sufficient to overwhelm recalcitrant groups. Rather, it
is derived from the state's strategic role as the indispensable linchpin that
holds the functioning units of society together and permits it to act in ways
that advance collective interests. Perhaps it can be called a "network"

or "relational" state in the sense that its power is largely derived from the nature of its relationship as central coordinator of strong constituent groups in society.

Its roles as societal linchpin is suggested by the choice of metaphors most commonly used to describe it: the symbolic embodiment of the house or family. Clifford Geertz (1981, p. 32) stresses the state's role in court ceremonialism as a means of demonstrating the status of noble houses. The Japanese state is to society what unbroken generations of the house is to the nuclear family (Haitani 1976, p. 39). It is not merely an administrative appendage, superimposed on society at large, in order to protect individual rights, optimize the individual's welfare, or ensure equity for constituent groups. Rather, state and society are parts of the same national polity; or put differently, the state both symbolizes and functionally affirms the nation's solidarity. The state derives its legitimacy from the fact that it is responsible for the well-being of the largest and most important collectively, Japanese society. Its prime responsibility is to enhance the nation's interests. This is in keeping with traditional cultural norms which, at all levels of social organization, place collective interests over those of constituent members (Bellah 1957, p. 39).

Japanese Industrial Organization: Access Points

In addition to the effectiveness of political institutions, MITI's ability to administer industrial policy is greatly facilitated by organizational characteristics of Japan's private sector; specifically, industrial associations and business federations, company specialization, *keiretsu* structures, close banking-industry ties, and extensive patterns of intercorporate stockholding. Most of these characteristics arise out of, and reflect, the penetration of distinctive organizational factors into the marketplace (Williamson 1975; Imai and Itami 1982; Dore 1983). Their significance from the standpoint of industrial policy is that they give MITI several convenient "points of entry or access" through which to intervene in the industrial economy.

In Japan, where collective interests have been pursued with greater success than in many Western states, industrial associations and business federations have tended to play a fairly important role in aggregating company interests, building intraindustry consensus, and serving as a vehicle of communications between industry and government. In explaining the effectiveness of government-business cooperation in Japanese society, William Ouchi stresses the decision role of trade associations (1984, pp. 32-61). The power of trade associations as autonomous organizations possessing binding authority over member firms is generally not great. In certain smokestack industries such as steel, with a relatively small number of companies, concentrated market shares, heavy capital investments, and limited leeway for product diversification and technological breakthroughs, industrial associations have made the task of implementing industrial policy simpler by exchanging information about such matters as market forecasts and adjusting intraindustry differences of opinion. Rapidly growing sectors such as the information industries, on the other hand, with a number of companies, low market concentration, potential for technological change, and leeway for product diversification tend to have less cohesive or active industrial associations. This constrains MITI's capacity to shift some of the burdens of intraindustry communication, interest aggregation, and consensus formation onto the shoulders of industrial associations.

MITI's relationship with Japan's biggest and most important association in the information industries, the EIAJ (Electronics Industry Association of Japan), made up of over six hundred companies, has been far from harmonious. For MITI the opportunity costs of its strained relationship with EIAJ have been significant but not debilitating. EIAJ still serves useful functions as a communications network. Moreover, MITI's interactions with other trade associations—such as the Japan Electronics Industry Development Association and the Japan Software Industry Association—have been closer and more cooperative. And to compensate for static in the EIAJ channel, MITI officials have relied more heavily on their own networks of informal contacts in the business community. The creation of special intermediate organizations for specific projects such as the VLSI Research Cooperative has also permitted MITI to work with, and through, a handful of leading corporations on cooperative endeavors of high national priority. Hence, the existence of self-regulating organizations that centralize communication channels within the private sector and aggregate intraindustry interests facilitates government-business cooperation (even when MITI's relations with one of the key trade associations happen to be strained).

One reason why industrial associations are more cohesive in Japan than, say, the United States, is because large Japanese corporations, in practicing permanent employment, take a more risk-averse, conservative approach to diversification, tending to stay within the clearly demarcated borders of a single industry (Clark 1979, pp. 55-64). Instead of diversifying through internal expansion or external acquisitions, Japanese companies prefer to "spin off" their own subsidiaries or affiliate with small firms in related industries. Vertical integration is commonly achieved through the creation of stable networks of subsidiaries and subcontractors, held together by fairly predictable transaction patterns and based on implicit long-term contracts, financing, and equity ownership.

For MITI, and the administration of industrial policy, company specialization is of significance, because dealing with industry is substantially simplified if each industry is comprised of a well-defined, relatively small set of companies. Japanese corporations maintain a clear, hierarchical sense of community, out of which emerges a shared perception of common industrial interests and goals. In the absence of hierarchy and shared interests, industries would have greater difficulty arriving at consensus, and this would make it harder for MITI to tailor industrial policy to fit the special needs of each sector. As it is, MITI can work with a manageable core of companies, organized hierarchically through industrial associations.

Perhaps the most conspicuous organizational "handle" in Japan is also the most talked about and distinctive: the *keiretsu,* or clusters of related companies organized under a loose umbrella structure. Corporate membership in a *keiretsu* such as Mitsubishi, Mitsui, or Sumitomo usually involves heavy reliance on the main *keiretsu* bank for debt financing, and extensive intra-*keiretsu* stockholdings. Contrary to stereotypes, *keiretsu* groups do not operate as self-contained, mutually exclusive enclaves. Significant cross-*keiretsu* ties in terms of financing, equity shareholdings, technological cross-licensing, and sales prevent *keiretsu* groups from degenerating into isolated enclaves, a fate that would sap the Japanese economy of much of its vigor. What exists instead is a loosely knit, permeable set of *keiretsu* groupings, interconnected by crosscutting linkages— or "quasi-tree stuctures" as Masahiko Aoki calls them (1983, p. 8). Under the twin forces of rapid technological change and financial deregulation, the boundaries between *keiretsu*—already blurred—are become increasingly hard to differentiate.

From the standpoint of economic efficiency, *keiretsu* structures—even of the nonexclusive variety—can impose certain costs, such as lower profit margins for member firms, the dangers of oligopolistic collusion, and wasteful duplication. However, from the standpoint of administering industrial policy, the existence of *keiretsu* offers a variety of advantages. Like trade associations, it provides a ready-made network for information gathering, sharing, and policy deliberations; unlike trade associations, that network cuts across industrial sectors, creating the kind of horizontal linkages that Nakane believes are so underdeveloped and hard to establish in Japan. In this sense, *keiretsu* groupings organize the private sector into horizontal structures that provide the government with yet another potential "point of access".

More important, *keiretsu* groupings serve to diffuse and reduce risks through intercorporate stockholding, financial ties of interdependence, and mutual assistance during difficult times (Nakatani 1984). This safety net eases the pressures that build up rather quickly for highly levered companies during business downturns, thereby relieving MITI of the headaches of having to step in directly to rescue firms from the brink of bankruptcy.

(Put differently, *keiretsu* affiliations discourage "exit" and bring out "voice" and "loyalty" in Albert Hirschman's terms; 1970, pp. 36-43.) The forward-looking orientation of Japanese industrial policy, as seen in its relative freedom from political "capturing," is made possible in part because of the existence of this safety net system within the private sector.

The extensive pattern of intercorporate shareholding within (and, to a lesser extent, between) *keiretsu* groups, a striking feature of Japanese capitalism, also facilitates the administration of industrial policy by relieving companies of the tyranny of following strategies for short-term profit maximization. Japanese companies seem to be under less compulsion to earn high rates of return on investments (ROI) than American and European firms, permitting them to pursue a market share, low-profit strategy. Without compelling pressures to yield high dividends or profits, Japanese companies have more flexibility to plow back a higher portion of retained earnings into R&D, marketing, and service—reinvestments that supply the fuel for continuous growth.

Not that Japanese stockholders have suffered. According to a study by the Boston Consulting Group, Japanese investors have fared better, on average, than their American counterparts in terms of stock appreciation plus cumulative dividends over a ten-year period, 1974-84—despite weaker ROI pressures. The differential is magnified after subtracting taxes (Stalk and Arbour 1984, p. 23). The findings are corroborated by a separate study that found, from 1972 to 1982, that Japanese stocks averaged better than a 14 percent annual return compounded, compared with only 7 percent by American and West German stocks (ibid.). The conundrum—less concern with ROI but higher overall rates of return—is cleared up by Japan's much faster rate of economic and corporate growth. Instead of expecting high dividends, Japanese investors clearly place their bets on stock appreciation through growth. Such priorities actually wind up fostering growth by freeing up funds for greater investments. Not only does this approach encourage corporate competition; it may also make it easier for companies to transcend narrow, short-term interests and reach industrywide consensus on collective longer-term goals.

Intercorporate stockholding has shielded companies from hostile outside acquisitions and takeovers, problems of mounting seriousness in the United States (Shad 1984). It has also had the effect of heightening barriers to new and foreign entry, obviating the need for the government to enact policies aimed at shielding domestic producers from certain forms of direct foreign investments. It also means that routine business transactions between companies holding stock in one another involve more than simply the price mechanism. Mutual trust, low transaction costs, delivery schedules, customer service, and other considerations enter into the calculus. The importance attached to extramarket considerations, which sometimes converts intercompany business into "quasi-internal" transactions, helps to explain foreign complaints about "buy Japanese" proclivities. The breadth and depth of such organizational penetration into the marketplace thus serves, unwittingly, to protect domestic producers and promote national interests—two explicit objectives on the industrial policy agenda of most states. The government hardly has to lift a finger.

Mention should be made, finally, of the special relationship of interdependence between Japanese banks and corporations, reflecting extensive patterns of bank lending and intercorporate shareholding. This relationship provides yet another organizational "handle" for the Japanese government to utilize when it wishes to intervene. Highly levered companies are open to inputs by lead banks, particularly when problems arise; and banks, in turn, can be influenced by the government and the priorities set forth in Japanese industrial policy.

What this all adds up to is a politico-economic structure remarkably well suited for selective state intervention and the administration of industrial policy. Japan's unique blend of public and private sector institutions, of markets and hierarchies, gives the government the leeway to choose from a broad array of industrial policy instruments. The distinctive characteristics of Japanese industrial organization help to reconcile what is otherwise a puzzle: contrasting images of the Japanese government as being an interventionist yet a minimalist state. The structure of Japan's political economy permits the government to do both by, first, working out a consensus vision of broad objectives for Japanese industry (in close consultation with the private sector); second, adopting market-conforming industrial policies that set limits on the scope of state intervention, while reserving the option of intervening selectively through the use of a variety of "handles" or "points of access"; and finally, retreating to "let the market operate," once the government accomplishes what it wants. Japan's political economy, in short, gives MITI extraordinary latitude to decide whether, when, and how to intervene, and in those situations when it decides to do so, the structural means, and specific policy instruments, by which to protect its power.

This chapter began by identifying the functional requisites of the information industries and by pointing out those regime characteristics of the Japanese political economy that facilitate state intervention. It has been argued that the regime characteristics of Japan's political economy, particularly the grafting of organizational structures onto the trunk of the market economy, have made it possible for the state to take a very active and effective role. This is why MITI has been able to do a comparatively competent job—where so many others have faltered—of administering industrial policy. Indeed, the many cases of industrial policy failure, or limited and mixed success, can usually be traced to structural constraints in the political economy of the countries attempting to use it. A facilitative institutional structure can thus be considered a necessary condition of industrial policy success. Having surveyed the functional requisites and set the political and economic context, let us turn to an in-depth examination of the instruments of Japanese industrial policy, starting with a brief discussion of the subject of industrial targeting.

Industrial "Targeting"

The Japanese government tries to cast crude molds for the shape of the country's industrial structure. If the composition of the emerging economy is left entirely in the hands of the market, the government runs the risk that finite resources will be diverted from key industries like semiconductors, computers, and telecommunications—on which Japan's future competitiveness hinges—and invested instead in sectors of less importance for the industrial economy (restaurants, coffee houses, and real estate speculation, for example). For Japan's collective well-being, therefore, MITI officials feel compelled to give shape to the emerging structure of its industrial economy—within the overarching framework of the market, hopefully without causing structural deformities. This is the rationale for industrial targeting.

A study by the U.S. International Trade Commission (USITC) defines "industrial targeting" as "coordinated government actions taken to direct productive resources to help domestic producers in selected industries become more competitive" (USITC 1983, p. 17). So defined, targeting entails four basic elements: (1) government initiatives to compensate for market failures, (2) singling out only certain industries for preferential treatment, (3) preferential allocation of finite resources, and (4) enhancing the competitiveness of domestic producers.

The USITC goes on to identify the use of five targeting techniques in Japan: (1) home market protection, (2) preferential tax treatment, (3) selective exemptions from antitrust, (4) promotion of science and technology, and (5) subsidies. In practicing industrial targeting, MITI has made its share of mistakes (even with the benefit of hindsight derived from observing the historical experiences of firstcomer states). In 1953, when a small company called. Tokyo Tsūshin Kōgyō sought permission to purchase Western Electric's transistor technology for $25,000, MITI was reluctant to grant approval, citing a shortage of foreign exchange. The use of scarce foreign exchange for a technology with uncertain commercial applicability seemed like a poor risk, especially since the supplicant company was only a small new start-up.

Only after a contract had been signed with Western Electric did MITI, in 1954, authorize the transfer of transistor technology (Nakagawa 1981, pp. 57-60). That small new start-up, subsequently renamed the Sony Corporation, went on to revolutionize the entire field of consumer electronics by successfully installing the transistor into a small, portable radio and later into television sets (pp. 62-68). The episode not only brings to light MITI's lack of prescience, notwithstanding its reputation for seldom making errors in judgment; but it shows that some of Japan's most successful industries, such as consumer electronics and precision equipment, have grown up outside MITI's incubator for "targeted" infant industries.

Although Japanese targeting techniques are often labeled "unfair" by leaders in the United States and Europe, they deviate far less from the world mean of government intervention than is usually believed outside Japan. Several policy tools—such as preferential tax provisions and R&D subsidies—are used nearly everywhere to promote high technology industries, while other methods—such as quotas and tariff rates—are taken to greater extremes in Europe. Of course, some of the policy measures adopted in Japan—such as the government's regulation of the financial system—go far beyond that of the United States and the United Kingdom. But, taken as a whole, the policy tools of Japanese industrial policy are not deviant cases in today's world of mixed economies and complex forms of government intervention. Let us examine the allegedly "unfair" measures associated with Japanese industrial policy, comparing them with American and European cases and assessing the accuracy of foreign allegations.

National Research Projects

For latecomer countries, national research projects that bring leading companies to work together on common projects of high national priority—avoiding wasteful duplication, pooling finite resources, and achieving research economies of scale—represent a cost-effective way of "leapfrogging" ahead. The problem is that not many countries are capable of organizing them. Either the companies are not sufficiently innovative to leapfrog ahead (France), or they are too competitive to cooperate, or antitrust is too strictly enforced (the United States).

Owing to regime characteristics identified earlier, especially MITI's capacity to persuade private companies to take a long-term view of their collective interests, Japan is one of the few countries in the world that has demonstrated an ability to organize a series of ambitious national research projects. Indeed, such projects have become a central part of Japan's overall efforts to promote high technology. One would expect Japan to take full advantage of this instrument of industrial policy (one seldom used in connection with the smokestack sectors).

National projects for the information industries began in earnest around the early 1970s, with the 3.75 Series Computer Development project

(1972-76), Japan's response to IBM's development of a third generation computer. A series of national projects followed in fairly rapid succession, the best-known of which was perhaps the Fifth Generation computer project scheduled for completion around 1990. Plans for a Sixth Generation are already under way, indicating that these projects may have become centerpieces for the government's industrial policy.

Interestingly, the number of R&D projects increased at around the time Japan was feeling foreign pressures to liberalize its import tariffs and quotas. MITI officials and industry leaders had feared liberalization would expose the competitive weaknesses of Japan's information industry. As foreign pressures could not be forestalled, they felt that the level of indigeneous technology simply had to be upgraded through a crash program of R&D projects designed to catapult Japanese industry ahead. The trade-offs seemed clear: either accelerate the pace of technological catchup through the organization of national projects or face up to the likelihood that domestic producers would lose out to foreign giants. The removal of tariff protection thus forced Japan to turn to national research projects as a means of quickly overcoming its backwardness. Fortunately for Japan, the information industry had already developed to a point where it was poised for a dramatic takeoff. Had it been farther behind, national projects would not have been enough to lift it to its present stage of world competitiveness.

As national research projects have proliferated, as they have become more ambitous, and as Japan has reached the frontiers of high technology, foreign competitors have come to express increasing concern about them. Some give them substantial credit for Japan's rapid technological progress (USITC 1979, p. 77). Others see them as unfair vehicles of government targeting in high technology—tangible evidence of "Japan, Inc." in action (SIA 1983). Almost everyone outside Japan, it seems, regards these projects as timely, important, effective, and unique in that they could be organized only in countries like Japan where the structure of government-business relations can accommodate limited, project-specific cooperation in the midst of fierce commercial competition. Many fear that Japan will vault ahead in most fields of high technology once the multiple projects currently under way are completed.

National research projects in Japan have several characteristics in common: identification of seminal or "seedling" technologies, long gestation periods, heavy capital outlays, great uncertainties, the development of precommercial prototype models, steep learning curves, and research economies of scale. Considering all these characteristics—several of which fall outside the scope of what the market can be expected to cover—the government is probably the only institution capable of mobilizing the resources necessary to administer such large-scale undertakings. If successful, these projects advance Japan's capabilities in key technologies like VLSI that promise not only to yield new products but also to enhance competitiveness in other sectors.

MITI feels it has a national responsibility to do whatever it can to give domestic industry a competitive edge against foreign competition. The organization of national projects is tangible evidence that it is doing something of high visibility and importance to promote Japanese industry and the public well-being. National projects also offer a concrete way of coaxing more money out of the Ministry of Finance. The level of funding is considered another indicator of the kind of job MITI is doing on behalf of private industry.

By identifying key technologies for the future, and providing modest seed money, national projects can also help research directors at various companies develop an internal consensus about where to focus their companies' research efforts. A whole industry can be mobilized in this way. By dividing up the research labor, moreover, national projects can prevent wasteful duplication. Making project patents available to all companies on a nondiscriminatory basis also ensures that key technologies will be diffused fairly widely in spite of limited cross-pollination resulting from Japan's relatively low labor mobility.

Leaving aside the theoretical rationale, however, how much have national research projects actually accomplished? Probably not as much as some foreign observers think. Certainly the most important R&D in Japan takes place outside the framework of national projects—within the confines of company laboratories (Kikuchi 1983, p. 6; Moritani 1982, pp. 151-58). At most, the work done for national projects supplements what individual companies are doing. What it provides is a firmer foundation of basic knowledge on which companies can compete. Corporate research in response to market demand is still the main driving force behind technological innovation in Japan (Okimoto 1984b, pp. 177-235).

While government subsidies relieve companies of some of the burdens of continuous R&D investments, leading companies are not always enthusiastic about participating in national projects, particularly if they possess more advanced technology than their competitors and feel there is little to be gained by participating. Successful organization of national projects is thus dependent on the relatively even distribution of technological capabilities among participating firms and the prospect that the project will yield substantial collective gains, particularly in relation to foreign frontrunners. The paucity of national projects in chemicals, pharmaceuticals, and machine tools—important high technology endeavors—can be understood in light of these and other necessary preconditions.

None of the national projects so far have led to momentous breakthroughs in state-of-the-art technology. Nearly all have been designed simply to close the gap with U.S. leaders. Some have not even achieved that modest goal. Except for R&D subsidies, which turned out to be of leverage value for participating companies, the 3.75 Series Computer Development project, the first of its kind organized, was considered a failure from a technical standpoint. Likewise, the Software Development Project (1976-80) failed to fulfill the specific mission for which it had been organized: to develop computer-written applications software. Although an effort was made to cast the results of the project in a positive light, referring to the "library of working aids for programmers" that had been developed, no amount of window dressing could disguise the fact that the project failed to acccomplish what it had set out to do—with high hopes and considerable public fanfare. Only about 20 percent of the software packages developed during the six-year project have turned out to be commercially useful (interview with MITI official, January 1984; USITC 1983, p. 138).

The VLSI project, trumpeted as Japan's greatest triumph, did propel the state of semiconductor technology forward, advancing in particular Japanese capabilities in production technology (i.e., electron beam lithography, design techniques, silicon crystal growth and processing, device testing). But the VLSI project failed to yield significant breakthroughs, except for its work in the use of liquid crystals (Weinstein et al. 1984, pp. 38-39). Skeptics believe most developments would have been achieved eventually anyway. All the VLSI project did was to hasten the process somewhat—a noteworthy but not earthshaking contribution. The project's most heralded achievement—collaborative research at four cooperative laboratories involving the five participating companies and specialists from MITI's Electrotechnical Laboratory—took several years of administrative massaging by the project's executive director before it could get on with the business of joint research. For the first several years, mutual suspicion and concerns about the leakage of proprietary information impeded the free exchange of information. "What I actually did (the) last four years," says the executive director, "was nothing but to chat with the staff over *sake*," so as to create the kind of atmosphere that would be conducive to joint research (Nebashi 1981; interview with Masato Nebashi, June 24, 1982). The fact that collaboration could be achieved at all should not be denigrated; whether it was worth the years of trial and error or whether the lessons can now be applied to future projects is not clear.

The work being conducted at ICOT (Institute for New Generation Computer Technology, the central laboratory for Japan's Fifth Generation computer project) suggests that meaningful collaboration is repeatable (Feigenbaum 1983). But since the hardest part of that project lies ahead, it is still too early to tell what useful results—to say nothing of technological breakthroughs—will emerge. Similarly, not enough information is in yet to evaluate the progess and likely contributions of Japan's other national projects—the fourth generation computer, basic technologies research and development, software development, optimal measurement and control systems, and so forth. Thus, assessing the technological value of national projects must await the outcome of the current—and most ambitious—research undertakings.

Nevertheless, on the basis of the track record so far, some tentative conclusions can be drawn. National research projects appear to have made their most noteworthy contributions in the following areas: (1) extensive generation and exchange of information involving industry, government, and the financial community; (2) reinforcement of close relations between government and industry; tangible evidence that MITI is positively promoting high technology and that industry is pursuing the national good; (3) consensus building concerning development of seminal technologies for Japan's future industrial economy; (4) mobilization of resources to implement consensus; (5) pooling of national R&D strengths; some reduction of duplication; and utilization of best research talent; (6) greater budgetary allocations for R&D in specific high techology industries; (7) "seed money" to reduce perceived risks and uncertainties and encourage riskaverse private corporations to invest more of their own capital; (8) diffusion of advanced technology throughout an economy where lifetime employment limits the speed and scope of diffusion; (9) a means of overcoming the shortcomings of the university-based research and the lack of military justification for massive funding of state-of-the-art R&D; and (10) leveling technological capabilities among leading firms, thus intensifying competition for the commercial development of new products and process technologies.

This list suggests that, quite apart from their technological successes or shortcomings, national research projects do serve a variety of instrumental functions; but the contribution they make is perhaps less in the area of generating quantum advances in state-of-the-art technology than in facilitating the policy processes, information circulation, budgetary allocations, technology diffusion, and market competition.

NTT-Related Research

The high visibility of national projects should not, however, cause one to lose sight of the important research simultaneously going on elsewhere in Japan—at such places at NTT's four large laboratories, the Electrotechnical Laboratories (ETL) of the Science and Technology Agency, and other research institutes. From the standpoint of microelectronics research, these government and public corporation laboratories—working in close conjunction with private industry—have probably done more to raise Japan's technological capabilities than any national project completed as of 1985. In the early 1950s, the Electrical Laboratory (*Denki shikenjō*), ETL's predecessor, and Electrical Communications Research Laboratory (*Denki tsūshin kenkyūjō*), forerunner of the NTT labs, laid much of the groundwork for Japan's introduction of transistor technology. The first transistor ever made in Japan, the point contact transistor (*ten-sesshoku-gata*), was developed at the Communcations Lab in October 1951 (Nakagawa 1981, pp. 22-32).

NTT operates four major laboratories, employing 3,000 scientists, engineers, and researchers. In 1983, NTT had a budget of 94 billion yen, or about $400 million (USITC 1983, p. 111). Of that amount, NTT spent around 35 billion yen ($146 million) for four major projects: information processing (12 billion yen), digital switching (8.1 billion yen), large scale integrated circuits (8.7 billion yen), and satellites (6.4 billion yen) (Little 1983, p. 24). Because of its excellent research facilities, large R&D budget, and prestige, NTT has been able to attract top-notch college graduates and conduct research of the highest quality in such fields as integrated circuits, electronic switching, power transmission, and data processing. Its laboratories have played a major role in advancing Japan's level of technology, as indicated by the fact that it has taken out nearly 8,000 patents.

The quality of NTT research—during the early postwar decades a cut above private sector standards—has had the effect of uplifting the level of corporate R&D. NTT works closely with family firms across a broad spectrum of technical tasks, contracting out research, exchanging information, and joining forces on certain technical problems. Over the years, like other government officals "descending from heaven" (*amakudari*) into high level positions in the private sector, a number of NTT research specialists have left to assume positions of high responsibility in the R&D divisions of leading family firms. The close relationship has thus functioned as a conduit for the transfer of technology from NTT to the private sector, and vice versa, mutually enriching the state of knowledge on both sides.

Japan's capacity to compete with U.S. manufacturers in mass memory chip markets is due in no small measure to joint research and the transfer of advanced NTT technology. NTT's groundwork in the development of the 64K RAM, the 256K dRAM, and the 1M ROM, encompassing device designs and production technology, has helped Japanese companies carve out large chunks of world markets. Certainly Japanese producers could not have become competitive so quickly without NTT.

To convey a crude notion of what NTT has meant to the Japanese electronics industry, imagine the impetus American companies would have received if AT&T had purchased all its supplies from the merchant market and if U.S. firms had been given the same opportunity to work as closely with Bell Laboratories as Japanese firms with NTT labs. But as AT&T's needs were met internally by Western Electric, its captive supplier, the direct benefits for the U.S. electronics industry turned out to be small. Nor did Bell Labs work intimately with leading private companies like NTT, even though top researchers left to join new ventures. To be sure, Bell Labs had to make its patents freely available at reasonable fees as part of the 1956 antitrust consent decree. The value of this transfusion of technology in terms of the nurturance and growth of the U.S. telecommunications, semiconductor, and computer industries can scarcely be overstated. But compulsory licensing not only invigorated America's information industries; it also helped to breathe life into Japan's fledgling information industries because Bell patents were also available for international transfer, and Japan took full advantage of this (Little 1983, pp. 35-39).

Hence, the bilateral implications of divergent U.S. and Japanese telecommunications structures and antitrust policies—each independently put in place on the basis of domestic considerations (without much thought given to the international repercussions)—were entirely fortuitous but far-reaching. AT&T's structure and the international diffusion of Bell technology kept the barriers to new entry low not only for U.S. companies but also for Japanese and other foreign latecomers. NTT's structure, particularly the lack of a Western Electric counterpart and the intimate give-and-take relationship between NTT labs and private Japanese companies, provided Japan's private sector the opportunity to speed up the process of industrial catch-up. Japan as a latecomer happened to be the beneficiary of America's open structure and strict antitrust enforcement. Had the situation been reversed, with Japan and NTT as the pioneer and the United States and AT&T as latecomer, the U.S. information industries would have had a much harder time overtaking the Japanese frontrunners, given their big headstart and their synergistic relationship with NTT.

The flow of benefits, though lopsidedly from NTT to the private sector, has not been entirely one way. NTT family companies also give something in return—such as proprietary information concerning technologies in which they may be comparatively advanced. One Japanese company, which we shall call Daimaru, started R&D work on fiber optics and gallium arsenide around the late 1960s, when most companies were hesitant to invest in these unproven technologies. The early start and sustained attention put Daimaru well ahead of virtually everyone else. When their commercial feasibility became apparent later, Daimaru willingly shared its cumulative knowledge with NTT on a confidential disclosure basis.

Working together with other family firms, NTT then succeeded in developing the vapor axial deposition (VAD) fiber optic production method, considered the most advanced in the world, as of 1985 (discussion with "Daimaru" executives, December 1983). To standardize fiber optic cables, NTT has licensed all Japanese cable makers to use VAD.

Daimaru was willing to disclose what it had learned through over fifteen years of sustained research, because its relationship with NTT is of overriding importance. Theirs is a give-and-take relationship, based on mutual trust and a strong sense of commitment—a perfect example of the infusion of organizational elements into market transactions (Williamson 1975). Like other family firms, Daimaru believed NTT would safeguard the confidential information shared, even though it realized that some portion of the proprietary information would eventually be diffused to competitor firms. Here is an illustration of what is organizationally fairly common in Japan, particulary between private corporations belonging to the same *keiretsu* or among firms linked to one another through complex stockholdings: close and enduring bonds that transcend ties of legal contract or short-term market considerations (Imai and Itami 1982). What is so unusual in Japan—compared with the United States or most European states—is the fact that confidentiality and mutual trust also bind private and public sectors.

In addition to bilateral relations with individual firms, NTT also organizes its own version of national research projects involving multifirm participation. It sponsored its own VLSI project in parallel with the better known MITI undertaking; NTT's VLSI project was oriented to applications in telecommunication equipment while MITI's concentrated on computer use. NTT coordinates R&D efforts in key areas of telecommunications technology such as switching systems, an area that requires large R&D investments, risk-taking, and the development of compatible equipment (Okimoto and Hayase 1985).

The typical multifirm project involves centralized NTT coordination of research through several stages: basic research, exploratory work on specific devices, experimentation with systems, field tests, and commercialization. At each stage, NTT provides at least some portion of the funding, constant feedback, and technical guidance. The whole process culminates with procurement contracts; firms that contributed the most at the various R&D stages are rewarded with the largest share of procurement contracts at premium prices (Okimoto and Hayase 1985).

The system of NTT-related R&D has greatly accelerated the pace of telecommunications technology, especially in such fields as switching systems. It has probably imparted more technological impetus than MITI's national projects to date. NTT family firms have become stronger, technology has been diffused, risks reduced, and costs lowered, with quality standards raised. NTT's former status as a public corporation gave the state a very effective means of directly influencing the information industries. But this lever has been lost, now that NTT has been converted into a private corporation. Privatization will undoubtedly mean that the old system of NTT-led R&D will disappear, with many of its advantages lost (though new ones will be gained).

The combination of national projects and NTT research—together with that conducted by a number of other government laboratories such as ETL and Tsukuba—has compensated to some extent for serious shortcomings in Japan's university-based research. Of course, the technological importance of NTT and government-sponsored research has been secondary relative to R&D in the private sector. But what is striking is the synergism—not simply the spillover effects—produced by the interplay between public and private sector R&D. NTT and government-led R&D has been designed to have precisely that kind of catalytic and synergistic effect. Public and private interests have converged in ways that have enhanced both sectors (Schultze 1977, pp. 1-15).

National R&D Systems: U.S. and Japan

The foregoing examination of "technology push" policies ought to be placed in the broader context of comparative, Japanese, and American R&D systems. Where the Japanese system differs from America's is in the government's almost exclusive focus on commercial instead of military objectives. Being largely free of onerous responsibility of having to provide for the defense of the Western alliance is a major asset for Japan if only because it permits the government to make more cost-effective use of the country's R&D resources.

To be sure, the military-oriented U.S. system has spawned nearly all postwar high technology industries. The early overlap of military and commercial technologies and the government's role as R&D contractor and first customer made the U.S. system marvelously well equipped to create one high tech industry after another. Each industrial progeny subsequently grew up on the nurturance of commercial demand provided by the U.S. market, the world's largest and most advanced (Okimoto 1983, pp. 3-20). The U.S. system worked very well until Japan suddenly emerged on the scene to challenge America's supremacy in high technology.

The inefficiencies, rigidities, and opportunity costs built into America's military R&D system, given the overwhelming importance of civilian markets for high tech industries, may render it less efficient and less adaptable than Japan's, even though the U.S. system overall—including university-based research and corporate R&D—appears to be more conducive to new product innovation. Because major defense-related undertakings such as the very high speed integrated circuit (VHSIC) and the supercomputer projects, America's response to Japan's VLSI and Fifth

Generation projects, are focused on military applications, they yield less in the way of civilian spillovers per dollar than the same dollars invested in projects aimed solely at the commercial marketplace. Thus Japan's industrially oriented R&D system, featuring a series of farsighted national projects, has come to be regarded as one of the country's major assests in the high technology sweepstakes. As pointed out, however, the strength of Japan's system lies less in the technological value of national projects than in the related functions that are served: the clear, singular commercial focus; the information shared; the building of consensus concerning technological objectives; mobilization of finite resources; reinforcement of government-industry cooperation; and, above all, the impetus the whole system gives to private sector R&D.

At the same time, however, Japan's R&D system suffers from several defects. Of these perhaps the most serious are the following ones: the second-rate quality of scientific research at Japanese universities; the relative neglect of basic research; the poor system of evaluating R&D projects and expenditures; the rigidities in standard operating procedures (e.g., having to spend government R&D allocations within the fiscal year, with little or no leeway to carry over unused sums); MITI's inability to raise massive amounts of R&D funds; a lack of central coordination in national R&D programs; the absence of a fully developed venture capital market; and, above all, the lag between the institutional structure of Japan's R&D system (still oriented to latecomer catch-up) and the changing circumstances and functional needs of the country's high technology industries. Such defects did not hinder Japan when it was still catching up through the acquisition of foreign technology; but at its currently advanced stage of development, they pose potentially serious stumbling blocks. Indeed, Japan's R&D deficiencies are precisely what has prompted the government to use industrial policy to overcome them and hasten the development of the information industries.

Government Financing and Capital Allocations

The government's use of another instrument of industrial policy—the channeling of scarce capital resources to targeted sectors—has been reduced largely by the maturation of Japan's economy and the abundance of investment capital. The proportion of government funds available to industry through the Fiscal Investment and Loan Program (FILP) has fallen steadily since the early 1950s. Whereas FILP used to account for nearly 30 percent of total capital to industry, its share in the 1980s has fallen to just over 10 percent, with only a tiny portion of that going to high technology. According to one estimate, the government's share of plant and equipment investments in the electronics equipment industry came to only 2.5

percent during the early 1960s and a mere 0.8 percent in the late 1970s (USITC 1983, p. 90). Compared with what the French government is pouring into its electronics industry, Japanese government financing is very modest.

As Japan's cup of investment capital now runneth over, there is little need to channel government funds to priority sectors. Large corporations in "targeted" industries are fully capable of meeting their own needs through a combination of retained earnings, bank loans, and stock and bond issuances. Naturally, they are happy to continue receiving financial support from the government. MITI officials continue to feel that the government bears a special responsibility to do whatever it can to promote the development of strategic industries considered central to Japan's industrial future. But "targeted" government financing is so small that it cannot be considered a major explanation for the international competitiveness of Japan's information industries.

Research Subsidies

In what forms, and to what extent, has the Japanese government subsidized research in the information industries? The common perception outside Japan is that the subsidies have been huge—so large, in fact, that a case could be filed against Japan for violating the Subsidies Code of the Tokyo Round agreement (Semiconductor Industry Association 1983, pp. 99-101). Is this the case? Does the Japanese government provide larger subsidies than most other countries?

The government can provide research subsidies from several sources: special grants budgeted by the Ministry of Finance for national research projects, internal allocations from MITI's own budget (including "hidden" funds available from energy-related taxes and bicycle racing proceeds), and funds from various other government ministries (Science and Technology, Education, Posts and Telecommunications, and Japan Defense Agency). Let us calculate the total subsidies by adding up the known categories of expenditures, beginning with the national research projects.

Government subsidies for national projects can be grouped into two periods: the era of frantic catch-up (1970-79), and the period of state-of-the-art development (1980-90). Government outlays from 1966 to 1980 amounted to around $565 million, or roughly $43 million per year; this represented less than 10 percent of total R&D expenditures for the information industry, the rest being shouldered by private enterprise. The main research projects are those listed in table 1. The sums were small, whether measured in the aggregate, averaged on an annual basis, or calculated as a proportion of total R&D in the information industry.

TABLE 1

Government Supported Research Projects in Japan, 1966–80

Period	Project	Amount (million $)
1966–71	High performance computer R&D	$ 42
1972–76	3.75 Series Computer development	228
1971–80	Pattern information processing system	115
1976–80	VLSI development	150
1976–80	Software development	30
	Total	$565

Source: Personal interviews.

In the United States, birthplace of the computer and integrated circuit, the government funneled far larger aggregate, annual, and percentage sums for R&D. In the year 1957, for example, the Air Force, Army, and National Aeronautics and Space Administration (NASA) provided $518 million for electronics and communications equipment, or roughly 70 percent of the total. Even as late as 1968, the U.S. government accounted for about $1.5 billion, or roughly 60 percent of total R&D (Okimoto 1983, p. 4). Of course, the U.S.-Japan comparison is a bit misleading, given the fact that the United States was the technological pioneer and Japan the follower. For firstcomers, the costs of R&D are usually far higher than those for latecomers, if only because the level of uncertainty is so much higher; failures and false starts are almost impossible to avoid. Latecomers have the advantage of knowing what has worked and often can license technologies. Nevertheless, the comparison brings to light the relatively modest sum of subsidies provided by the Japanese government from the mid-1960s to the end of the 1970s.

The small sum shrinks even further when one notes that most of the early subsidies were conditional loans, or *hōjōkin*, for which repayment was contingent on the success of the project. Although contingency loans would seem to create perverse incentives either to "cheat" on repayments—what Oliver Williamson calls "opportunism" (1975, pp. 26-31) or "self-seeking with guile"—a surprisingly high percentage of loans have been repaid. Of the *hōjōkin* grants made by MITI's Agency for Industrial Science and Technology (AIST) over the five-year period 1974-78, nearly half, or 43.6 percent, had been repaid by 1982 (USITC 1983, p. 105). This record of *hōjōkin* repayment thus reduces the net R&D subsidy to an unspecified amount well below the aggregate figure cited for national research projects. (The reduction cannot be specified because the data on repayment are not broken down by research project, making it impossible to ascertain which of the information industries projects had been repaid.) It can be calculated in terms of the unpaid principle plus the uncharged commercial interest rates.

MITI chooses which projects to organize and subsidize very carefully, in close consultations with industry. To qualify for government assistance, a project must meet four criteria: (1) the proposed project must be of seminal importance for Japan's technological progress and future economic well-being; (2) the research must be of the precommercial variety, so that participating companies do not gain decisive advantage over excluded firms; (3) government assistance must be indispensable for the project to get under way and be completed; (4) the time frame for the project's completion must be realistic. Government financing supplies the critical missing ingredient for launching projects of high capital costs and risks, relatively long gestation, fundamental technological importance, and broad commercial applicability.

MITI prefers to put up only a portion of the total capital necessary to finance a national project (interviews with MITI officials, September 1983). Usually the sum is around half the total costs, based on the rationale that the seed money not only makes the project feasible but also forces industry to invest some of its own capital. If MITI bore the full costs and risks, incentives to be efficient might be dampened. MITI might then be strapped with the same problems that plague contract research elsewhere: padded expenses, unanticipated delays, huge cost overruns, and failure to meet technical specifications and development targets. Other things being equal, therefore, MITI's clear preference is to insist on cost sharing through the extension of *hōjōkin*, or low interest loans repayable from the profits made on commercial applications.

Having closed the gap with American frontrunners in most areas of high technology, the Japanese government turned its attention to the organization of more ambitious national research projects aimed at achieving state-of-the-art technology. The 1980s have witnessed the organization of nine major projects related to the information industries designed to propel Japan beyond the frontiers of knowledge (see table 2).

Unlike the funding arrangements for most of the national projects during the catch-up phase, many of the state-of-the-art projects listed above, with the notable exception of the Fourth Generation computer, involve the government's assumption of all expenses. Such financing, referred to as *itakuhi*, is more akin to contract research in the United States. The reason *itakuhi* has come to be used more than *hōjōkin* is because state-of-the-art projects are by definition substantially more costly, risky, uncertain, and of longer gestation. Private companies are far more hesitant about committing their own resources.

For several of these ambitious projects, MITI has had to seize the initiative. Had it not done so, the projects might never have materialized; private firms might never have been willing to bear the costs of precommercial

TABLE 2

Government Supported Research Projects in Japan, 1980s

Period	Project	Amount (billion yen)
1979–83	Software for VLSI hardware	22.5
1976–82	Software production technology	6.6
1979–86	Optoelectronics applied system	18.0
1981–89	Fourth Generation high speed computer	51.5
1981–91	Fifth Generation computer 1981–84:	10.5
1981–90	Next Generation industries technology	25.0
1977–84	Flexible manufacturing	13.0
Continuous	Important technology	2.1
1983–90	Critical work robot	17.5
	Total	166.7

Sources: U.S. Embassy, Tokyo, unclassified telegram, May 1982; Little 1983.

research. An employee of one of the companies that agreed to participate in the Fifth Generation project explained the financial arrangements from the private sector's point of view: "At first, MITI wanted to support this project at only 50 percent for the first three years, with private firms supplying the other 50 percent of the funding, but we in the companies said no. We can't afford to support such a high-risk project, even at 50 percent, plus contribute researchers' time. When they saw we meant it, they agreed to support it 100 percent, at least for the first three years. After that, we'll see" (Feigenbaum and McCorduck 1983, p. 109).

The shift from *hōjōkin* to *itakuhi* has increased the actual amount of subsidies significantly. Over 60 percent of R&D subsidies from 1976 to 1982 were *hōjōkin*, subject to eventual repayment. But for the nine projects listed above, *itakuhi* support has come to surpass *hōjōkin* by a wide margin.

The government's willingness to underwrite the full costs of a number of the frontier R&D projects, however, should not be misinterpreted. It does not mean that all private companies are eager to jump on the bandwagon and reap the benefits of the government's free ride. Consider the case of the Fifth Generation project: several firms had to be coaxed into participating, and several openly groused about it. On their visits to Japan, Edward A. Feigenbaum and Pamela McCorduck have observed: "Resentment and hostility are hardly strong enough to describe the attitudes of another firm's managers toward the Fifth Generation. They told us frankly that they had not wanted to participate and only under duress (whose nature we couldn't ascertain) did they finally contribute their researchers to ICOT" (ibid.).

Quite apart from having to divert research personnel, Japanese corporations often have the same reservations about *itakuhi* as American companies do about government contract research: mounds of paperwork, minute and irritating regulations, rigid accounting procedures, constant government monitoring, strict technical specifications, no guaranteed markets for commercializable products, and so forth. Sometimes it does not seem worth the hassle.

On top of the bureaucratic red tape, contracting companies in Japan are usually not allowed to retain proprietary rights over the research results. Patents automatically revert to the sponsoring government agency, which makes them available on a nondiscriminatory basis to nonparticipating companies (for a patent license fee). Despite full financial coverage, therefore, *itakuhi* is not as attractive to private companies as the notion of a "free ride" suggests. Administrative costs alone are hardly trivial.

The aggregate sum for all Japanese national research projects—166 billion yen spread over more than a ten-year period—sounds enormous, and the figure does not include costs for the second half of the Fifth Generation computer project. Nor does it include internal MITI funds that require no special Ministry of Finance authorization, such as revenues from bicycle racing and special energy tax revenues which can be used for energy-related R&D (capable of being defined to include a variety of research projects). In 1982, for example, MITI was able to allocate around 2 billion yen (about $8.5 million) from its regular budget for high tech R&D support. In addition, discretionary funds are available every year from revenues gained through regulated bicycle racing gambling. The amount varies from year to year, but in 1982 it came to around 27 billion yen (about $112 million), or slightly more than 5 percent of MITI's budget. Most of that money is used to support miscellaneous activities such as trade fairs, public relations activities, and trade associations; but some can be used to underwrite research in advanced technology.

From MITI's standpoint, the advantage of drawing on bicycle racing revenues, instead of special funds from the Ministry of Finance, is that administrative entanglements are averted. MITI does not have to go through the time-consuming process of submitting formal budget proposals for financing, and companies are not burdened with heavy reporting requirements. MITI is completely free to choose which research projects to support. In 1982, it allocated 800 million yen (about $3.3 million) for research in computer software and data processing, an area of pressing need where Japanese companies were thought to be lagging far behind the U.S. leaders.

The real value of discretionary funds is not so much the additional money available, therefore, but the flexibility it gives. MITI drew on these funds, for example, when the Ministry of Finance initially balked at the idea of underwriting the risky Fifth Generation computer project. By putting up its own funds, MITI was able to get the project launched. Once its feasibility and long-term value were demonstrated, the project received substantial funding from the Ministry of Finance. Without discretionary funds at MITI's disposal, the Fifth Generation computer project, Japan's best-known and perhaps most important to date, might never have moved beyond the planning stage.

If NTT's R&D expenditures are included at roughly 94 billion yen (1983) per year over a ten-year period, an estimate that fails to take annual increases into account, the grand total for research subsidies comes to 516 billion yen (roughly $2.3 billion, estimated at a yen-dollar exchange rate of 230 yen to the dollar). Although the figure seems enormous, it averages out to be only 51.6 billion yen per year over a ten-year period ($230 million per year). For any given year, that figure represents only a fraction of national R&D expenditures. Compared with Bell Laboratories' yearly budget of $2 billion as of 1983 ("Bell Labs: The Threatened Star of U.S. Research," *Business Week*, July 5, 1982, p. 47), or IBM's budget of over $1.6 billion ("A Research Spending Surge Defies Recession," *Business Week*, July 5, 1982, p. 54), the size of Japan's $230 million subsidy seems modest indeed, especially remembering that the latter figure includes the principal on contingent loans that have to be repaid and thus overestimates the actual subsidies. This brings us back to a point made earlier: the purpose of government subsidies is to compensate for market failures by serving as catalysts, not substitutes, for private sector investments and activities in basic research.

American and European Research Subsidies

What about U.S. government support for R&D in the information industries sector? How does it compare with Japan's? Let us start by looking at only a few of the U.S. government's highly publicized projects, most of them sponsored by the Department of Defense (DOD). The very high speed integrated circuit (VHSIC) project, launched in 1980 and scheduled for completion by the end of 1988, calls for DOD to put up an estimated $500 million in contract research (Fong 1983). In partial response to Japan's Fifth Generation project, DOD has also launched its own "Strategic Computer Project" designed to advance the frontiers of artificial intelligence, software, and computer architecture, with a projected budget of around $600 million for the first five years, and perhaps another $900 million for the final five years. Two other DOD projects of note are its $100 million program for the development of gallium arsenide circuits and a seven-year, $250 million project called Software Initiative. Adding up the allocations for just these four projects, U.S. government financing comes to $2.35 billion, or roughly the same as the the aggregate Japan Development Bank, MITI, and NTT total. Since virtually all the money is in the form of contract research (none of it repayable loans), the actual level of subsidies in the United States for the four projects is higher than Japan's. Including subsidies for all other projects (for which full statistics are not available), the U.S. level is undoubtedly several times higher.

As a percentage of R&D expenditures, the U.S. government accounted for over 18 percent in the category of office machinery (SIC code 357) and 40 percent in communication equipment (SIC code 361-64, 369) in 1980 (National Science Foundation 1981, p. 2). The figures exceed those in Japan by a substantial margin. But it should be pointed out that most of the U.S. government money goes to support military-related R&D projects, only a portion of which lead to direct commercial applications. From a purely commercial point of view, therefore, the U.S. government total is not nearly as cost effective as Japan's, and to the extent that it is not, the amount of federal subsidies should be discounted. Nevertheless, U.S. criticisms of Japanese subsidies—even allowing for low commercial spillovers—sound hollow in light of the federal government's much greater R&D expenditures (Wilson et al. 1980, p. 154).

Certain countries in the European Community also provide far more in the way of research subsidies than Japan. Take, for example, semiconductor research: government financing in the United Kingdom alone exceeds that in Japan (Hazewindus 1982, p. 121). The government in France has subsidized its electronics industry more heavily. Under President François Mitterrand, the state embarked on an ambitious, crash program to upgrade France's capabilities in electronics and other high technology industries. It set aside $1 billion for investment in France's electronics industry over a five-year period, 1982-1986, with $600 million earmarked for R&D and $400 million for expanding manufacturing facilities (Jones 1982, p. 88). The $1 billion represented only a small part of a massive $17 billion package in public and private funds Mitterrand has committed to the development of electronics. Nor is that all. The troubling inability of the computer industry to compete effectively against American and Japanese companies has prompted the French government to take the ultimate step: nationalization of major parts of the computer industry and its organization into four autonomous subsidiaries under the control of one holding company, Compagnie des Machines Bull (Jones 1983, pp. 37-38; "Can Mitterrand Remake France's Economy?" *Business Week*, January 10, 1983, p. 58).

On top of subsidies supplied by individual countries, the European Commission has launched a major, five-year research project called Esprit, aimed at thrusting Europe's level of technology forward in microelectronics, software, artificial intelligence, office automation, and computer-aided design and manufacturing ("Europe's Desperate Try for High-Tech Teamwork," *Business Week*, May 30, 1983, p. 45). The EC is also seeking to streamline research across the European continent in order to achieve the benefits of scale economies and to curtail the waste that results from extensive duplication of R&D. By one estimate, the total amount of public and private money invested in European R&D in 1982 was more than double that of Japan (USITC 1983). And should projected spending levels stay on track through the end of the 1980s, the gap will widen. Such spending levels are especially high relative to the overall size of Europe's electronics industry. In 1982, Europe's share of the world's market for integrated circuits was a mere 7 percent, and European-built computers accounted for only 10 percent of world production. Government subsidies in Europe as a percentage of total electronics output, therefore, exceed Japan's by a wide margin.

Accordingly, Japanese government subsidies to the information industries—whether measured domestically in terms of total investments or internationally in comparison with American and European outlays—cannot be considered abnormal. It is, as this discussion has conveyed, exceedingly difficult to standardize measures for international comparisons of government subsidies. How can Japan, the United States, and Europe be compared when there is not even agreement on what constitutes a subsidy? Is it best simply to add up loans, outright grants, and contract research? Or is it more accurate to adjust for differences in the specific terms of the subsidies, taking into account, for example, only the interest rate differential between the government and commercial loans and considering that differential as the effective subsidy? Perhaps the most revealing measure is one referred to as "marginal subsidy equivalent," or the value obtained when a company produces an additional unit of output as a function of a given subsidy input (USITC 1983). The problem is, as the USITC study admits, accurate quantification of marginal subsidy equivalents is "virtually impossible" (ibid.). What we are left with, then, is aggregate data that provide only crude evidence of government R&D assistance. The weight of that evidence indicates that the Japanese state is hardly alone in thinking that the market mechanism must be supplemented with subsidies if society is to reap the full fruits of innovation and growth in high technology industries.

If anything, the level of Japanese subsidies is located toward the lower end of the bell-shaped curve of world distribution, with the United States, France, and the United Kingdom standing at the higher tail. It is still too early to tell whether the massive government subsidies will propel Europe to the technological forefront. But if past patterns hold true, the likelihood is that simply pumping more subsidies into the R&D effort will not remedy whatever it is that ails Europe. Commercial competitiveness hinges on far more than the quantity of government subsidies. Indeed, subsidies not only seem to have a point of diminishing returns but, taken to excess, may actually dull a country's competitive edge.

If this is the case, why do some countries rely so heavily on subsidies? The answer seems to lie in the inability of private corporations to compete in international markets and the lack of viable policy alternatives. Finding themselves falling farther behind, certain European countries have had few alternative policy instruments at hand to arrest the slide. Providing subsidies, in one form or another, is often the simplest and most direct instrument of industrial policy. Regime characteristics in countries such as the United Kingdom make outright subsidies and import protection politically easier than, say, the organization of national research projects, which few seem capable of administering effectively.

The problem is that the impact of government subsidies depends less on quantity (though larger subsidies can be advantageous) than on such qualitative factors as industry's capacity to convert public assistance into technological and commercial progress. Japanese industry has demonstrated time and again that it has the capacity to derive the most from government assistance. The cooperative structure of government-business relations seems to lend itself to cost-effective utilization of what is, by international standards, relatively modest R&D subsidies.

The fact that all countries subsidize—in different degrees— suggests that various forces are pushing governments to assist the emerging information industries: (1) the pronounced learning-curve effects that interpose formidable obstacles in the way of latecomers seeking to close the technological and commercial lead opened up by firstcomers (Warnecke 1978); (2) the crucial importance of achieving increasing returns to scale in production; (3) the exceedingly high technological, economic, and international stakes prompting advanced industrial states to enter, and stay, in the competitive sweepstakes as long as possible; and (4) deep-seated problems in many of the old-line manufacturing sectors—sluggish growth, large plant overcapacity, loss of comparative cost advantages, and so forth—which intensify the need for innovation to stimulate new products, demand, and growth.

Placed in the context of such universal forces at work, the proliferation of government R&D subsidies is not hard to understand, even though it introduces vexing problems for international trade. For latecomers, especially those dependent on free trade, relying on research subsidies could very well be preferable to falling back on import protection, if domestic producers have no other way of competing against foreign frontrunners. We have noted, in fact, that government subsidies for R&D rose dramatically when foreign pressures forced Japan to lower tariff barriers during the early seventies. When faced with a choice between subsidizing or protecting domestic industries, many governments will opt for subsidization as the less costly, more palatable course of action, particularly in terms of the norms of free trade.

The problem is that desperate governments may feel compelled to combine subsidies with trade protection—as is the case in Europe's semiconductor industry—if domestic producers lag so far behind that subsidies alone cannot compensate for their competitive shortcomings. Moreover, the problem is exacerbated by the fact that R&D subsidies for high technology are widespread not only among the states that find themselves behind but also even among those—like Japan and the United States—that are far out in front of the pack and involved in a hotly contested, two-way race.

The universality of research subsidization indicates that all governments consider it a necessary but not sufficient condition for innovating and competing in high technology. The perception that it is necessary stems, in large part, from the failure of the market to stimulate risk-taking and sustain levels of capital investments required to achieve optimal rates of innovation. Escalating capital costs and risks; short product cycles, rapid second sourcing (i.e., licensing other firms to manufacture proprietary products), and the problems of capturing profits to cover up-front costs; long periods of technological gestation; the complexity and multidisciplinary character of much of high technology research; the benefits of research economies of scale (in certain fields); evidence of widespread and wasteful duplication; and lack of central coordination—all appear to make government intervention mandatory.

Tax Policies

For most countries, tax policies represent perhaps the most ubiquitous instrument of industrial "targeting." Tax provisions that discriminate between sectors offer an immediate means of bestowing special assistance and encouragement to specific industries. From a political standpoint, the virtue of using taxes is that it requires no direct or visible drain on budgets and can usually be hidden from the spotlight of public scrutiny and insulated from the usual pressures of political accountability. It is thus a convenient tool of industrial policy, especially as a "quick fix" solution to quiet the clamor of short-term lobbyist demands. Powerful interest groups can be "bought off" by generous tax provisions, without the din of public criticism that might accompany, say, zero-sum budgetary allocations.

The danger is that tax policies can become the handmaiden of political expediency, with short-term solutions exacting heavy costs in long-run macroeconomic efficiency; this is particularly problematic if interest groups with the most political clout also happen to be economically inefficient, as is often the case in advanced industrial states. Old-line industries, supporting large, organized labor forces, tend to maintain their political influence long past their economic prime. There is almost always a lag or disjunction between the political power and the economic growth potential of interest groups with respect to policies that directly affect their vital interests. Generous tax treatment for old-line declining industries can also be justified as constituting an alternative to the costly consequences of trade protectionism or widespread unemployment.

This helps to explain why, in the case of the United States and most European states, intersectoral tax policies are skewed in favor of economically inefficient industries. Without strong institutions of interest aggregation, tax policies tend to fall captive to organized lobbyist groups. Instead of channeling capital to high growth sectors, tax measures wind up funneling resources to the "wrong places"—the inefficient and declining sectors. This introduces serious shortfalls and distortions into the government's revenue base. Even when the U.S. Congress, principal locus of tax policy making, tries to facilitate the growth of high tech industries by formulating generous provisions for accelerated depreciation allowances, capital gains, or investment credits, the provisions often lead to unforeseen, perverse effects. (Included among the sometimes undesirable side effects are leveraged "buy outs," hostile takeovers, stepped-up use of debt financing, overextension, and vulnerability to cyclical recession.)

Congress is also apt to grant across-the-board incentives to all sectors, even though the circumstances and needs of each industry differ. It may want to avoid the appearance of playing favorites because of its commitment to the principles of equity and impartiality. Certain businesses like real estate wind up reaping the windfall benefits of generous capital gains provisions, at substantial costs to the U.S. economy in lost tax revenues and the distortions caused by misinvestments in the less productive sectors. Thus the U.S. Congress tends to treat inefficient industries overly generously on two fronts: through preferential corporate tax breaks and through tax incentives designed with high tech industries in mind but applied indiscriminately. What is in the abstract a potentially effective tool of industrial policy, therefore, turns out to be a blunt and sometimes harmful instrument of economic inefficiency.

Despite intense lobbying by various business interests, the Japanese government has managed to maintain some coherence in its approach to corporate taxation, thanks largely to the capacity of the Finance Ministry to stay in relatively firm, depoliticized control of the policy-making processes. With only a few notable exceptions, it has not allowed very many inefficient industries to obtain grossly inequitable concessions. The apportionment of the tax burden is more evenly distributed between industrial sectors in Japan than in either the United States or the United Kingdom (Saxonhouse 1982). Not only does this mean that Japan's tax structure is less distorted by politicized discrimination; it also indicates that the "targeted" sectors receive less preferential treatment than is commonly believed. Indeed, the high tech sectors may be better off, overall, by virtue of the smaller distortions caused by preferential treatment of smokestack sectors.

The effective capital taxation in Japan (1973), as Gary Saxonhouse points out, varied from 34.7 percent (nonferrous metals) to 49 percent (electrical machinery), compared with the much wider amplitude of variation in the United States—from 19.7 percent (petroleum) to 131.2 percent (electrical machinery). Yet the average corporate tax rate, including state and local levies, is the same in both countries: 53.2 percent in Japan, 51.2 percent in the U.S. Thus "targeted" taxation is in some senses practiced less widely in Japan than in the United States (except that the "wrong" sectors—the declining industries—tend to be targeted in the United States). Again, the contrast can be attributed to differences in political regime characteristics, most notably Japan's stronger institutions for dealing with interest group demands.

Every year, after extended negotiations, MOF and MITI agree on an aggregate ceiling for special tax measures. MITI is free to grant tax incentives in whatever amounts to industries of its choosing, so long as it stays within the limits of the aggregate ceiling. Various divisions and bureaus within MITI vie with one another to win special tax provisions for industries under their jurisdictions. The Business Behavior Division (*Kigyō kōdō-ka*) of the Industrial Policy Bureau (*Sangyō seisaku-kyoku*) decides which industries deserve to receive tax incentives, and in what amounts, after consulting with each division and bureau, and especially with the Accounting Division (*Kaikei-ka*) and General Coordinating Division (*Sōmu-ka*) of the Minister's Secretariat (*Daijin kanbō*).

In the complicated aggregation of interests within MITI, special tax provisions are considered one of four interrelated policy measures designed for each industry; the others are subsidies, legislative measures, and administrative guidance. The General Coordinating Division tries to blend all four ingredients, each in appropriate measure, into an effective recipe that meets the needs and peculiar circumstances of each industry. Declining industries may get a stronger dose of administrative guidance and subsidies, while for high tech industries, greater tax incentives and research support may be the most effective instruments of promotion.

The strength of Japan's system is that it (1) keeps a cap on the estimated losses due to special tax incentives, (2) forces all industries to compete with one another for special tax treatment on the basis of what lies in the best interests of the industrial economy as a whole, (3) gives MITI the leeway and authority to determine the optimal uses of special tax incentives, (4) holds parochial politicking in check, and (5) uses tax policies in relation to other tools of industrial policy. Tax "targeting" is thus subsumed within the broad framework of macroeconomic policy, not utilized in isolation as an easy and elastic solution to short-term political lobbying. That Japanese industrial tax policies come out bearing fewer signs of obvious inconsistencies is therefore hardly surprising.

With respect to specific tax incentives for R&D investments—a matter of obvious importance for high tech industries—the stereotype of extensive and unfair Japanese targeting is again belied by comparisons with the United States. Whereas Japan grants tax credits of 20 percent for all R&D expenditures that exceed the highest annual rate in a corporation's past, with a ceiling of 10 percent of the corporation's taxes, the United States allows tax credits of 25 percent for all R&D expenditures exceeding the *average* over the past three years, with no ceiling on the amount deductible and the flexibility to continue carrying the tax credit over a fifteen-year period. Japanese corporations saved 27 billion yen (roughly $122 million) in 1981 thanks to this R&D tax credit; no comparable data have been found for the United States, but given the larger amount of R&D investments, it is likely that the figure was significantly higher.

The United States also offers investment tax credits of up to 6 percent of the value of new equipment on depreciation schedules as short as three years, and up to 10 percent for equipment with a longer life. Japan offers nothing comparable. Such provisions indicate that Japanese high tech industries receive less preferential treatment than is widely assumed, whether compared with other Japanese or foreign firms.

High tech companies in Japan do, however, enjoy some important advantages. The most significant is that the effective tax rate on Japanese corporations, taking into account national price factors, is lower than comparable rates for U.S. companies, thanks to lower inflation (USITC 1983, p. 76). America's high rate of inflation since the mid-1970s has had the effect of raising real corporate taxes. The negative interaction between inflation and taxes has also inhibited capital investments in the United States. It should be pointed out, however, that this advantage stems from macroeconomic, not industrial, policies and is systemic in nature, not the product of government targeting. In national tax policies, as in R&D subsidies and national projects, Japanese industrial policy per se does not appear to confer grossly unfair advantages on high tech sectors over competitors from other advanced countries. To the extent that there are discrepancies in Japan's favor, they can be better explained by reference to regime characteristics than to deviant policy practices.

Antitrust Policy

Two other areas where Japan differs from the United States are the less stringent enforcement of antitrust law and the use of administrative guidance as a tool of industrial policy. Although antitrust law is not usually considered an integral part of industrial policy, the strictness or laxness with which it is enforced has a bearing on the government's flexibility to make use of certain policy tools.

National research projects, Japanese style, would be harder to organize in the United States because of weightier concerns about the possibility of anticompetitive effects. Japan's FTC (Fair Trade Commission) seems to feel that national projects pose little threat to market competition as long as most of the major firms participate. Inviting most of the large corporations, however, would appear to give rise to a slightly different set of potential antitrust implications. Would it not, for example, have the effect of strengthening the hand of the already dominant firms, accentuating oligopolistic patterns of market concentration, raising barriers to new entry, and keeping excluded firms relegated to second-class status?

If so—and such concerns are not without foundation—the Japanese government does not appear to be overly concerned. Market concentration in high tech sectors—though higher than in the United States—remain sufficiently low, particularly in such industries as information processing, that the FTC worries little about the dangers of oligopoly. Moreover, since demand is still on a steep upward ascent—with technology constantly advancing, new products continually hitting the market, and considerable leeway for horizontal entry from outside but related industries—fears of excessive market concentration appear much less worrisome than is the case for smokestack industries. Hence the Japanese government is confident that high tech sectors face little danger of stagnancy or slack competition.

The basic, precommercial nature of research also makes national projects palatable from an antimonopoly point of view. Similarly, the availability of patents on a nondiscriminatory basis to all firms neutralizes the most serious objections excluded companies might raise. The principal advantages gained by participation in national projects are therefore confined to two areas: (1) government funding, which can be used to supplement the firm's research investments, and (2) direct research experience, which goes beyond the know-how obtainable through patent licensing. While these advantages are certainly not minor, neither are they so decisive that firms, by participating, gain an insurmountable edge. This helps to explain why second-tier companies like Sanyo and Sharp express few complaints about being excluded from the select circle of national project participants.

It should be pointed out, furthermore, that U.S. antitrust policies do not rule out all forms of cooperative research. Every year a few dozen or so requests, usually involving small-size firms, to engage in joint research are approved. So long as cooperation does not seriously inhibit competition, joint research can be accommodated under the provisions of U.S. antimonopoly law. Collaboration is, in fact, often encouraged by DOD projects. VHSIC, for example, has organized companies into several distinct contract teams in order to bring about an efficient division of labor and encourage research cooperation. Hughes, RCA, and Rockwell standardized their computer-aided design system and exchanged information on mask designs, design rules, and patents in working together to develop CMOS/SOS technology (Fong 1983). Perkin-Elmer and Hughes Research Labs also joined forces in the development of electron beam lithography, exchanging very sensitive company information in order to achieve better joint results. Collaboration was also necessary to ensure compatibility for important technological systems such as the signal processor chip set. Hence interfirm collaboration and cooperation do take place in the United States under the aegis of government projects (though much less extensively).

If collaboration is reasonably common in defense-related research, is U.S. antitrust more stringent in the commercial domain? The answer is yes, but the seriousness of the competitive threat posed by Japan appears to have had some effect on notions of legitimate cooperation in purely commercial research, especially since the commercial viability of high tech industries is perceived to be crucial to the country's economic—and ultimately national—security.

In 1983 a potentially big step forward was taken when the Microelectronics and Computer Technology Corporation (MCC), a consortium of thirteen major U.S. companies, was granted permission to undertake joint research on advanced computer architecture, software, artificial intelligence, component packaging, computer-aided design and computer-aided manufacturing technologies. MCC is, to some extent, an organizational response to the competitive challenge posed by Japanese national projects. Each member company sends researchers to MCC headquarters in Austin, Texas, where they work alongside representatives from the twelve other firms. The thirteen companies bear the costs of research and share in its fruits.

MCC is the first consortium of its kind ever to be given the go-ahead to operate as a corporate entity. It performs some of the same functions as Japanese national projects: judicious identification of long-range technological objectives, mobilization of collective resources, research economies of scale, facilitation of information exchange and technological diffusion among member firms, and avoidance of wasteful duplication. The Justice Department has warned that it will monitor MCC's activities closely, and approval could conceivably be rescinded if there is evidence of anticompetitive consequences. Even in the commercial domain, therefore, cooperative research in the United States has been permitted, albeit under stricter constraints and closer monitoring than comparable projects in Japan.

The passage of special development laws in Japan to promote high tech industries does exempt certain circumscribed areas from antitrust prosecution. But the exemptions only apply to such matters as standardized specifications for electronics components. Special development laws, in effect for only a limited duration, do not give high tech industries license to engage freely in collaborative research, much less to divide up product and overseas markets, as some charge (interview with Silicon Valley executive, September 1982; looking at the pattern of Japanese semiconductor exports, this executive speculated that Japanese electronics companies might be engaging in tacit division of overseas markets among themselves). The VLSI project, for example, did not qualify for special exemption from antitrust; it fell into the standard category of "laws concerning public enterprise research associations" (interview with Masato Nebashi, former executive director, VLSI project, June 24, 1982, Tokyo).

Where antitrust leniency, based originally on the Law Concerning Temporary Measures for the Promotion of the Electronics Industry (1957), had a major impact was in the creation of the Japan Electronic Computer Corporation (JECC) in 1961. JECC is a semigovernmental joint venture comprising Japan's seven leading computer manufacturers which arranges favorable financing for computer rentals and purchases (Nihon Denshi Keisanki Kabushiki Kaisha 1983). It has played a central role in consolidating the competitive staying power of Japan's computer industry, particularly during the 1960s and early 1970s, when IBM threatened to overwhelm Japan's domestic market. Something like JECC would be hard to imagine in the United States. In all likelihood, it would not receive approval from the Justice Department or FTC. Here is an instance where greater leniency in the application of antitrust law has had far-reaching consequences.

The overall picture is therefore complicated: while antitrust policy in Japan has not permitted Japanese high tech companies to collude or fix prices, it has given them more leeway for collaborative research than U.S. antitrust policy. Moreover, the creation of JECC has had a big impact on the development of the fledgling Japanese computer industry.

Administrative Guidance

One of the most talked about instruments of Japanese industrial policy which has no counterpart in the United States is administrative guidance (*gyosei-shidō*)—informal guidelines issued by MITI and other government ministries to help specific industries deal with vexing problems that threaten to harm their collective interests. Unlike formal legislation, administrative guidance is not backed by legal sanctions. Its effectiveness depends on voluntary compliance. To ensure compliance, the government carefully consults with industry before issuing administrative guidance; sometimes private industry approaches government ministries with what it wishes to have issued. Administrative guidance can sometimes carry almost the same weight as statutory laws in terms of getting things done.

For MITI, administrative guidance has served as a versatile tool for microindustrial fine-tuning, particularly during the era of high-speed growth. (For the most authoritative discussion of administrative guidance in the English language, see Johnson 1982, pp. 242-74.) It has offered MITI the flexibility of tailoring policies to fit ever-changing circumstances without having to pass a batch of laws in the Diet. Over time such laws tend to clog and constrict the range of policy options, endangering the health of the industrial economy. By avoiding heavy dependence on formal legislation, MITI has been able to protect industrial policy from parochial interest groups and partisan politicking. It also enables MITI to intervene quietly and selectively and then pull back. Few, if any, other states can elicit compliance simply by issuing nonbinding guidelines. The reason Japan can do this is again because of the structural characteristics of its political economy, particularly close government-business relations.

Like other older tools of industrial targeting (e.g., antirecession cartels), administrative guidance has come to be used less and less as Japan's economy has matured. For administrative guidance to be effective, several prior conditions have usually had to be met: (1) a relatively small number of homogeneous companies in a given industry, (2) preferably one clear leader among them, (3) a fairly high degree of market concentration, (4) a mature stage (or beyond that) in the industry's life cycle, (5) either a relatively cohesive and strong industrial association or effective mechanisms of industrywide consensus formation, (6) a high degree of dependence on MITI, or a history of closeness, and (7) common problems of sufficient severity to coax individual companies into cooperating, rather than "cheating," in order to advance collective interests.

Except for the last two, none of the prior conditions pertain to the high tech industries. Consider, for example, the software industry. There are far too many companies, competing against one another, with no clear leader, in a very dispersed market still in the early phases of growth. This makes it very difficult either to arrive at industrywide consensus or to close ranks to pursue collective goals. It is not surprising, therefore, that administrative guidance has hardly been used for high tech industries. One of the few areas where it has been used is international trade. MITI has sought to reduce temptations to engage in predatory price cutting abroad because such behavior is almost certain to trigger antidumping procedures; but in few other areas of high technology has administrative guidance been practiced.

It is most commonly used for sunset or declining industries characterized by stagnant or severely fluctuating demand, serious plant overcapacity, and problems of international competitiveness. But even for these
industries the practice of issuing administrative guidance had been cur-
tailed. In a landmark 1974 decision, the Tokyo High Court ruled price
fixing illegal in the petroleum industry (the result, in part, of private sector response to administrative guidance), and while stopping short of
declaring administrative guidance illegal, noted that limits had to be
imposed on its use. Hence, though well known as one of Japan's unique
targeting tools, administrative guidance is no longer relied on extensively
even for old-line industries, much less for high tech enterprise. Like credit
allocation and cartelization, it reveals how a number of Japan's old instruments of industrial policy have waned in effectiveness over the years. The
erosion has not been very damaging, because new policy tools, more
appropriate for high growth industries, have emerged in their place, and
also because the maturation of Japan's high tech industries appears to
have rendered industrial targeting progressively less necessary.

Market Demand

Technological innovation, production efficiency, and sound finances—
the *sine qua non* of high tech competitiveness—rest at least as much, some
say even more, on demand factors than on supply-promoting measures
(Kamien and Schwartz 1982, pp. 35-48). Yet, except at the infant and
declining phases of an industry's life cycle, the range and effectiveness
of industrial policy instruments available for government use in the domain
of market demand tend to be more restricted than is the case for supply
measures. They include: government procurements, home market protection, export promotion, and the encouragement of "buy national" propen-
sities. Each, if handled clumsily or taken to extremes, is capable of giving
rise to serious problems, such as violations of GATT-based agreements
and principles, bilateral trade frictions, threats of retaliation, counterproductive costs of inefficiency, and, perhaps above all, the loss of long-
term, commercial competitiveness. The dangers of corruption, interest-
group capturing, fiscal rigor mortis, and partisan politicization loom large,
because huge public expenditures are at stake. (Mancur Olson refers to
the stultifying effects of "distributional coalitions" on economic growth
rates. See Olson 1982, pp. 36-73.)

This suggests that in the area of market demand, industrial policy is
constrained in what it can do effectively to shape outcomes. Industrial
progress depends largely on private sector responsiveness to market forces.
Where government is poised to have its biggest impact is in the stimula-

tion of greater overall demand through macroeconomic management; the artifical generation of demand for targeted sectors through protectionism, closed procurements, and rigid "buy national" programs is much less likely to have positive consequences. It usually turns out to be self-defeating, because it tends to thwart competition and breed inefficiency. (Exceptions might include temporary infant industry protection and short-term national security objectives.)

Japanese high tech industries have benefited greatly from the country's growth in aggregate demand, fastest of all the major industrial states over the postwar period. While macroeconomic measures are not aimed at promoting specific industries, the effects are differentially felt. The information industries, for example, can be counted among the prime beneficiaries of rapid growth, as can other high tech sectors characterized by high income elasticity of demand. One can argue, therefore, that insofar as demand-side factors are concerned, Japan's high tech companies have advanced commercially and technologically as a result far more of macroeconomic than of industrial policies.

Where guaranteed demand as an instrument of industrial policy can make a substantial difference is in the early stages of an industry's or new product's life cycle. The assurance of defense procurement, for example, has had very positive effects on technological innovation during the toddler years of the U.S. microelectronics industry (Levin 1982). The offer of R&D support, by itself, may not be enough to take major investment risks, since the R&D investment might not lead to commercial products that make the effort worthwhile. Knowing that there is a customer willing to buy new products before a commercial market has taken shape often provides the kind of certainty companies need to invest manpower and resources in state-of-the-art technology. A military market is especially alluring if it is perceived as the first wave in what promises to be a second and much bigger wave of commercial demand (interview with Elliott Levinthal, formerly of the Defense Advanced Research Project Agency, U.S. Department of Defense, September 1983). Often the lure of government procurements as the forerunner of a potentially large commercial market is coupled with government research contracts or R&D subsidies, so that demand-pull and technology-push, in combination, reduce enough of the risks to make forays into the unknown palatable (Nelson 1982, pp. 471-72). The history of innovation in the U.S. computer, microelectronics, and telecommunications industries reveals that the government as guaranteed first purchaser played a crucial initial role, only to be overwhelmed by the subsequent development of commercial markets. Government procurements today account for only a fraction of aggregate demand in these industries.

MITI: The Lack of Procurement

One of the most striking and significant features of Japanese industrial policy is that MITI possesses practically no budget for public procurement. Nothing in the Japanese government is even remotely akin to DOD's or NASA's huge procurement budgets. Japan's Defense Agency operates on one of the world's lowest proportional budgets—roughly 1 percent of GNP—of which only about 25 percent is devoted to weapons acquisition. The implications of MITI's lack of procurement power are far-reaching. Among other consequences, it had meant that:

1. MITI has had to rely heavily on supply-related policies; what it has been able to do on the demand side has been confined to measures other than procurement: home market protection, "buy Japanese" encouragement, and tax incentives for private sector purchases.

2. Macroeconomic policies aimed at expanding aggregate demand have been of far greater importance than industrial policy in stimulating demand for high tech products.

3. MITI's power has been circumscribed by the lack of a budget for procurements.

4. Japanese industrial policy has been less politicized and perhaps more effective than would have been the case if large-scale state procurements had been involved.

5. As latecomers, Japan's high tech companies have had to concentrate on establishing an early base at the lower end of the value-added spectrum from which they have gradually worked up the ladder of technological sophistication.

6. This has sometimes meant that Japanese companies have had to choose consumer-oriented mass market niches (e.g., hand-held calculators for the early development of mass volume memory chips) instead of more sophisticated products for military and industrial applications, which they developed later.

7. Japanese corporations have had to recoup upfront R&D and other capital investments quickly through profits made from newly developed mass volume products sold in the commercial marketplace.

8. Having no assurance of government demand for new products, Japanese companies have lacked compelling incentives to take greater risks in exploring the technological unknown, Japanese companies have tended to follow a comparatively conservative approach to R&D, one with reasonably high prospects of commercial feasibility; this is one reason that the Japanese have not been noted for bold new product innovation.

9. The large size of Japan's domestic market, the capacity of Japanese producers to dominate it, and the commitment to penetrate over-

seas markets have permitted Japan to come from behind in high technology and catch up with U.S. frontrunners, using increasing returns to scale.

10. Japanese engineers and scientists have not had to be diverted from commercially oriented R&D to do highly specialized work for military and space projects; the technological spillover benefits of national security-related research and procurements for the commercial interests of U.S. high tech companies have probably fallen far below the commercial returns that would have been gained had the U.S. research work force not been engaged in security-related endeavors.

Estimating the spillover benefits of national security R&D for commercial purposes is obviously difficult and controversial; but there seems to be general agreement that the spillovers have come to much less than the yields that would have been made if the same time, resources, and manpower had been devoted to commercial R&D. That MITI has lacked the power to wave the magic wand of government procurements thus has had major consequences for government-business relations, industrial policy, corporate strategy, and technological innovation.

Other government agencies such as the Ministry of Construction have had substantial procurement budgets, and it is no coincidence that Construction is one of the most politicized ministries in Japan. The Ministry of Transportation, which also has procurement powers, has used some of its funds to stabilize the ups and downs of shipbuilding demand; not only has this strengthened the ministry's hand, but it has also facilitated the emergence of Japan's shipbuilding industry as the largest and most technologically advanced in the world, though by the late 1970s its world preeminence was ebbing (Vogel 1983). The Japanese government, like France's and the United Kingdom's, has tried to advance the development of Japanese producers by purchasing domestically made computers and other high tech equipment for use in the myriad of local, prefectural, and central government offices and public corporations; until 1975, IBM and other foreign manufacturers had been excluded from this procurement circle.

But almost all industrial states use the power of procurement purchases to strengthen the position of domestic producers. Japan is no exception. U.S. computer companies in the United Kingdom have gone to court over the British government's discriminatory procurement practices (Muller 1982). U.S. government agencies also discriminate against foreign companies. What is unusual about Japan is that the level of demand generated by government procurements is relatively small, accounting in 1980 for less than 4 percent of the number of computers sold, and less than 14 percent of the total value of all computers used in Japan (Nihon Jōhō Shori Kaihatsu Kyōkai 1981, pp.95-105).

NTT Procurements

NTT (Nippon Telegraph and Telephone) used to be one of the few public institutions in Japan with substantial procurement power for the information industries. In 1981, NTT's procurement budget came to about $2.7 billion. For NEC, NTT's largest and most important supplier, procurements exceeded $500 million, representing 12 percent of total company sales. Assured sales of telecommunications equipment gave NTT-family firms the leeway to take advantage of the following benefits: economies of scale; greater learning by doing; advances in production technology; cost and risk reduction; profits and fungible resources to plow back into R&D; experience that could be used to enter related technologies or new product markets; and the capacity to raise more capital.

Until 1981, this procurement bonanza had been closed to foreign bidders; in 1984, three years after liberalization, foreign manufacturers had still managed to win less than 5 percent of NTT procurements, and that mostly in the lower value-added products, not in areas of clear U.S. superiority. Foreign firms, excluded from NTT contracts, maintain that the closed system has funneled de facto subsidies to domestic producers, with competitive fallout effects felt not only in telecommunications but also in the semiconductor and computer industries.

Demand for telecommunications equipment is expected to keep climbing through the end of the century, as NTT implements an ambitious plan to expand and upgrade the nation's entire telecommunications infrastructure through the Information Network System (INS). Over a twenty-year period, INS is expected to generate upwards of 30 trillion yen (roughly $130 billion at 1984 exchange rates) in procurement demand, or an average of about $6.5 billion per year. If Japanese companies garner all but a small share, the technological and commercial impetus imparted to such areas as voice recognition and storage, high speed and mass volume information processing, and facsimile equipment is bound to be enormous (Kitahara 1983, pp. 80-103).

Conceivably, the combination of NTT and Japan Defense Agency demand could facilitate bolder risk-taking and state-of-the-art breakthroughs by Japanese corporations in the future, perhaps in a manner similar to that of DOD and NASA procurements. Now that Japan's information industries have reached the frontiers of technology, state-of-the-art research support, backed by guaranteed government procurements, may become increasingly useful in reducing the risks and costs of new product development and keeping the pace of technological and commercial growth moving briskly ahead. But defense-related R&D is likely to remain small for the foreseeable future, and the conversion of NTT from a public to private corporation has transformed ties between NTT and family firms, shifting the nexus from organizational arrangements for joint R&D and procurements to a more market type of buyer-and-seller relationship.

Indirect Demand Stimulation

Without the power of procurements, MITI has had to rely on a variety of indirect instruments of demand stimulation: tax incentives, export facilitation, organizations for rental or leasing, and home market protection. Until 1983, MITI used special tax incentives to encourage Japanese manufacturers to purchase and install robots, numerically controlled (NC) machine tools, and other automated assembly line equipment. While the primary objectives were to increase output, lower costs, heighten productivity, and reduce hazardous working conditions, the switch to automated facilities had the effect of boosting demand for high tech equipment. During 1982-83, companies buying robots and NC machine tools received a 13 percent tax credit on the purchasing price—on top of regularly scheduled depreciation allowances. Of course, other governments, including the U.S., have also offered generous depreciation allowances; hence, whether and to what extent special Japanese tax credits have boosted sales is unclear. Would Japanese companies have purchased and installed robots and NC machine tools without tax credits?

MITI has also exhorted domestic producers to move down the learning curve by exporting to open overseas markets. Although Japanese trading companies and most individual companies are well equipped to handle the logistics of exporting, the government provides encouragement, valuable information about markets, and constant feedback and advice. MITI has probably done more to remind Japanese companies of the importance of taking a global view of market share and to facilitate exports as any government in the world. In addition to information, probably its most valuable service, MITI also helps to make arrangements for export insurance and financing through the Japan Export-Import Bank.

Lacking the wherewithal to purchase high tech equipment, MITI often comes up with clever ways of accomplishing perhaps the next best thing: organizing nonprofit companies to purchase, rent, or lease costly and continually changing high tech equipment. The Japan Electronic Computer Corporation (JECC), created in 1961 as a semigovernmental joint venture involving the seven leading computer manufacturers, is perhaps the best-known example. Drawing on a pool of funds, including low interest loans from the Japan Development Bank, JECC had purchased a cumulative total of over $7.25 billion worth of computer equipment, by 1981, with rental revenues of $5.6 billion. Its role in helping Japan's computer industry establish a secure foothold in the expanding leasing market was critical, especially during the early years when IBM appeared on the verge of taking control of the Japanese market and Japanese computer companies lacked the financial resources, individually, to compete (Nihon Denshi Keisanki Kabushiki Kaisha 1983).

The Japan Robot Leasing Company (JAROL), organized in 1980, is another joint venture (comprising twenty-four robot manufacturers, ten insurance companies, and seven general leasing firms) which leases robots to small- and medium-size companies. As of 1982, it had leased nearly eight hundred robots, worth over $25 million. Furthermore, the Small Business Finance Corporation, a government institution, provided loans to small-medium companies for robot installation. Thus even without a procurement budget, MITI has been able to make use of several policy instruments that can be thought of as indirect and limited functional substitutes. While they have not had as much impact as large-scale procurements, these policy instruments have boosted demand in ways that would not otherwise have been possible.

Home Market Protection

Another instrument of indirect demand stimulation on which MITI has relied heavily in the past (but less so since the late 1970s) is the protection of home markets and domestic producers against foreign competition through formal import duties, quotas, restrictions on foreign direct investments, and a variety of nontariff barriers. Formal tariffs, which used to be very high, have been lowered substantially since the mid-1970s. In 1963 dutiable imports carried a 20.9 percent average levy; by 1983 it had fallen to 4.3 percent. Import duties for high tech products conformed to the national pattern. From 1972 to 1983, computer peripheral duties fell from 22.5 percent to 6 percent; computer mainframes were lowered from 13.5 percent to 4.9 percent; semiconductors dropped from 15 percent to 4.2 percent, with complete elimination scheduled by 1987. Such reductions have brought Japan in line with U.S. levels, and far below the European Community.

Although formal barriers have come down, Japanese industries are still shielded from the full force of foreign competition by various nontariff barriers, ranging from a maze of intercorporate stockholdings to a politicized retail distribution network. Indeed, it may be that the Japanese government has been willing to clear away formal barriers in part because it realizes that full foreign access to Japan's lucrative home market continues to be impeded by structural barriers in the private sector. Hiroshi Okumura (1982, p. 61) draws attention to the fact that the impact of capital liberalization has been neutralized by developments within the realm of the intercorporate stockholding: "As it turned out, while the government went about the liberalization of capital, Japanese companies were busily implementing their own plans for keeping foreign capital out by means of stock-securing maneuvers. As mentioned, these involved the placement of a large bloc of the stock issued by one company in the hands of other companies—typically its bank and leading partners. The companies thus entrusted with stock did not accept it merely because they were asked to. They became stockholders to enhance intercorporate cohesion and to bind the group together more firmly. The main reason almost no Japanese companies have been absorbed by foreign capital is that each corporate group met the capital liberalization program with its own stock-defense program" (Okumura 1982). The government encouraged the trend toward intercorporate stock concentration, according to Okumura; lax antitrust enforcement permitted corporate entities to expand their share of outstanding stocks to over 70 percent, and occasional administrative guidance facilitated the process.

Not only has this obstructed foreign acquisitions and takeovers; it has also contained foreign penetration of Japanese markets. Buying and selling within a self-contained circle of Japanese companies owning stock in one another makes sense from the standpoint of implicit long-term contracts. Purchasing intermediate goods from subsidiaries, closely affiliated subcontractors, or members of the same *keiretsu* can almost be considered quasi-internal transactions. It is not surprising therefore that the complex structure of Japanese industrial organization—with its maze of vertical and horizontal groupings and the logic of stable, long-term relations and low transaction costs—has thus limited foreign penetration of lucrative Japanese markets.

Sales of foreign-made intermediate goods are limited further by the diverse vertically integrated nature of Japanese corporations. Instead of relying on merchant houses, Japanese computer companies make their own components and sell what they do not use. U.S. semiconductor producers complain that Japanese companies tend to purchase only those highly sophisticated components that they themselves cannot make: state-of-the-art microprocessors and custom-made logic devices, for example (interviews with several Silicon Valley executives, October 1983). And once Japanese corporations learn how to produce the more advanced devices, the demand for American-made products drops. Americans suspect that a well-orchestrated "buy Japanese" policy lies behind their inability to expand exports to Japan; but there are other plausible explanations which do not hinge of conspiratorial theories, such as captive, in-house production, *keiretsu* membership, subcontracting and subsidiary networks. The point is that the nature of Japanese industrial organization makes foreign penetration into Japanese markets harder than the obverse.

Japanese companies in electronics, and probably most other fields, conduct business within a clear hierarchy of corporate customers, based on the length, magnitude, and overall importance of the business relationship. Priority in financing, commodity supplies, and services is given to customers that rank toward the top of the hierarchy. Should there be a shortfall of supplies—as, for example, 256K RAMs—Japanese corporations will distribute available commodities in accordance with their hierarchical priorities. Customers lowest on the list come out on the short end. To underscore the point: the importance of extramarket considerations—especially the preferance for stable, predictable, long-term business relations, based on mutual trust—has had the effect of raising barriers to foreign (as well as new Japanese company) entry. Such structural, nontariff barriers embedded deeply in the private sector are not directly connected with industrial policy; but their existence serves basically the same function as formal measures of home market protection.

Conclusions

There is no witchcraft involved in MITI's formula for successful industrial policy. Most of its policies can be found on any standard list used by states seeking to promote their high tech industries. The dosages and mixes may vary, depending on the circumstances, but the prescription is fairly standard. Japanese industrial policy measures for high technology can be grouped into four categories: (1) general, (2) selective omissions, (3) distinctive but not decisive, and (4) distinctive and critical. Let us conclude by grouping the policy measures discussed in this chapter into these categories, noting parenthetically other countries that have relied on the same policy measures.

1. *General Policies*
    Funding for university-based R&D (U.S.)
    R&D subsidies (France, U.S., U.K.)
        Contract research
        Loans at preferential interest rates
        R&D tax credits
    National research projects (U.S., France, EC)
    Procurements (U.S., France, W. Germany, U.K.)
        Preferential treatment for domestic producers
        Telecommunications
        Central and local governments and public corporations
        Defense procurements
    Tax incentives (U.S., France, W. Germany)
        Government loans for exports (France, W. Germany, U.S.)

Credit insurance guarantees (France, W. Germany, U.S.)
Foreign exchange loss guarantees (France, Sweden, U.K.)
Tax-free reserve for marketing costs overseas (Belgium)
Accelerated depreciation for new facilities (U.S., W. Germany)
Accelerated depreciation for overseas investment (W. Germany)
Tax deferrals for overseas investment (France, W. Germany)
Export facilitation (France, W. Germany, U.K., Sweden, U.S.)
Information and promotion (U.K., W. Germany, France)
Incentives for small businesses (U.K., W. Germany, France)
Home market protection (EC)
Residual tariffs (lower than EC)
Nontariff barriers
Industrial location (Italy, France, W. Germany)
Prefecture and state policies
Central-local coordination

2. *Selective Omissions*
Large defense and space procurements (U.S.)
Diversion of engineering and scientific manpower from
commercial R&D
Reduced resource allocation cost effectiveness
Limited commercial spillovers
Prestige projects of limited commercial payoff (France, U.K.)
Example: supersonic jet, Concorde
Selection of "national champions" (France, W. Germany)
Nationalization (France, Italy)
Government-controlled venture investments (U.K., France)
Strict antitrust enforcement (U.S., W. Germany)
On joint research
Cumbersome and restrictive controls on technology exports (U.S.)
Export Administration Act (U.S., 1979)
Sustained protection of sunset industries (Italy, U.K., U.S.)
Defiance of shifting international comparative advantage
Misallocation of capital and labor
Overly blunt policy instruments (U.S.)
Across-the-board tax incentives for all industries
Domestic International Sales Corporation (DISC)

As the list of selective omissions indicates, the Japanese government
has sought to keep the discipline of market forces alive (operating within
the framework of organizational arrangements). It has withstood the temp-
tation (to which some European states have succumbed) of trying to make
the transition from smokestacks to high technology by pouring vast sums

of public money into R&D. It has not extended as visible a hand as other states in setting up life-support systems for dying industries. Nor has it ever considered nationalizing leading high tech corporations à la Thomson and Cii-Honeywell Bull in France. And without having to bear America's heavy burdens of military security, Japan has not had to divert manpower and resources away from commercially oriented R&D. The net result of these selective omissions is that Japanese industrial policy has probably created fewer economic distortions than industrial policy intervention in most other countries. What else sets Japanese industrial policy for high technology apart?

3. *Distinctive But Not Decisive Policies*
    Special Temporary Development Laws for priority industries
        Authorization for MITI to devise special programs to
            facilitate and accelerate development of priority areas
        Selective exemption from antitrust
    Administrative guidance
        Concerning especially exports
    Nontariff barriers
        Difficulties of foreign acquisition of Japanese firms
        Extensive intercorporate ownership of firms
        Retail distribution network
        Keiretsu membership
    Rental and leasing arrangements
        Preferential financing
        Tax-free reserves for rental equipment losses
    Tax incentives
        Performance bond coverage (U.K.)
        Tax-free reserves for retirement payments
    Antitrust
        Consideration of international competitiveness (France, Italy)
        Tolerance for extensive intercorporate stockholdings
        Permission for joint research as long as competition among
            major companies is not diminished
        Research cooperatives
        Legality of administrative guidance
    Preferential treatment for large blue-chip corporations
        NTT family and national research project participation
        R&D subsidies

The previous two categories of policy measures, however important, still do not provide a sufficient explanation of why Japanese industrial policy is comparatively effective. What factors can be cited as distinctive and critical?

4. *Distinctive and Critical Policies*
   Positive adjustment policies
       Gradual phase-out of declining sectors
       Search for higher value-added production
       Adjustment to changing international comparative advantage
   Nonpoliticized industrial policies
       Primacy of collective, national interests and goals
   Market-conforming nature of industrial policies
       Concern with keeping market forces and discipline strong
   Synergism between R&D activities of government and industry
   Sustained cooperative R&D between NTT and NTT family firms
       Joint and contract research
       Information exchange on confidential disclosure basis
   Nonlegalistic nature of industrial policies
       MITI reliance on persuasion and incentives, not coercion
       Industry dependence on MITI for policy support
       Minimal MITI recourse to formal legislation
   Compatibility of industrial and macroecomonic policies
       Loose integration of industrial policy within macroeconomic
           framework
       Example: special tax provisions for "targeted" sectors
   Extensive information gathering and analysis
       MITI: communication center
       Private-public sources of information
   MITI "vision": economic forecasting and goal-setting
       Annual, medium, and long-term plans
       Concern for broad social implications of high technology
   MITI-industry consensus: mobilization and objectives
       Comparative harmony of government-business interests and
           goals
       Probusiness policy orientation

Of the characteristics listed above, probably the three rarest and hardest to achieve are the low level of politicization, nonlegalistic and generally market-conforming policies, and synergistic working relationship between government and private enterprise. The three characteristics go farthest in explaining the comparative effectiveness of the government's use of industrial policy instruments. No other large, industrial state has managed to combine these and other policy characteristics to quite the extent that Japan has.

How has Japan done it? To explain the country's capacity to administer a relatively successful industrial policy requires returning to the structural characteristics of the Japanese political economy. For it is the structure of the regime that provides the overall context within which industrial policy is administered—advantageously or at the cost of considerable, sometimes irreparable, collateral damage. At the regime level, there are several characteristics that stand out as more or less unique to Japan and decisive in explaining why Japanese industrial policy has not failed or had more mixed success.

Structural Features of Japan's Political Economy
    Macrosocietal factors:
        Organization into groups as basic units of society
        Nation as ultimate collectivity
        State as symbol, goal-definer, coordinator
        Consensual norms
    Electoral politics:
        Liberal Democratic Party's continuous control over the
            Diet
        Broad base of electoral support for LDP
        Factional fragmentation of LDP
        Probusiness orientation
        Relative weakness of organized labor
        Weakness of opposition parties
        Absence of deep ideological cleavages
    Bureaucratic administration:
        Scope of MITI policy-making power
        MITI's internal organization
        Legitimacy from tradition, track record, and coordinating
            role
    Political-bureaucratic relationship:
        Close LDP-MITI working relations
        Interpenetration of personnel (ex-bureaucrats in politics)
        Structure of LDP informal caucuses, policy committees, and
            Diet committees
        Interest aggregation capacity
    Private corporations:
        Specialization and cohesion of Japanese companies
        Permanent employment
        Combination of merit and ascription
    Industrial organization: the fusion of market and organization
        Keiretsu groupings
            Horizontal ties
        Vertical networks
            Subcontracting
            Subsidiaries

Corporate financing
  Bank-business ties
  Intercorporate stockholding
  Hierarchical, long-term business relationships
Public-private interface:
  Industrial associations: intraindustry
  Business federations: interindustry
Public-private interpenetration:
    Public corporations
    Special nonprofit corporations
    Mixed, public-private enterprises
    Informal policy networks
MITI-industry's capacity to forge consensus

Some of the institutions—an active and elite bureaucracy, consensual procedures, and public corporations—can be found elsewhere. Others—like the LDP's long dominance over the legislature, the scope of MITI's jurisdiction and the nature of its internal organization, and extensive *keiretsu* structures—are more distinctively Japanese. The uniqueness of Japan's political economy cannot be understood solely by comparing one institution with another outside Japan, though such a comparison would bring to light subtle differences in degree as well as in kind. What makes the Japanese system different is the way the individual institutions fit together as parts of an integrated, mutually reinforcing whole. The whole is much greater than the sum of its parts.

Consider high debt financing and lifetime employment, two of the most significant practices among Japanese corporations. The combination would spell disaster if Japanese corporations had to function within the context of related institutions which happened to be incompatible: for example, militant craft unions prone to carry out prolonged strikes; or rigidly bureaucratic banks disposed to lend only on the basis of strict market criteria; or arm's-length transactions with subcontractors; or a legalistic government not especially supportive of business interests.

Or consider Japan's educational system, a harshly criticized system based on a series of fiercely competitive examinations beginning with kindergarten and culminating in college entrance examinations. Leaving aside the human costs of "examination hell," the educational system generates an extraordinary level of competition, reaffirms the principle of merit as the basis of upward mobility, supplies industry with a large supply of talented manpower, permits companies to intermingle merit and ascription (seniority), and channels the "best and brightest" to elite organizations and the key sectors of the economy. In these and other ways, it greatly facilitates the implementation of industrial policy.

Perhaps the system's most striking feature, and a central explanation for its well-integrated nature, dynamism, and stability, is its particular mix of market and organization. Market forces supply the energy and dynamism, organization the structure and stability. Each compensates for the shortcomings of the other, with a delicate but dynamic balance being struck between the two. Compared with the United States, in Japan organizational elements permeate the economy and structure market forces more extensively; compared with France, in Japan the market is more vibrant, driving firms to compete more vigorously. By giving structure to regime characteristics, the delicate interaction between market and organization also accounts in large measure for what must be considered a relatively successful industrial policy for high technology.

As this paper has repeatedly pointed out, however, Japan's political economy is undergoing change as the country's industrial structure shifts from the old-line industries to high technology. The nature and role of such institutions as *keiretsu* groups, subsidiaries and subcontracting networks, and banking-industry relations are changing under the impact of such external forces as financial deregulation and fast-moving technology. A number of these changes are adaptations to the different functional requisites of high technology. The proliferation of small subsidiaries and the increasing shift of R&D from parent firm to subsidiaries, for example, ought to be understood as structural adaptations to the requisites of innovation and compensation for the absence of a venture capital market. This raises the as yet unanswerable question whether Japanese institutions, marvelously well suited for latecomer catch-up in the old-line industries, can adjust quickly enough to facilitate, rather than impede, the transition to high technology. Nothing brings to light more clearly the broader significance of the historic transition Japan's whole political economy is passing through.

Despite Japan's past successes, and despite the comparative effectiveness of Japanese industrial policy to date, Japan is by no means guaranteed to shift smoothly from latecomer to pioneer. As Japan's regime characteristics change, the state's capacity to administer industrial policy will probably also undergo change. But as the need for, and effectiveness of, industrial policy also seems to be diminishing, the change may not be nearly as damaging for high technology as it might have been for the old-line industries.

Indeed, technological and commercial change is moving ahead so fast that public policy simply cannot keep up. The private sector is being called upon to make more of the necessary adjustments, thus lightening the burden that used to fall on the state. This suggests that as Japan rises to meet the challenge of high technology, the delicate balance between market and organization will be altered. Perhaps the balance will be tilted in the direction of stronger and less fettered market forces. Perhaps the best measure of success with respect to Japanese industrial policy will be the extent to which it renders itself progressively unnecessary.

REFERENCES

Aoki, Masahiko. 1983. "Innovative Adaptation Through the Quasi-Tree Structure: An Emerging Aspect of Japanese Entrepreneurship." Unpublished paper.

Arrow, Kenneth J. 1962. "The Economic Implications of Learning by Doing." *Review of Economic Studies* 29(1):155-73.

Bellah, Robert N. 1957. *Tokugawa Religions: The Values of Pre-Industrial Japan.* Glencoe: The Free Press.

Clark, Rodney. 1979. *The Japanese Company.* New Haven: Yale University Press.

Dore, Ronald. 1983. "Goodwill and the Spirit of Market Capitalism." *British Journal of Sociology* 34(4):459-82.

Eads, George C. 1983. "The Political Experience in Allocating Investment: Lessons from the United States and Elsewhere." In Michael L. Wachter and Susan M. Wachter, eds., *Toward a New U.S. Industrial Policy?* pp. 453-82. Philadelphia: University of Pennsylvania Press.

Feigenbaum, Edward A. 1983. Presentation at the U.S.-Japan High Technology Project, Northeast Asia–United States Forum, Stanford University, November 21.

Feigenbaum, Edward A., and Pamela McCorduck. 1983. *The Fifth Generation: Artificial Intelligence and Japan's Computer Challenge to the World.* Reading, Mass. and Menlo Park, Calif.: Addison-Wesley.

Fellner, William. 1969. "Specific Implications of Learning by Doing." *Journal of Economic Theory* 1(2):119-40.

Fong, Glenn R. 1983. "Industrial Policy Innovation in the United States: Lessons from the Very High Speed Integrated Circuit Program." Unpublished paper presented at the 1983 Annual Meeting of the American Political Science Association, Chicago, September 1-4.

Geertz, Clifford. 1981. *Negara: The Theatre State in Nineteenth Century Bali.* Princeton: Princeton University Press.

Haitani, Kanji. 1976. *The Japanese Economic System.* Lexington, Mass.: Lexington Books.

Hazewindus, Nico, with John Tooker. 1982. *The U.S. Microelectronics Industry.* New York: Pergamon Press.

Hirschman, Albert. 1970. *Exit, Voice, and Loyalty.* Cambridge: Harvard University Press.

Imai, Ken-ichi, and Hiroyuki Itami. 1982. "The Firm and Market in Japan: Mutual Penetration of the Market Principle and Organization Principle." Unpublished paper.

Imai Ken-ichi, Itami Hiroyuki, and Koike Kazuo. 1982. *Naibu soshiki no keizaigaku* [The economics of internal organizations]. Tokyo: Tōyō Keizai Shimpōsha.

Johnson, Chalmers. 1978. *Japan's Public Policy Companies.* Washington, D.C.: American Enterprise Institute for Public Policy Research.

Johnson, Chalmers. 1982. *MITI and the Japanese Miracle: The Growth of Industrial Policy, 1925-1975*. Stanford: Stanford University Press.

Jones, Keith. 1982. "French and U.S. Interests Intertwine Around ICs." *Electronic Business* 8(7):88.

Jones, Keith. 1983. "Nationalized French Computer Industry Sparks Controversy." *Electronic Business* 9(4):37-38.

Kamien, Morton I., and Nancy L. Schwartz. 1982. *Market Structure and Innovation*. Cambridge: Cambridge University Press.

✓ Katzenstein, Peter J. 1985. *Small States in World Markets: Industrial Policy in Europe*. Ithaca: Cornell University Press.

Kikuchi, Makoto. 1983. *Japanese Electronics*. Tokyo: Simul Press.

Kitahara, Yasusada. 1983. *Information Network System: Telecommunications in the Twenty-first Century*. London: Heinemann Educational Books.

Kotler, Philip, Liam Fahey, S. Jatusripititak. 1985. *The New Competition: What Theory Z Didn't Tell You About—Marketing*. Englewood Cliffs, N.J.: Prentice Hall.

Levin, Richard C. 1982. "The Semiconductor Industry." In Richard R. Nelson, ed., *Government and Technical Progress*, pp. 9-100. New York: Pergamon Press.

Lijphart, Arend. 1977. *Democracy in Plural Societies*. New Haven: Yale University Press.

Little, Arthur D., Inc. (Japan). 1983. "Summary of Major Projects in Japan for R&D of Information Processing Technology." Unpublished study.

Moritani, Masanori. 1982. *Japanese Technology*. Tokyo: Simul Press.

Muller, Robert L. 1982. "U.S. Computer Firms in Britain Suspect U.K. Agencies Favor Home Companies." *Wall Street Journal*, August 12.

Nakagawa Yasuzo. 1981. *Nihon no handōtai kaihatsu* [Japan's semiconductor development]. Tokyo: Daiyamondosha.

Nakane, Chie. 1970. *Japanese Society*. Berkeley and Los Angeles: University of California Press.

Nakatani, Iwao. 1984. "The Economic Role of Financial Corporate Grouping in Japan." In Masahiko Aoki, ed., *The Economic Analysis of the Japanese Firm*, pp. 227-58. Amsterdam: North Holland.

National Science Foundation. 1981. "Industrial R&D Expenditures in 1980 Show Real Growth for Fifth Consecutive Year." *Highlights*, December 31, 1981. NSF 81-331.

Nebashi, Masato. 1981. "VLSI Technology Research Association." Unpublished paper.

Nelson, Richard R. 1982. "Government Stimulus of Technological Progress: Lessons from American History." In Richard R. Nelson, ed., *Government and Technical Progress*, pp. 451-82. New York: Pergamon Press.

Nihon Denshi Keisanki Kabushiki Kaisha, ed. 1983. *JECC: Computer Handbook*. Tokyo.

Nihon Jōhō Shori Kaihatsu Kyōkai. 1981. *Conpyuuta hakusho 1981* [Computer White Paper 1981]. Tokyo.

Okimoto, Daniel I. 1983. *Pioneer and Pursuer: The Role of the State in the Evolution of the Japanese and American Semiconductor Industries*. Stanford: An Occasional Paper of the Northeast Asian-United States Forum on International Policy, Stanford University.

Okimoto, Daniel I. 1984a. "Political Context." In Daniel I. Okimoto, Takuo Sugano, and Franklin B. Weinstein, eds., *Competitive Edge: The Semiconductor Industry in the U.S. and Japan*, pp. 78-133. Stanford: Stanford University Press.

Okimoto, Daniel I. 1984b. "Conclusions." In Okimoto, Sugano, and Weinstein,

eds., *Competitive Edge*, pp. 177-235. Stanford: Stanford University Press.
Okimoto, Daniel I. Forthcoming. *Between MITI and the Market: Japanese Industrial Policy for High Technology*. Stanford: Stanford University Press.
Okimoto, Daniel, and Henry K. Hayase. 1985. "Organizing for Innovation."
Okumura, Hiroshi. 1982. "The Closed Nature of Japanese Intercorporate Relations." *Japan Echo* 9(3):53-61.
Olson, Mancur. 1982. *The Rise and Decline of Nations*. New Haven: Yale University Press.
Ouchi, William. 1984. *The M-Form Society: How American Teamwork Can Recapture the Competitive Edge*. Reading, Mass.: Addison-Wesley.
Patrick, Hugh, and Hideo Sato. 1982. "The Political Economy of United States-Japan Trade in Steel." In Kozo Yamamura, ed., *Policy and Trade Issues of the Japanese Economy*, pp. 197-238. Seattle: University of Washington Press.
Price, Victoria Curzon. 1981. *Industrial Policies in the European Community*. London: St. Martin's Press, 1981.
Saxonhouse, Gary R. 1982. "Japanese High Technology, Government Policy, and Evolving Comparative Advantage in Goods and Services." Unpublished paper.
Schultze, Charles L. 1977. *The Public Use of Private Interest*. Washington, D.C.: Brookings Institution.
Semiconductor Industry Association. 1983. *The Effect of Government Targeting on World Semiconductor Competition*. Cupertino: Semiconductor Industry Association.
Shad, John S. R. 1984. "The Leveraging of America." *Wall Street Journal*, June 8.
Stalk, George, and Kenneth Arbour. 1984. "Your Can Stop Pitying the Japanese Stockholder." *Wall Street Journal*, June 11.
U.S. International Trade Commission (USITC). 1977. *Staff Report on the United States Steel Industry and Its International Rivals: Trends and Factors Determining International Competitiveness*. Washington, D.C.: U.S. Government Printing Office.
U.S. International Trade Commission. 1979. *Competitive Factors Influencing World Trade in Integrated Circuits*. Report to the subcommittee on Trade of the Committee on Finance and the Subcommittee on International Finance of the Committee on Banking, Housing, and Urban Affairs of the U.S. Senate. Washington, D.C.: U.S. Government Printing Office.
U.S. International Trade Commission. 1983. *Foreign Industrial Targeting and Its Effects on U.S. Industries, Phase I: Japan*. Washington, D.C.: U.S. Government Printing Office.
Vogel, Ezra F. 1983. "Shipbuilding: Basic Industry." Unpublished manuscript.
Wachter, Michael L., and Susan M. Wachter, eds. 1983. *Toward a New U.S. Industrial Policy?* Philadelphia: University of Pennsylvania Press.
Wakasugi Takahira. 1984. "Sentangijutsu sangyō no kenkyū kaihatsu katsudō" [The R&D activities of high technology industries]. *Bijenesu rebyuu* 31(3):59-62.
Warnecke, Steven J., ed. 1978. *International Trade and Industrial Policies*. New York: Holmes and Meier Publishers, Inc.
Weinstein, Franklin B., Michiyuki Uenohara, and John G. Linvill. 1984. In Daniel I. Okimoto, Takuo Sugano, and Franklin B. Weinstein, eds., *Competitive Edge: The Semiconductor Industry in the U.S. and Japan*, pp. 35-77. Stanford: Stanford University Press.
Williamson, Oliver E. 1975. *Markets and Hierarchies: Analysis and Antitrust Implications*. New York: The Free Press.
Wilson, Robert W., Peter K. Ashton, and Thomas P. Egan. 1980. *Innovation, Competition, and Government Policy in the Semiconductor Industry*. Lexington, Mass.: D.C. Heath, 1980.

Chapter 3

Industrial Policy and Factor Markets: Biotechnology in Japan and the United States

Gary R. Saxonhouse

"The latest example of Japan's industrial development strategy is the biotechnology field. . . . With this drive underway, U.S. biotechnology firms believe they will have limited access in selling genetic engineering products to Japan" (Hufbauer 1982).

There is a widespread feeling that the Japanese government is unfairly acquiring for its economy the few really good tickets to prosperity in the twenty-first century. Foreign reactions to Japanese targeting have ranged from concern that such practices are unfair and inconsistent with the international economic system, and that Japan should be forced to eliminate them, to intense admiration and a hope the United States can somehow emulate Japan. Understanding Japanese practices, particularly as they relate to high technology industries, requires an analysis not only of relations between government and business in Japan, but also of those between government and education and between education and business. From the perspective of an analysis of these interrelationships it is possible to understand the character of the market distortions and market failures that Japanese policy has sought to cope with. It should also then be possible to assess whether the United States faces similar problems requiring similar interventions. These analyses will proceed with particular focus on the development of the biotechnology industry in Japan and the United States.

Government and Business: Japanese Government
Policy Instruments in American Perspective

A consensus has been reached at the highest government levels in Japan that biotechnology is of substantial importance to the future of the Japanese economy. From an American perspective the most picturesque manifestation of this consensus came at the 1983 Economic Summit in

Williamsburg, where in the glare of global publicity, Prime Minister Nakasone commended biotechnology to President Reagan and proceeded to attempt to enlighten him on the character and significance of recombinant DNA. This interest in biotechnology arises not because Japan faces unique problems for which biotechnology promises solutions, though such problems and solutions do exist. Rather biotechnology is viewed as reaching a stage of development at which, during the next five, ten, and twenty years, its many commercial applications, together with complementary developments, will yield an extremely high rate of return on resources committed. When biotechnology is commonly defined to include the industrial use of recombinant DNA, cell fusion, and novel bioprocessing techniques, under even the most optimistic appraisals of the future market size of biotechnology related projects, the future development of this industry cannot, by itself, have a significant impact on the aggregate growth and productivity of large industrialized economies. Nonetheless, as an element in a broader strategy of emphasizing knowledge-intensive high technology industries and emulating American interest, biotechnology is well regarded by Japanese government officials. Characteristically, many Japanese government agencies believe that public policy working both through and outside of market processes can affect the timing and form of biotechnology's impact on the economy.

From as early as April 1971 when the Science and Technology Council (*Kagaku gijutsu kaigi*), a group of government, business, and academic leaders, serving in an advisory capacity to Japan's Science and Technology Agency (*Kagaku gijutsu chō*), identified the life sciences as an area worthy of special government and private sector assistance, there has been a steady stream of government reports and statements by leaders of business groups regarding the future of biotechnology in Japan (KGK 1971).

While the areas that came to be known as biotechnology elicited Japanese government interest before such historic events as the first gene cloning in 1973, the first expression of a gene cloned from a different species in bacteria in 1974, and the creation of the first hybridoma in 1975, systematic consideration of biotechnology's place in the future of the Japanese economy by policy makers in either the private sector or the public sector is no more recent than late 1980. This acceleration in interest was fueled first by the extraordinarily favorable reception received by biotechnology-related companies in the American equity markets. In October 1980 the initial public offering by Genentech, the first American firm founded to exploit recombinant DNA technology, set a Wall Street record for fastest price per share increase by going from $35 a share to $89 a share in twenty minutes.

At the same time that it became apparent that there were widely held extremely optimistic expectations regarding biotechnology's future potential it also became apparent that access to these technologies might not be so easy. In 1980 in the landmark case *Diamond* v. *Chakrabarty*, the Supreme Court held that the inventor of a new microorganism, whose invention otherwise met the legal requirements for obtaining a patent, could not be denied a patent solely because the invention was alive. This decision made possible the granting of what appeared at the time to be an extremely inclusive patent to Stanford University and the University of California at Berkeley for the work of Herbert Boyer and Stanley Cohen. Where earlier antitrust concerns and the 1956 Consent Decree with American Telephone and Telegraph had allowed the benefits of the research and development at Bell Laboratories to flow to Japanese firms at nominal or zero costs (U.S. Commerce Department 1977), there was now concern in Japan that at just the time biology looked most promising American technology policies were about to change.

The Cohen-Boyer patent was issued six weeks after the Genentech offering. Two weeks after that, in early December 1980, a hurriedly called meeting of the Committee on Life Sciences of the Japan Federation of Economic Organizations (Keidanren) was held. The stated purpose of this meeting was to help frame a Japanese response to these new developments. Attending were the president of Mitsubishi Chemicals, the chairman of Kyowa Hakkō (a chemical company with significant involvement in pharmaceuticals), the president of Tōray (a leading synthetic fiber producer), and representatives of thirty other Japanese companies with an interest in biotechnology. The Cohen-Boyer patent was seen as a matter of enormous concern because those attending the meeting had been advised that the patent would affect almost any product application of genetic engineering. Ironically, it was claimed at this meeting that the United States was designating biotechnology, in the wake of the Genentech success, as a strategic national industry and was weaving about it a new and unprecedented network of protective patents (Tatara 1981).

While the very existence of such a committee in Keidanren reflected long-standing Japanese policy concern with biotechnology, the December 1980 meeting marked the first attempt to give high profile attention to this new industry. In the wake of this meeting, what had been a steady stream now turned into a veritable flood of authoritative statements by both public and private sector bodies as to what actions ought to be taken by Japan to ensure Japanese participation in this promising new industry. This remarkable upsurge in interest was noted by a distinguished Japanese molecular biologist whose professional career had been in the United States but who happened to be in Japan in 1981: "When I went back to Japan five years ago, I explained to Japanese scholars, government officials and businessmen, the importance of genetic engineering. However, most of them were not interested in genetic engineering at all. Now everyone is talking about it. This is a typical Japanese phenomenon, isn't it?" (Susumu 1982, p. 126).

Because of the rather heterogeneous character and the potentially far-reaching impact of what is called biotechnology, the breadth of both public and private interest is not surprising. What did, however, mark 1981 as the Year of Biotechnology in Japan was establishment by the Ministry of International Trade and Industry (MITI) in September 1981 of the *Baiotekunoroji sangyō chōki bishon sakuei iinkai* (Biotechnology Industry Long-term Vision Discussion Group), its plans to establish the following year the *Baiotekunoroji shinkō shitsu* (Office of Biotechnology Promotion), and its inclusion of three major biotechnology projects within its *Jisedai sangyō kiban gijutsu kenkyū kaihatsu seido* (Program for Next Generation Basic Industrial Technology).

While the Ministry of Education, the Science and Technology Agency, the Ministry of Agriculture, Forestry and Fisheries, and the Environmental Protection Agency had previously had an interest in this area, apart from some energy-related interest in the development and use of biomass, 1981 marked the beginning of a major interest by MITI in this area. MITI's bureaucratic entry into high visibility strategic planning for biotechnology signaled the beginning of spirited jockeying among a wide array of government entities for influence. It should be noted that the emergence of high profile Japanese concern with biotechnology was certainly no earlier than and probably lagged slightly the manifestation of high profile government interest in biotechnology in West Germany, France, and the United Kingdom (Jasonoff 1983; Vaquin 1982a and 1982b).

With the establishment of the Office of Biotechnology Promotion in May 1982, MITI officials hoped special legislation might be passed in the Diet that would single out the biotechnology industry for special attention that would be similar qualitatively, if not quantitatively, to earlier special attention given by the Diet to computers and to structurally depressed industries. To this end, a "biotechnology caucus" (*Baio-saiensu gi-in kondan kai*) of Liberal Democratic Party Diet members was organized especially to promote a new set of government programs in this area which would be entirely immune from the sharp budget restraint associated with the Suzuki Administrative Reform Program. (On the specific Diet legislation on behalf of the computer industry see KGC 1972; on legislation to help structurally depressed industries in Japan, see Saxonhouse 1979.)

Despite continuing MITI interest in such legislation, in the five years since the Diet biotechnology caucus and the Office of Biotechnology Promotion were organized, no major special legislation has yet been forthcoming. In the face of a continuing large budget deficit and a general disinclination to give special subsidies to nonagricultural activities, the political will has not existed in the Diet to make any special commitment of resources either directly or indirectly for the promotion of biotechnology in Japan.

The absence of major special legislation for biotechnology does not necessarily mean that this industry is not receiving large amounts of special aid and comfort from the Japanese government. The political will may not exist for the Diet to give high profile, special help to any particular industry, but the bureaucracy may already have enough authority for the rapid promotion of biotechnology through existing policy instruments: tariffs, quotas, and nontariff barriers; grants and subsidy programs; tax expenditures; loans from government financial institutions; special aid through government procurement; and regulation of market structure, financial markets and intellectual properties, and the government's role in education. In order to get a full assessment of what targeting biotechnology for special development might mean in Japan, the use of each of these instruments will be examined in comparison with the use of similar instruments on biotechnology's behalf in the United States.

Upon examination of each of these instruments, it will be seen that, on the whole, for reasons seemingly more of domestic politics than international pressure, it has been difficult for the Japanese government to take major overt steps to aid any industry other than agriculture. This is particularly so for high technology industries and is particularly true compared with the United States. The subtler and less financially onerous steps that the Japanese government has taken to guide high technology industries, such as biotechnology, and that have made such a vivid impression on foreign observers, can be seen as limited compensation for the absence in Japan of a number of market processes and institutions, found in the United States, particularly beneficial to the development of high technology industries. This does not necessarily mean Japan is handicapped in high technology competition with the United States. Paradoxically, Japanese high technology, particularly biotechnology, draws significant direct benefits from America's own high technology policy.

Tariffs and Quotas

Japan no longer makes much use of such traditional instruments of direct protection as tariffs and quotas for aiding its nonagricultural sectors. In 1982, the import share weighted average level of tariffs on industrial and mining products in Japan was lower than the average tariff level for the United States and for all members of the European Economic Community (ECC). By 1984 Japan had implemented virtually all the tariff cuts related to nonsunset industries agreed to in the Multilateral Trade Negotiations (MTN) and its average level of tariffs on all industrial and mining products had already fallen to no more than 2.9 percent. This level, which includes some unilateral reductions beyond the rates agreed to at Geneva, is not only lower than the levels of all other major market-oriented industrial economies, it is also lower than the average tariff level of any of these economies even after 1987 when all Tokyo Round agreements will have been phased in. (In 1987, U.S. average tariff levels will still be 4.4 percent. Among the nine members of ECC, average rates will vary from 5.2 percent to 6.9 percent; Deardorff and Stern 1983.)

What is true for industrial and mining products generally is true specifically for high technology products. Although during the 1970s there had been some special tariff protection on computers and integrated circuits, on becoming a signatory to the MTN in 1979 Japan gave up such special protection. The tariff rates on these items are now comparable to American rates and considerably lower than EEC rates. It should be noted that there is no tariff at all on imported machine tools.

The situation for import quotas is much the same as for tariffs. Japan maintains fewer import quotas on industrial products than does the United States or France (Keizai Kikakuchō 1981). Rather than protecting high technology products, manufactures under formal Japanese quota include nothing more exciting than coal briquettes and four types of leather products (USTR 1982, pp. 10-14). (Apart from formal quotas, only Japan's sunset silk industry benefits from foreign voluntary restraint on competitive imports. This limited use of VRA's contrasts dramatically with the practices of Japan's trading partners.) Note that although manufacturing receives little protection, Japanese agriculture does remain heavily protected from foreign competition by a network of tariffs and quotas.

Considering the present character of biotechnology—an industry producing mostly knowledge and relatively little product—it is hardly surprising that tariffs and quotas cannot be found which protect this industry. Moreover, in view of Japanese government policy toward other high technology sectors, it is most unlikely that Japanese firms that have commenced research and development efforts in this area can believe protection will come from this source when tangible products are ready for manufacture.

Product Standards in Pharmaceuticals

For most conventionally defined high technology sectors, the use by Japan of product standards as a nontariff barrier has not yet emerged as a major issue. Pharmaceuticals, which is and will continue to be a major application area of the new biotechnologies, is an important exception. Pharmaceuticals is regularly cited as an instance of nontariff barriers being used to frustrate the liberal international economic arrangements which Japan, in other forums, has agreed to support.

American and European pharmaceutical companies have bitterly criticized Ministry of Welfare product approval policies, product standards, and testing procedures as being designed to protect Japanese companies. Most, but not all, Japanese pharmaceutical companies are widely recognized as not being fully internationally competitive. American companies, supported by the Office of the U.S. Trade Representative, have argued since at least the mid-1970s that the Ministry of Welfare procedures are extremely time consuming and work to make it difficult and costly for foreign drug manufacturers to introduce new products into the Japanese market.

American complaints on approval, standards, and testing procedures in pharmaceuticals have reached the highest levels of the Japanese government. On May 28, 1982, in the course of a public response to foreign criticism of the lack of reciprocity in Japan's international economic relations, the prime minister's office felt compelled to address this issue. The government defended its practice of not accepting foreign clinical test data for the approval of new pharmaceuticals by arguing that physiological differences between Japanese and foreigners required testing anew in Japan. Copious reference was made to differing data between Japanese and other ethnic groups in tests of a number of pharmaceuticals. No defense, however, was made of such other practices as requiring entirely new product approval when import agents are changed.

Further diplomatic pressure by the United States did finally result in the Japanese Diet passing new legislation in the spring of 1983 amending sixteen Japanese standard and certification laws. In addition to the amendments of the Pharmaceutical Affairs Law, amendments to the Agricultural Chemicals Law and to the Toxic Chemicals Law have particular pertinence for the future of biotechnology. The amendments are designed to give foreign producers direct access to the certification system, including direct ownership of approvals. Foreign manufacturers may apply for, and be granted, factory inspection and U.S. product type approval. It is anticipated that the Ministry of Welfare will allow these factory inspections to be carried out by U.S. testing firms. These amendments will bring Japanese practices into line with practices in other countries.

In addition to the amendments passed in the Diet, the Ministry of Welfare, as part of Japan's July 1985 market access package, has agreed to accept foreign clinical test data not done on Japanese nationals where there is evidence that ethnic and dietary differences could have no bearing on the test outcome. Another very significant change in procedure will allow product approvals to be transferred from one importer to another.

These changes in product approval procedures still leave Japan with a system that can delay approvals for years and is extremely expensive. With the changes outlined above, however, it is difficult to argue that Japanese pharmaceuticals are being particularly protected by Japanese regulatory procedures. For example, for all the concern about the length of the approval process in the Pharmaceutical Division of the Ministry of Welfare, the delays are, on average, no longer than those resulting from Food and Drug Administration procedures in the United States. Moreover, there is no concrete evidence that Japanese and foreign companies are being subjected to different standards. In the last fifteen years, in response to consumer pressure, the testing and approval processes of pharmaceutical regulatory authorities the world over have become more demanding, resulting in much more expensive and time-consuming processes in most countries.

It is thus hard to envision Japanese product standards being readied for use as a protective device when commercially viable biotechnology-derived products do enter the marketplace in large amounts. Japan's National Institute of Health, a unit of the Ministry of Welfare, has had a committee, with an annual budget of over $100,000, studying the framing of approval standards for products derived from recombinant DNA technology. While the formation of such committees are routine when approval standards are being developed, the committee's agenda is supposed to reflect a special sensitivity to the international ramifications of the standards recommended. In light of regulatory changes since 1983 and those projected, Japanese firms are unlikely to be making commitments to biotechnology industry in the expectation of government protection by such instruments.

Direct Subsidies and Grants

In striking contrast to the policies of some European countries, where large sectors of the economy are publicly owned and where large subsidies may be given such enterprises in order to maintain employment in otherwise unprofitable enterprises, there is little in the way of direct subsidies and grants given to manufacturing industries in Japan. (On European policies, see Hager 1982.) In a study done on Japanese government subsidy policy covering 1977 and 1978, for thirteen major manufacturing sectors in Japan, only one received direct subsidies greater than 0.1 percent of gross domestic product originating in that sector. The sector targeted for special attention was food processing, which received subsidies equal to 0.6 percent of gross domestic·product originating in that sector.

Where there are large subsidies provided by the Japanese government, they go to agriculture, mining, and transportation. Aid given the agriculture, forestry, and fisheries industries dwarfs that to all other sectors of the Japanese economy. In absolute amount, the actual subsidies given agriculture are almost half again the total amount of subsidies given the rest of Japanese economy. The rate of subsidy given agriculture is fully 12.3 percent of gross domestic product originating in that sector (Ueno and Goto n.d.).

What is true about direct subsidies in general is also true of research and development grants. In 1984, the Japanese government funded only 1.8 percent of all research and development undertaken by private sector industry. This contrasts with West Germany funding 16.9 percent of private sector R&D, France funding 24.5 percent, the United Kingdom funding 29.2 percent, and with the United States so actively involved in private sector industry R&D as to fund fully 32.3 percent of all research and development undertaken by private sector industry in the American economy (Kagaku Gijutsu Chō 1984).

These aggregate research and development figures are reflected in Japanese government policies toward most leading edge technology sectors. The communications and electrical machinery industries receive research and development contracts, grants, and subsidies equal to no more than 1.1 percent of their total research and development expenditures. Sectors such as pharmaceuticals, machinery (excluding electrical), and precision equipment receive such funds from the Japanese government equivalent only to 0.1, 1.0, and 0.2 percent, respectively, of their total research and development expenditures.

These figures do not mean that some sectors of the Japanese economy are not targeted for substantial research and development support. As might have been expected from the previous discussion of subsidies, 18 percent of agriculture's research and development expenditures are funded by the Japanese government. In this instance, agriculture is not alone in receiving such substantial aid: 10 percent of mining's R&D expenditures, and 15 percent of the railway, aircraft, and shipbuilding industries' R&D is funded by the Japanese government. (What makes these figures for the nonautomobile transportation sector so high is the continuing large R&D funding for Japan's structurally depressed shipbuilding industry. These figures also include continuing unsucccessful efforts by the Japanese government to develop a broadly based domestic aircraft industry. All ratios on Japanese government funding as a proportion of sectoral research and development expenditures have been estimated with data from Sōmuchō 1985.) By contrast, in France the government funds 72 percent of all aircraft R&D, 26 percent of all electronics R&D, and 12 percent of all chemicals industries' R&D. In the United States, individual sectoral support can be such that almost half the R&D undertaken by the electrical machinery industry is funded by the government (Kagaku Gijutsu Chō 1981, pp. 43 and 82).

Because of the multidisciplinary character of biotechnology, it is difficult to speak with precision about the exact amount of government funding. Various Japanese government and private estimates regularly add, subtract, and reassign programs to biotechnology depending on the perspective desired. A recent estimate of direct Japanese government funding of biotechnology research of $35 million is presented in table 3.

The Japanese government's expenditure on biotechnology research and development is a rather simple reflection of Japanese R&D policy as a whole: (1) The amounts involved are relatively small. (2) A large proportion is energy related. (3) Agriculture receives a large amount relative to its size in the economy and relative to the importance of biotechnology R&D specific to agriculture's interests. (4) Much of MITI's interest in biotechnology is motivated by a desire to help the structurally depressed chemical, pulp and paper, and textile industries. (5) Much of the research builds on traditional Japanese strengths in bioprocesses, such as fermentation. (6) The timing of programs seems to be a reaction to foreign developments.

Japanese Government Programs in Biotechnology. In common with the experience of flexible manufacturing systems, semiconductors, and computers (described in Saxonhouse 1983b), and despite the importance that even Prime Minister Nakasone has attached to this industry, Japanese government funding of biotechnology is exceedingly modest even by comparison with the programs of other countries. While funding has been increasing at an average annual rate of almost 30 percent in recent years, in fiscal 1984 total government funding was still no more than $35 million. (The U.S. Office of Technology Assessment estimates Japanese government funding about double the figures in table 3. The source is a manuscript of mine, "Biotechnology in Japan." OTA has taken the estimates in table 2.1 of "Biotechnology in Japan," which are similar to those in this chapter's table 3, and effectively doubled them by wrongly assigning the *total* for all Japanese government funding of biotechnology in place of the otherwise small amount of research and development funded by the Ministry of Education, Ministry of Welfare, and the Environmental Protection Agency, and then adding this figure to itself! Unfortunately, publications such as *Science* [Dibner 1985] have already cited these incorrect OTA estimates.)

By contrast with Japan, the U.S. Office of Technology Assessment (1984, p. 317) estimates that the West German government funds from $49 million to $70 million in research projects related to biotechnology, the British spend upwards of $60 million, estimates for the French range from $35 to $60 million, and the U.S. federal government funds $522.3 million of biotechnology R&D (table 4). In other words, the United States funds more than double the high estimates of biotechnology R&D

expenditures for the West German, British, French, and Japanese governments combined.

It is often suggested that comparisons between the enormous scale and scope of U.S. government funded R&D and the much smaller governmental efforts elsewhere are misleading. It is generally argued that while the U.S. government mainly funds basic research, foreign governments fund research that has an applied character to it and is designed primarily to enhance directly the competitiveness of one or another national industry (USOTA 1984, pp. 323-24).

Such generalizations are difficult to substantiate except with much more detailed analysis. In biotechnology, where circumstances may be quite special, such a distinction seems unhelpful. Hundreds of millions of dollars in venture capital resources in the United States have been attracted to small private firms whose primary assets are scientists with university positions and who characteristically recently have completed so-called basic research projects with long-term funding from the National Institutes of Health, or who may even retain such funding as they engage in more commercially oriented activities.

A more helpful distinction may be the degree of dissemination of knowledge derived from the research and development funded by the government. In this regard there is probably a major difference between Japanese and American government activities. Relatively more U.S. funding goes to universities than in Japan. There is a much greater incidence of active publishing among American scientists and engineers compared with their Japanese counterparts, so it is fair to say there is wide dissemination of a relatively high proportion of the results of biotechnology research funded by the U.S. government. Indeed, U.S. government funding may be of considerable benefit to the Japanese biotechnology industry, but it is unlikely Japanese programs are of much benefit to the American biotechnology industry.

Alternative Energy Sources and Japanese Government Programs in Biotechnology. The Japanese government's first commitment of new resources to biotechnology research and development came as part of a broader response to widespread concerns about the availability and price of future sources of energy. The release of energy as a by-product of enhanced biological reactions in organic matter is known loosely as biomass. Biomass has attracted the Japanese government as one of a number of alternative energy strategies. Government funding of biomass is, however, a very small part of energy-related R&D, which has focused primarily on nuclear reactors, and it seems noteworthy only because Japanese government funding of R&D for other areas of biotechnology is so modest in comparison.

From as early as 1971, when OPEC's Teheran Conference first

TABLE 3

Major Biotechnology-related Projects in 1983 and 1984 Budget (million yen)

Ministry/Agency	Topic/Project	1983	1984
Ministry of International Trade and Industry	1. Planning and promotion of biotechnology	13	52
	2. Biotechnology projects in the Next Generation basic technologies program	1,191	1,201
	• recombinant DNA	364	
	• bioreactor	452	
	• mass cell culture	375	
	(ten-year plan with a total budget of 20 billion yen, started in 1981)		
	3. Biomass-related R&D (alcohol production from cellulose resources such as garbage) (seven-year plan with a total budget of 35 billion yen, started in 1980)	1,071	1,284
	4. Biotechnology R&D except items 2 and 3, (biotechnology portion of special R&D expenses at the Science and Technology Agency)	311	935
	5. Expansion of the storage program for patented microorganisms and the construction of a new laboratory at the Fermentation Research Institute	20	22
	6. R&D cooperation with developing countries on the production technology for palm oil	15	105
	Subtotal	2,621	3,599
Science and Technology Agency	7. Life sciences R&D at the Institute of Physical and Chemical Research	1,134	1,281
	• development of bioreactors		
	• research on enzyme production technology		
	• development of new medicines		
	• screening and breeding of new microorganisms with recombinant DNA methods		
	• construction of P4 facility at Tsukuba		
	8. Biotechnology-related budget of New Technology Promotion and Commissioned Research on New Technologies	1,070	1,480

Ministry	Item		
	9. Biotechnology-related other New Technology Promotion Fund	390	740
	Subtotal	2,594	3,501
Ministry of Agriculture, Forestry and Fisheries	10. Coordination of government, industry, and academic biotechnology R&D	0	14
	11. Basic R&D expenses for biotechnology at Ministry of Agriculture, Forestry and Fisheries affiliated national research laboratories	416	612
	12. Commissioned research at private companies	41	395
	13. Comprehensive system for genetic information on crops and breeding	174	182
	Subtotal	631	1,203
Ministry of Education	14. Research on recombinant DNA techniques	73	85
Ministry of Welfare	15. Securing biological resources	1,044	undecided
	16. 10-year War on Cancer program	—	1,507
	17. Study group for the application of DNA-related technologies to health care and medical practice	31	undecided
	18. Establishing approval standards for the pharmaceutical applications of DNA technologies	27	undecided
	Subtotal	1,175	1,592
Environment Protection Agency	19. Environmental impact of the development of new microorganisms	8	8
	Total (excluding 15, 17, and 18)	5,927	9,903

Source: *Nikkei baioteku*, January 30, 1984.

TABLE 4
U.S. Federally Funded Research in Biotechnology (million $)

Agency/Topic	Fiscal Year	Amount
National Institutes of Health		
Molecular biology,		
generic manipulation,		
hybridoma, monoclonal antibodies	1982	378.0
Immobilized enzymes	1982	2.0
National Science Foundation		
Recombinant DNA research	1982	12.8
Bioprocess engineering	1982	1.7
Other biotechnology research	1982	38.6
Department of Agriculture		
Agricultural Reserve Service		
Plant biotechnology	1983	7.2
Animal biotechnology	1983	6.4
Other	1982	20.4
Department of Defense		
DARPA	1983	2.2
Army/Navy/Air Force		
Recombinant DNA research	1983	3.3
Other biotechnology	1983	2.0
Department of Energy		
Photosynthesis, stress mechanisms of		
plants and microorganisms, genetic		
mechanisms and methanogensis	1983	9.9
Conservation and Renewal Energy Program	1983	23.7
Biocatalysis research	1983	0.5
Others	1983	2.0
	Total	522.3

Source: U.S. Office of Technology Assessment.

substantially raised the price of oil, MITI has been a major bureaucratic force shaping Japanese energy policy. It is within this context that MITI has shown continuing and substantial interest in research and development of biomass as an alternative energy source. Most recently, this R&D has been sponsored as part of MITI's *Shin nenryō kenkyū kaihatsu* (New

Fuels Research and Development). As shown in table 3, the amount of 1.3 billion yen devoted to this single area of biotechnology is more than what is being spent on any other MITI biotechnology promotion activity (including the high profile Next Generation technologies biotechnology projects). Little connection has been made between these biotechnology efforts and other MITI projects, and little liaison exists among them.

MITI biomass activities are housed in the Petroleum Refining Section of the Agency for Natural Resources and Energy. In common with the Next Generation projects, much of the biomass research and development work that MITI is promoting is being conducted by private sector laboratories. Of the eighteen firms whose laboratories are participating in the biomass portion of MITI's New Fuels Research and Development program only one, Kyowa Hakkō, is also participating in any of MITI's other biotechnology projects. In common with Japanese government practice in cooperative projects these eighteen firms are also organized into a research association. This association is not exclusively concerned with biomass R&D, since it includes all firms participating in any New Fuels Research and Development project. As is most typical of such research and development associations, except for a program office, there are no interfirm or suprafirm facilities.

Like MITI, MOAFF's (Ministry of Agriculture, Forestry and Fisheries) interest in the new biotechnologies first came as a by-product of an interest in alternative energy sources. In 1978, MOAFF, through its Institute of Agricultural Technology, inaugurated a ten-year Green Energy Program. This project was supplemented in 1981 with yet another ten-year project, the Biomass Conversion Program. Together the Green Energy Program and the Biomass Conversion Program account for more than half of MOAFF's budget for biotechnology R&D. Despite the similarity of the topics covered and the research strategies pursued, there is no formal or informal coordination of the MITI and MOAFF programs.

Nonenergy Related Biotechnology Programs of the Ministry of Agriculture, Forestry and Fisheries. Cell fusion is a basic process among the new biotechnologies. Cell fusion, by artificially joining cells, attempts to combine the desirable characteristics of different types of cells into one cell. As a technique it shows as much promise as recombinant DNA, bioreactors, and mass cell cultures. What interest MOAFF has had in the new biotechnologies outside of alternative energy sources has been concentrated in this area. In 1982, MOAFF prevailed on MITI to remove cell fusion technologies from MITI's projected Next Generation Technologies program in favor of MOAFF's then-started effort in cell fusion.

Elementary hybridization has long been a technique to improve crop species. For all the work done with this technique, limits to its use arise rather quickly. MOAFF hopes fusion of cells from two different plant species can be used to overcome these barriers. While this rationale has legitimized MOAFF's new lead role within the government in sponsoring cell fusion techniques, the hybridoma (the hybrid cell that results from cell fusion) has far broader application and can be used for many other purposes, including the diagnosis and treatment of a wide variety of nonagricultural diseases.

The Ministry of International Trade and Industry's Interest in Biotechnology. It is generally found in surveys of Japanese businessmen that while the new biotechnologies will have broad use, the most immediately promising application areas are in pharmaceuticals. Despite such prospects and doubtless because MITI has never had a role in regulating the pharmaceutical industry, MITI's high profile research projects in biotechnology have not involved existing pharmaceutical companies.

MITI's biotechnology interest that is not focused on energy has been concentrated in a trio of seven-year projects on recombinant DNA, bioreactors, and mass cell cultures involving a combined research effort by Japanese government laboratories (including the Fermentation Research Institute, the Research Institute of Textiles and Polymers, and the National Chemical Laboratory for Industry) and private firms. These three projects are in turn part of MITI's Next Generation industrial technologies program. These projects are housed within MITI's Basic Industries Division, which has oversight responsibility for such industries as steel, nonferrous metals, and chemicals. The locus of MITI's administrative responsibility for biotechnology reflects MITI's predominant interest in biotechnology as part of a general program of structural adjustment for the extremely depressed basic chemicals industry. While the application areas from MITI's three projects run the gamut from pharmaceuticals and food processing to textiles, eleven of the fourteen private sector participants in MITI's biotechnology cooperative research projects have been drawn from the chemical industry.

Tax Expenditures

In common with foreign commercial policy, Japanese tax policy was once used as a major instrument to stimulate the growth of new industries. For example, in the 1950s, half the cost of a new automobile factory could be written off in the first year the factory was in operation. Today such industry-specific largess is much less common. If agriculture and food processing are excluded, Japanese effective sectoral tax rates on capital and labor are much more uniform than those of the United States and the United Kingdom, and this has been the case from as long ago as 1973.

In 1973 in Great Britain, when tax policy was clearly used to channel resources between industries, the effective tax rate on capital ranged from a low of 6.3 percent on iron and steel products through a confiscatory rate of 285.5 percent on electrical machinery to a still higher of 390.2 percent on nonelectrical machinery. In the United States, effective incidence of capital taxation ranged from a low of 19.7 percent on petroleum and related products through a rate of 131.2 percent of electrical machinery to a high of 144.7 percent on rubber products. Since 1985, a special 10 percent bonus depreciation on equipment used in biotechnology research has also been allowed. By comparison in Japan effective capital taxation ranged from a low of 34.7 percent on nonferrous metals to a high of 49 percent on electrical machinery (Saxonhouse 1983b). Since at least the early 1970s, Japanese tax policy has, in practice, seemed more concerned with removing distortions between sectors than giving special help to any particular sector. In the early 1980s, effective tax rates in Japan remain far more uniform than the U.S. Recovery Act of 1981 rates, as shown in table 5.

Again what is true at the aggregate level is true in high technology sectors. Tax credits and special depreciation allowances designed to stimulate these activities are less generous in Japan than in other major market-oriented industrialized countries, particularly the United States. For example, the American and the Japanese tax codes both maintain a tax credit for encouraging increased private sector research and development expenditures. In Japan, a 20 percent tax credit is given for R&D expenditures over and above a company's previous and highest level of R&D expenditure since 1972. This credit is limited to 10 percent of a company's corporate income tax liability, which limits its value to small R&D oriented firms in Japan. Since 1985, a special 10 percent bonus depreciation on equipment used in biotechnology research has also been allowed. By comparison, in the United States, a 25 percent tax credit is given on current R&D expenditures over and above the average of the previous three years. Quite apart from the absence of an American ceiling on the size of the credit, with continually growing expenditures, the U.S. provisions effectively allow a 25 percent credit on the difference between the current year's R&D expenditures and those of two years ago, while the Japanese allow only a 20 percent credit on the difference between the current year's and last year's expenditures. A National Science Foundation study (Collins 1983) finds the U.S. research and development credit resulting in a tax expenditure of $2 billion annually. (Eisner, Albert, and Sullivan 1984 put the tax expenditure for the U.S R&D tax credit at $1.3 billion annually.) By contrast, the Ōkurashō (1983, p. 188) estimates that the Japanese R&D credit results in a tax expenditure of the equivalent of no more than $140 million annually.

TABLE 5

Effective Tax Rates by Industry in the United States (1982) and Japan (1981)

United States		Japan	
Sector	Tax Rate	Sector	Tax Rate
Traded Goods			
Agricultural production: agricultural services, horticultural services, forestry and fisheries	14.7	Agriculture, forestry, and fisheries	17.4
Food and kindred products	27.0	Food, beverages, and tobacco	49.3
Tobacco manufactures	24.3		
Textile products	22.3	Textile products	31.1
Apparel and other fabricated textile products	25.3	Wearing apparel	31.1
Leather and leather products	27.4	Leather products	37.1
Lumber and wood products	25.3	Wood products	37.1
Furniture and fixtures	28.6	Furniture and fixtures	32.1
Paper and allied products	18.3	Paper and paper products	32.7
Printing, publishing, and allied industries	28.1	Printing and publishing	32.7
Chemicals and allied products	20.1	Chemicals	36.2
Petroleum and coal products	33.2	Petroleum and related products	36.2
Rubber and miscellaneous plastic products	17.8	Rubber products	36.2
		Nonmetal miscellaneous products	33.4
Stone, clay and glass products	24.6	Glass and glass products	33.4
Primary metal products	26.0	Iron and steel	29.7
		Nonferrous metals	27.4
Fabricated metal industries	23.3	Metal products	35.0
Machinery, except electrical	24.6	Machinery, except electrical	37.2

Electrical machinery, equipment, and supplies	24.7
Transportation equipment except motor vehicles	30.4
Motor vehicles and motor vehicle equipment	21.3
Professional photographic equipment and watches	27.0
Miscellaneous manufacturing industries	25.8

Nontraded Goods

Metal mining	34.3
Coal mining	19.1
Crude petroleum and natural gas extraction	32.2
Nonmetallic mining and quarrying, except fuel	15.6
Electrical utilities	25.0
Gas utilities	20.0
Water supply, sanitary services, and other utilities	39.4
Construction	13.1
Wholesale trade, retail trade	18.7
Railways and railway express service	21.4
Street railway, bus lines, and taxicab service	10.0
Trucking service and storage	14.7
Water transportation	6.3
Air transportation	11.5
Pipelines, except natural gas	27.9
Services incidental to transportation	17.1
Telephone, telegraph, and miscellaneous communication services	19.7
Radio broadcasting and television	25.8
Finance, insurance, and real estate	37.3
Services	23.9

Electrical machinery	38.6
Transportation equipment	36.1
Miscellaneous manufacturing	35.0
Mining and quarrying	46.0
Electric, gas and water	25.9
Construction	33.4
Wholesale and retail trade	26.1
Transportation, storage, and communication	31.5
Finance, insurance, and real estate	36.1
Community, social, and personal services	25.3

Sources: Alan J. Auerbach, "Corporate Taxation in the United States," *Brookings Papers in Economic Activity 1983:2*; Nihon Ginkō Tōkei Kyoku, *Omō kigyō keiei bunseki*; Ōkurashō, *Hōjōkin benran*.

The American tax code goes well beyond the R&D credit in providing encouragement to R&D oriented firms. The lowering of long-term capital gains tax in 1978 is widely credited with substantially increasing the pool of venture capital for start-up firms. (While Auten and Clotfelter 1982, Minarik 1984, and Feldstein, Slemrod, and Yitzhaki 1984 debate the size of long-term impact of this change, none doubt its immediate impact.) The 1979 change in the interpretation of the Employee Retirement Income Security Act (ERISA) has also allowed substantial amounts of pension fund money to flow into venture capital investments. And about the same time, the Securities and Exchange Commission changed Rule 144 to allow early investors in new companies to dispose of their restricted holdings much sooner than had been the case. This, in turn, has created a major new incentive for the provision of venture capital.

Still more important than changes in the tax code, the Supreme Court held in *Snow* v. *Commissioners* that limited partners could offset whatever other income they might have with partnership research or other experimental expenses. At that time, the Court extended the reach of Section 174 of the IRS code, which covers deductions for research and experimental expenditures to include business not yet offering products for sale. Prior to this, such expenditures had to be capitalized. Almost as beneficial is the continuing treatment of the outputs of limited R&D partnerships under Section 1235 of the IRS code. While investment in an R&D partnership can be written off against income, royalty income from any patent produced can be treated as a capital gain.

The elements of the American tax code just described have had a profound impact on the form and quite possibly the volume of biotechnology R&D in the United States. In marked contrast with Japanese tax provisions, and prior to the many changes that may occur in 1986, there have been numerous U.S. tax incentives that particularly encourage R&D in small firms. Since 1979, American equity markets have raised $1.5 billion for American biotechnology firms with net worths of less then $5 million (*Manhattan Report on Economic Policy* 1983, p. 17). Almost one-third of this financing, about $500 million, took the form of the limited R&D partnership (USOTA 1984, p. 282). This is an extraordinary response for a sector that has yet to generate significant commercially viable products.

Capital Availability

Given the character of the Japanese financial system, Japanese industrial targeting of an industry such as biotechnology could be pursued by government manipulation of the availability and terms of access to industrial finance. Capital is much more concentrated in Japan than in the United States. Decades of Ministry of Finance regulation have insulated Japan's finance-poor corporations from direct contact with Japan's savings-rich households. (This is an increasingly controversial point for some Japanese economists. See, for example, Horiuchi 1980 attacking this point of view, and Iwata and Hamada 1980 defending it. See the general summary of this literature in Murakami 1982, pp. 11-18.) In Japan, external financing is characteristically done as bank loans. Although the Federal Republic of Germany is similar, in the United States, France, and the United Kingdom direct financing is much more important. (For example, in 1985 in the United States bank loans accounted for only 3.3 percent of new corporate finance. By contrast, in Japan, even with the great changes that have taken place in recent years, bank loans still accounted for 30.3 percent of new corporate finance.)

Japanese corporations, when they wish financing, quite regularly turn to the few, large banks dominating the domestic financial system. These banks are closely regulated by the Ministry of Finance. The large banks are not the only corporate source for loans in Japan. Some 13 to 14 percent of corporate financing comes from government financial institutions (Noguchi 1982). The same financial regulation that has limited the direct financial relationship between households and corporations makes postal savings accounts, government-sponsored life insurance programs, and government pension plans favored assets for Japanese households.

The financial resources accumulated in this way by the government are in turn lent by such government financial institutions as the Japan Development Bank and its sister institution, the Small Business Finance Corporation. These institutions have government-business-academic policy committees that shape the sectoral allocation of loans, and in this context the financial needs of promising new industries do play an important role.

Is this, however, the real locus of Japanese industrial policy for high technology? In practice, the largest portion of the resources of these government financial institutions are not used for promising new industries, and the loans made to these new industries are granted on terms that are hardly different from what would be available from private banks. Indeed, the high profile biotechnology industry, identified in a survey by the *Nihon keizai shimbun* (December 28, 1982) (Japan's equivalent of the *Wall Street Journal*) as the sector with the greatest future growth potential, as late as March 1984 had yet to receive any funding from either the Japan Development Bank or the Small Business Finance Corporation.

If, in Japan, firms pursuing biotechnology projects have not been able to receive financing from government financial institutions, in the United States, biotechnology firms have found far more accommodating circumstances. SBICs (Small Business Investment Corporations), licensed by the Small Business Administration (SBA), have already made available more than $7 million for twenty-two small biotechnology firms in 1981 and 1982 at rates 300 or 400 basis points below prime. Loans on such favorable terms have been possible because U.S. law allows the SBA to lend SBICs up to three times its equity on extremely favorable terms. As an incentive for investing in SBICs, stockholders can treat losses from disposal of SBIC stock or SBIC convertible debentures as offsets to ordinary income, while any gain is taxed as capital gain. Also, SBIC stockholders can get generous long-term dividend exclusions. Although SBICs are the principal vehicle by which small and medium size firms in the United States can receive direct government financing, substantial indirect financing for such firms is provided by the Subchapter S Act and the Subchapter S Revision Act of 1982. Under the requirements of these acts, which include the stipulation that the number of shareholders not be greater than thirty-five, corporation owners have the advantage of limited liability for debts, and the corporation's income can be taxed at the shareholder's tax rate. Shareholders investing in R&D-intensive corporations that have large initial losses can use these losses as offsets against other income.

Regulation of Market Structure

Japanese pharmaceutical companies, most of whom have a substantial interest in biotechnology, have been subject to a form of price regulation that has had the potential for creating large implicit subsidies. Close to 90 percent of the drugs sold in Japan are available under prescription from the Japanese national health plan, and the Ministry of Welfare sets standard prices for each of these. This system is now applied to new products from abroad as well as to Japanese pharmaceutical manufactures. The possibility that this price regulation might be used as an instrument either directly against foreign competition or indirectly by arranging large implicit subsidies certainly exists in theory. In practice, in the past eight years the opposite appears to have happened, as the Ministry regularly has cut its posted prices. The price controls have no explicit basis in law and in the last analysis are ineffectual. Pharmaceutical companies have regularly undercut government regulation by varying the effective discount given buyers, and by varying the quantity of sample drugs being offered. Recognizing that this system of regulation is contentious but ineffectual, and hoping nonetheless that burgeoning health care costs could be lowered otherwise, the Ministry of Welfare now plans to further accelerate cuts in the prices of most of the drugs that it regulates. Pharmaceutical price regulation is unlikely to serve in the future as a source of new subsidies for a government-targeted biotechnology industry.

Different Institutions:
Similar Functions? Similar Outcomes?

It is possible to argue that a policy-instrument by policy-instrument survey of the pecuniary incentives given Japanese industry by the Japanese government misses the true manner by which competitive advantage in an industry is created. The whole may be bigger than the sum of its parts. Possibly, it is not necessary for the Japanese government to make large formal interventions in private sector activities in order for the government to achieve its ends. In the industrial targeting context, there are four strands to this argument. First, it is possible that it is not the total amount and terms of Japanese government financial institution loans or R&D grants that are important but rather that such loans or grants are given at all. In this way, it is argued, the Japanese government communicates to the closely regulated private financial system that an industry, such as biotechnology, is of considerable future importance to the Japanese economy, that the government stands behind this industry, and that the private financial system should actively participate in the development of this industry.

A second strand suggests it is not proper to measure the impact of Japanese government research and development project by the size of government expenditure. Even in a case as prominent as the VLSI project, by the standards of the Subsidies Code negotiated at the Tokyo Round the amount of direct government aid is trivial and is not a possible subject of a countervailing duty. What is important, it is argued, is that a small dose of government aid and a large dose of government involvement helps diverse Japanese companies coordinate their research. By preventing duplication of effort and by sharing information, the true impact of government involvement is the sum of all the relevant R&D expeditures of private companies participating in a project *and* the government R&D expenditures, not just the government expenditures alone. This is a contention of the American Semiconductor Industry Association (1983).

The third strand, which was partly dealt with earlier, emphasizes that the link between total R&D spending on any program and future commercial success is in any event weak. In every high technology area, American government R&D expenditure is much higher than in Japan, but American expenditure is concentrated on basic research, the results of which are available to all, including Japanese competitors, at nominal cost, or it is defense related. By contrast, Japanese funding is small but concentrated in applied research and in product development. In short, it is carefully targeted.

The fourth strand, which won't be pursued in detail here, views Japanese targeting as a misleading tactic in the oligopolistic rivalry between

American and Japanese high tech industries. For example, the Japanese semiconductor industry stresses what is in fact an inaccurate account of the closeness of its relations with Japanese government in order to divert venture capital and other resources from American rivals (Dixit 1983; the October 1982 issue of *Scientific American* contains a lengthy advertising insert by the Electronic Industries Association of Japan extolling the special advantages of good government-business relations and interfirm cooperation).

Japanese Government Financial Institutions and Signaling

A spate of loans from the Japan Development Bank to a promising new sector may be a signal to private finance to get involved, but in doing this it may be simply compensating, and not very well for that matter, for the absence in Japan of American-style equity markets.

American equity markets have a history of great success in concentrating large resources on promising but risky ventures on the technological frontier. Indeed, given the American legislative, judical, and regulatory decisions of the last ten years, over and above historic precedents, an enormous array of incentives now exist for the American economy to direct resources to R&D intensive activities. These incentives may well be justified on the grounds of the substantial externalities associated with these activities, but it is also important to point out that most of these incentives are not offered in the Japanese economy.

As the case of biotechnology seems to confirm, these incentives are having a considerable impact. Between 1977 and 1983, 111 new American firms were formed with the explicit intention of exploiting biotechnology. In addition, 108 established firms entered the field. As pointed out earlier, since 1979, American equity markets have raised $1.5 billion for American biotechnology firms having a net worth of less than $5 million, and almost $500 million went into R&D partnerships. Established U.S. firms had invested almost $400 million through July 1983 in new biotechnology companies. The market value of the equity of the largest new biotechnology firms has reached almost $3.5 billion (USOTA 1984, p. 282).

Quite apart from the entry of new firms into the American biotechnology industry on a flood of venture capital, and quite apart from investments in these new firms by established companies, many established companies within the American economy have also made significant commitments of resources within their own firms to this new field. For example, four large American chemical and pharmaceutical companies, Schering-Plough, Eli Lilly, Monsanto, and DuPont, have annual R&D budgets for biotechnology which together came to over $300 million for 1982 (USOTA 1984, p. 78).

By contrast with the American situation, in Japan the government has regularly announced that the development of biotechnology is a priority, yet despite enormous discussion, resources have been relatively slow to move into this area. In 1985, according to an authoritative *Nihon keizai shimbum* survey, Japanese private concerns invested the equivalent of $402 million in biotechnology research and development. This figure was up from $140 million in 1981. This reflects a swift 30 percent average annual increase in R&D expenditures, but it in no way compares with the explosive increase in the U.S. commitment. While the four largest established American companies active in biotechnology spent $468 million, which is 15 percent more than the entire private Japanese biotechnology R&D expenditure, public and private, the four largest Japanese companies active in biotechnology spent no more than $98 million. This comparison is particularly compelling because while the Japanese industry is being developed exclusively by established firms, the distinctive feature of the American industry is the important role played by newly established biotechnology firms. For example, the four largest newly established American biotechnology firms in 1985 spent more than twice what the four most active established Japanese companies spent on biotechnology R&D.

Whether the characteristic American response indicates a bold, farsighted commitment of resources through the marketplace to ensure an important role in the dynamic industries of the twenty-first century or a faddish overreaction; and whether the Japanese response indicates a prudent assessment of the level of resources actually required now to participate in the future growth of a new technology or instead an inevitably inadequate response because of cumbersome financial bureaucracies, remains an issue to be discussed. It is clear, however, that whatever Japanese industrial policy may accomplish, it does not provide the Japanese economy with a unique capacity to search out promising new technologies and concentrate large new resources on their development. Indeed, in the biotechnology case the American economy seems better able to grasp these opportunities.

The relatively limited Japanese response to the opportunities presented by the new biotechnologies does require some explanation, particularly in light of the high profile attention given this new industry by the Japanese media. The different Japanese response is a result of different policies by the Japanese government and a different financial, industrial, and R&D structure in Japan. Government policy in Japan has left potential Japanese entrants into biotechnology without an uncapped R&D tax credit and limited R&D partnership arrangements. Their presence in the United States has allowed new entrants into biotechnology to obtain financing and retain their autonomy while allowing some other entity to take immediate benefits from the tax write-offs associated with biotechnology's relatively long gestation period.

The Japanese response to the opportunities presented by biotechnology has also been more limited than it otherwise might have been because of the character of Japan's industrial structure. The single most attractive opportunity for commercially viable products in the near future within biotechnology is in pharmaceuticals. Chemicals are a distant second. Large American and European pharmaceutical companies have made enormous new commitments to biotechnology as a defensive strategy to protect existing market shares. Japan's smaller and much less successful pharmaceutical firms have not had the need to make investment anywhere on such a scale. Even though biotechnology will in the future yield important applications in chemicals, textiles, agriculture, paper and pulp, and food processing, most Japanese companies already in these areas are interested in biotechnology as a means of diversification, most often into pharmaceuticals. In the Japanese context, this motive, by itself, has not been enough to call forth large private resources.

Venture Capital Institutions in Japan

Quite apart from tax advantages and considerations of existing industrial structure, Japan's still heavily regulated financial system, where venture capital remains unimportant and where the supply of capital is not fully competitive, must bear a considerable share of the blame or praise for the biotechnology outcome. Where the supply of capital is not fully competitive and where even private resource allocations are made bureaucratically, government-business decision making has had limited capacity to move quickly. (The press release issued when the U.S. Office of Technology Assessment published its report, *Commercial Biotechnology: An International Analysis*, alleged that in the early 1980s the Japanese government was arranging large low interest loans for its biotechnology firms. This allegation is not documented and does not appear in the OTA report itself or in the contract report on Japan which I did for OTA.) Small wonder that not a single entrepreneur or research scientist in Japan has been willing to give up permanent status at an existing firm and assume the risks of starting a new biotechnology firm. In consequence, entirely unlike the U.S. case, almost no new firms have come into existence to exploit this special new opportunity.

It is even possible to argue that it is the information provided by American equity markets that provides much of the glue for what Japanese government-business consensus building there is in the allocation of new resources. Indeed, industrial policy in Japan may hinge on the existence of relatively unregulated and competitive capital markets in the

United States. In an era when Japan was well away from the global technological frontier, observation of what other, more advanced economies had already accomplished provided a guide for such consensus building. That is past now. With Japan at the technological frontier, what other countries will do—not what they have already done—is most interesting. In Japan, equity markets play too marginal a role in capital allocation to serve as an ultimate arbiter of future prospects. In the United States, where they do play a central role, values determined by capital markets serve as an extremely rich source of information on the future prospects of industries. As each wave of American venture capital and over-the-counter market interest has converged on one or another new technology, it has started a boom in Japanese government-business interest in the same sector.

If industrial policy in Japan appears as no more than a substitute for what could be accomplished equally well or better by the institution of efficient capital markets in Japan, why does industrial policy persist? In fact, the deregulation of some financial markets has become an explicit objective of a fading Japanese industrial policy. Indeed, eyeing the almost $6 billion in venture capital now current in the United States, of which some 25 percent is biotechnology related, and the 13,000 security issues now traded over the counter, MITI is once again showing interest in developing a venture-capital market in Japan. Paralleling the creation of the Office of Biotechnology Promotion, MITI has also set up a new Office of Venture Enterprise Promotion. Whether the development of such venture capital institutions as an over-the-counter market for company equities will be successful remains to be seen.

This is not the first time that MITI has shown an interest in venture capital institutions. In the early 1970s MITI made an effort similar to what is taking place right now. While widely publicized, this effort yielded little in the way of tangible accomplishments. As late as 1981, only 111 companies had their securities traded over the counter, and total venture capital investments amounted to no more than $84 million. In its current phase of interest, MITI is attempting to change the regulations on Japan's over-the-counter market to greatly ease the requirements for listing a security. Since regulation of securities markets is vested in the Securities Bureau of the Ministry of Finance and not in MITI, how important any changes in regulations might be is not clear. The Ministry of Finance is the architect of the present financial system and retains considerable influence through its continued existence. Numerous cosmetic steps in deference to MITI are likely, but it remains to be seen the extent to which the Ministry of Finance will allow significant steps toward this kind of direct financing of new investment and research.

Quite apart from the Ministry of Finance, there is a more deep-seated view in Japan that unregulated capital markets are unreliable. Japanese inspired criticism of American performance relies heavily on this mistrust (Pascale and Athos 1981). Such critiques complain that American corporate managers are excessively short-sighted in their decision making because of American corporations' overly heavy reliance on equity markets. Decisions are allegedly made with undue concern regarding how any given action will affect the next quarterly earnings statement. Reliance on equity financing has led to compensation packages for top-level American managers that tie bonus payments to the market performance of company equities. (The 10K filings with the Securities and Exchange Commission by publicly traded companies in the United States must contain detailed statements on the compensation agreements with top corporate officers.) This, however, need not lead to an excessively short-run outlook for corporate managers. Tying compensation to equity market evaluation rather than directly to earnings should help the longer-term view to prevail. Efficiently working equity markets should distinguish between ephemeral manipulation and long-term structural improvements. Only if it is accepted that there is pervasive and persistent destabilizing speculation is it possible to argue that preoccupation with quarterly earning reports by top management will enhance equity values at the expense of the long-term performance of the firm (Flavin 1983).

In point of fact, the Japanese mistrust of equity financing, which has very nearly taken on the status of an issue in the bilateral economic diplomacy between Japan and the United States, is rooted in the experience of many Japanese business leaders with equity financing during the pre-Pacific War period but has little to do with current conditions in the United States. In prewar Japan, new investment was commonly equity financed. Equities in major industries, such as textiles, were characteristically pledged by owners as collateral for the bank loans that permitted their purchase. The interests of equity holders that dominated the prewar boards of directors of Japanese enterprises often demanded that unrealistically high dividends be paid out so that equity holders' bank loans might be serviced.

Japanese Government-Business
Cooperative Research and Development Program

In light of actual industrial performance in Japan, it is hard to imagine Japanese government-sponsored research and development projects, such as those organized for biotechnology, as the pivot around which all industry research and development expenditure revolves. Consider, for example, first the performance of such projects in some other sectors. For example, between 1977 and 1983 the Japanese machine tool industry was the beneficiary of a $44 million MITI-sponsored cooperative research project on laser-using complex manufacturing systems. This project, large by Japanese standards, was one of ten during the late 1970s that MITI had given special priority, designating it a Large Scale National Research and Development Project. It is unlikely, however, that such a project, despite involving the cooperative efforts of twenty Japanese firms, could really be the centerpiece for the intimate coordination of collusive activities by members of the Japan machine tool industry.

In fact, during the six-year period mentioned above during which this National Research and Development Program was active, the Japanese machine tool industry experienced extremely rapid growth, which created as much upheaval domestically as it did among its foreign competitors. The leading machine tool producer in 1981, with almost twice as much production as the number two, was not even among the top five producers in Japan in 1975. Among the top six machine tool producers in 1970, only two were still among the top six in 1981. During this period, a new group of Japanese machine tool companies, some of which had been small, family owned firms in the early 1970s and others of which had not participated in the MITI-sponsored project, assumed positions of technological leadership. And some of the firms dominant in 1970 were forced to undergo painful readjustment in capacity and labor force.

If the high profile Japanese government-sponsored cooperative R&D projects are not research pivots around which an industry cartel functions, what is their role? Cooperative R&D projects are important in Japan only because in Japan, relative to other industrialized countries and particularly the United States, there is much less informal communication and cooperation among scientists and engineers working at different firms. As Japanese government survey after survey shows, Japanese firms rarely look to other firms and individuals in their own industry as a source of new technological information (Kagaku Gijutsu Chō 1979). In the United States, the diffusion of useful research results across firms is possible because of the high degree of professional orientation among firm scientists and engineers. This pattern has developed in the United States because of the strong, common theoretical background of university-trained R&D staff, which not only facilitates communication but also creates labor market related incentives for communicating effectively with R&D workers at other firms.

Between Japan and the United States, the roots of these different patterns of communication lie in the very different means of financing education and training. In the United States, from the beginning of the postwar period several extremely significant programs have subsidized skill accumulation directly or facilitated use of financial intermediaries for financing such accumulation. These programs began with the G.I. Bill of Rights and include Veterans Educational Benefits and Guaranteed

Student Loans. Most require training in educational institutions that are in some fashion officially accredited. In consequence, these programs have helped to increase the demand and therefore, in time, the supply of vocational, undergraduate, and, in this context what is most important, graduate education in the United States.

In Japan, in the postwar period, skill accumulation has been institutionalized in a rather different way. There have been no major government programs directly subsidizing individual education. Instead there has been a relatively modest increase in the number of heavily subsidized public institutions, which provide education at a very low tuition. For the most part, however, the large increase in the number of Japanese receiving higher education has been at private universities which finance themselves largely out of tuition charges (Horiuchi 1973). These major differences between Japan and the United States in the financing of higher education have led to major differences in the character of educational institutions in the two countries, to major differences in the character of education, and, ultimately, to major differences between the Japanese and American labor forces.

In the United States, government programs have almost exclusively subsidized training that takes place outside the firm. This has resulted in the development in the United States of a large number of graduate research institutions and professional schools. American firm managers and scientific personnel receive a large amount of their training outside the firm. Relatively speaking, this training is general and theoretical in character. Such training is consistent with the academic character of the institutions imparting it. By contrast, in Japan, most advanced managerial and scientific training is done under firm auspices.

While a Ph.D. is almost a prerequisite for active participation in a U.S. corporate R&D laboratory, such an advanced degree is much less common in otherwise comparable Japanese facilities. For example, while a number of subsidized public universities including Tokyo, Kyoto, Osaka, and Kyushu have significant programs in biotechnology, the role of these programs as a source of advanced research personnel for Japan's industry is limited. More than 1,200 Ph.D. scientists and engineers work in U.S. biogenetic engineering according to a 1982 survey by the Office of Technology Assessment and National Academy of Sciences. In contrast, a Keidanren survey found only 161 Ph.D. scientists and engineers doing firm-based research and development work in biotechnology in Japan in 1982, including Japanese with Ph.D.'s from American universities. It is not surprising that in a dynamic, high technology industry like biotechnology, 80 percent of the research personnel in a MITI sample of 104 firms have been trained in biotechnology methods exclusively in their own firms. At the same time, in surveys conducted in 1981 and 1982, over

40 percent of Japanese biotechnology firms indicated that some engineering and scientific personnel would be sent abroad for either primary or supplementary training.

Japanese industry has apparently discovered that there are cheaper ways of obtaining the relevant R&D skills than sending large numbers of employees through doctoral programs. Often the right mix of skills and information can be obtained by using foreign consultants on a temporary basis. The resulting training that Japanese personnel receive is less general and less theoretical than what might be received in extrafirm institutions in the United States, but it is more closely coordinated with the Japanese firm's actual needs. There is little or no emphasis on turning out well-rounded members of a profession, occupation, or craft (Dore 1973). It is commonplace to note how few lawyers per capita there are in Japan relative to the United States and Western Europe. While this is often incorrectly attributed to a homogeneous Japanese society that has informal mechanisms for conflict resolution, it is rather the simple consequence of the Japanese educational system not offering many opportunities for advanced professional training. The United States has thirty times the number of lawyers as Japan, but each year it also graduates thirty-six times the number of Ph.D.'s in biology and ten times the number of Ph.D.'s in chemistry (Mombushō 1979; National Center for Educational Statistics 1982).

The difference in locus and emphasis of training in Japan has led to much lower mobility between firms than in the United States or even Western Europe. It has also led to much less of a professional and occupational orientation in Japan relative to the United States. The American economy's pervasive extra firm training programs and the American economy's market allocation of skilled and experienced labor also means that by contrast with Japan much potentially proprietary scientific information readily becomes public goods. Both the prospective American employer and the prospective American employee may operate under strong incentives to disclose some proprietary information as a means of signaling quality. Such disclosure can be done directly or in the context of professional association activities. Strong professional identity makes possible the use of professional association activities as a lever to job mobility.

Professionally oriented, potentially mobile managers and technical personnel might be implicity disclosing proprietary information to enhance their employment prospects, but they also might be disclosing such information to receive in exchange, albeit informally, information of commensurable value. Such trading could make everyone better off (Rogers 1981 and Nelson 1982). And such information swapping can be quite complementary to explicit market transactions in information. Actually, in many instances, such informal trading is a necessary prerequisite to more formal market transactions.

To the extent informal exchanges are useful and are facilitated by having professionally oriented technical and managerial personnel, it is quite possible that Japan by virtue of its employment system does have a competitive handicap. On average, senior research personnel in the American biotechnology industry meet with scientists from other other firms in an information-sharing context, such as a professional association meeting, fourteen times a year. In Japan, even including government-sponsored projects, the average in biotechnology is no more than six. More narrowly, the Japanese government's interfirm cooperative research projects can be viewed as an effort to ensure that Japanese R&D efforts do not become still more narrowly firm specific than they are because of the permanent employment system. Rather than an effort to pool R&D resources to create special competitive strength in a way not possible in the United States, such projects are best viewed as a substitute for the unusual degree of informal interfirm communication which takes place among the more professionally oriented R&D personnel in the United States. The importance of the government role here can be seen in a 1982 survey, where it was found that on average 40 percent of the interfirm professional scientific and engineering interaction in biotechnology in Japan took place under government auspices (Saxonhouse 1983b).

Cooperation among firms in Japan does not come easily, as is illustrated by the difficulties the government has had in securing participation. In biotechnology, while most of the major firms in the chemical industry are participating in MITI's three cooperative research programs, most have also been careful to avoid joining the biotechnology group researching its own specialty area. For example, Kyowa Hakkō and a number of other companies with advanced research expertise in DNA are not participating in the cooperative Recombinant DNA group. Tanabe, a medium-size pharmaceutical company noted for product development and a leader in bioreactor work, has decided not to participate in any of the cooperative MITI projects. Many firms that have joined are quite ambivalent about their participation. Progress in biotechnology has outstripped government planning. The Next Generation project is often derisively called the "This Generation" project, for firms outside MITI's supervision have regularly beaten government-aided firms in reaching recombinant DNA, cell fusion, and bioreactor goals. Many MITI project participants complain that they would be better off cooperating with firms outside the project or with foreign firms (*Nikkei baiotekunoroji*, January 16, 1984).

The interfirm cooperation that does take place in Japan is secondary to research and development each firm conducts independently. Government-sponsored projects characteristically absorb only a small amount of the resources devoted to R&D in the area in which the project is undertaken. Quite apart from the already documented small amount of government expenditures on these projects, another indication of the scope of these efforts is the limited fiscal participation in the cooperative research associations that are characteristically created to coordinate firm cooperation and to hold patents resulting from joint activities. The assets that member firms use in connection with R&D done under association auspices can be written down for tax purposes 100 percent in the first year, yet the Ministry of Finance (Ōkurashō 1983, p. 192) estimates that only $17 million of tax revenue was lost in 1982 from the use of this provision.

American R&D—A Public Good?
Japanese R&D—A Private Good

In case after case, high technology sectors of the Japanese economy seem to be globally competitive despite research and development expenditures modest by comparison with efforts in Western Europe and particularly in the United States. This may result from much of overseas R&D benefiting Japan about as much as the economies in which it is conducted and from so much overseas R&D being defense related.

At the level first of privately sponsored firm-conducted R&D, it is true that the same mechanisms that encourage the diffusion of potentially proprietary information among American firms also make probable the leakage of at least some of this information to Japanese firms. Such leakage is facilitated by sophisticated information gathering programs by Japanese firms and by the Japanese government. Since, in general, the same sorts of information do not diffuse among Japanese firms, except with the aid of formal programs, it is doubtful that the development of Japanese style information gathering programs in Japan by foreign government entities and foreign firms would yield rates of return comparable to what the Japanese have experienced.

Of at least equal importance to what has been learned through informal channels at American professional association meetings, from American technological consultants, from American professional journals, and from Japanese firm-sponsored graduate students studying in American research facilities, is what has been learned from technology held directly by the American government. Unless it is defense related and classified, the results of the very large amount of contract research sponsored by the American government are available globally on demand. Patents resulting from contract research have been held by the American government and characteristically have been licensed at a fixed rate to all comers. Japanese firms have been avid consumers of reports issued by the National Technical Information Service and other information agencies of the

American government, and they have licensed many American government-held patents.

In marked contrast, in Japan the results of the relatively small amount of corporate research funded by the Japanese government generally have been held privately. For example, most of the thousand patents generated by MITI's VLSI project have come to be held by the VLSI Research Association, whose members are the companies participating in the VLSI joint project; no more than fifty patents are held jointly or individually by the Japanese government.

In the last several years there have been important changes in the policies of the Japanese and American governments regarding the results of the research they fund. In the United States, rather than belonging to the public, patents developed under American government grants or contracts now belong to the grantors or contracting companies that use federal funds to develop new technologies. Moreover, unless a specific government waiver is obtained, the right to sell or use any government patent in the United States may be limited only to firms "manufacturing substantially in the United States." In particular see the changes embodied in Government Patent Policy, Memorandum from the President, 19 Weekly Compilation Presidential Documents 252 (Februrary 21, 1983).

At just the time U.S. technology policy is becoming markedly more protectionist, Japanese technology policies are beginning to approximate some important elements of U.S. policies of the 1970s. At Ministry of Finance insistence, MITI's practice of giving research subsidies (*hōjōkin*) and then allowing the recipient of the subsidy to hold the patent is ending. In MITI's Next Generation program, by contrast with the VLSI project, all firm participation is on contract (*itaku*) basis. All the biotechnology patents resulting from projects under this program will be held by the Japanese government. MITI has stated that these patents will be licensed on a nondiscriminating basis to both foreign and domestic firms. Given that research progress has been faster by Japanese firms outside this project than by firms in it, there have been complaints that *itaku* financing is dulling the incentive to rapid progress.

Japanese Economic Performance

If there is little Japanese government use of the conventional instruments of industrial policy and if much of the government high profile but largely informal involvement in private resource allocation and research and development is a substitute for, not a complement to, market institutions that work successfully overseas, why is Japanese industrial and trade structure so distinctive by international standards? And why has Japanese economic growth been so rapid by international standards?

In fact, it is possible to answer both these questions on the basis of economic considerations that have little to do with a distinctively successful Japanese industrial policy. What is distinctive about the Japanese trade structure is its low share of manufactured imports as a proportion of GNP and total imports. Japan does have a distinctive trade structure by comparison with other advanced industrial economies, but only because the Japanese economy's other attributes are also distinctive. No other advanced industrialized economy of its large size combines such high quality labor with such poor natural resources at such a great distance from its trading partners. It is these distinctive characteristics and not, for example, an industrial policy that other countries might or might not wish to emulate which gives Japan a robust comparative advantage in so many manufactured products. It is the natural resource wealth of the United States and the natural resource poverty of Japan that accounts for the relative Japanese success in so many manufacturing lines. It is the large size of the Japanese economy relative to its East Asian neighbor, Korea, that explains why as a percentage of GNP Japan imports are so much lower than Korean imports. It is the short distance of the resource-poor Italian economy from its major trading partners relative to the Japanese case that helps explain why its imports of manufactures are high relative to Japan. (These preceding paragraphs are a summary of the econometric analysis performed in Gary Saxonhouse 1983.)

If when the Japanese experience is properly normalized for capital stock, labor force, geographic position, and material resource endowment, there is little variance left to be explained by industrial policy, there is still the matter of explaining why, for example, over so much of the postwar period Japan's capital stock grew so rapidly, and this in turn changed Japan's trade and industrial structure rapidly, if normally. The same financial regulation that both necessitated and limited the supply of financial intermediaries and, in turn, did require of the government an industrial policy, if only to emulate the allocation decisions of other economies, did have a major influence on the scale of capital stock growth. During much of the period when Japan was experiencing particularly rapid growth in its capital stock resources, on the average of 8 to 9 percent of GNP was annually transferred from the household sector to the corporate sector.

Quite apart from the historical thriftiness of the Japanese household, the Ministry of Finance has worked assiduously to create and maintain this flow. For much of the postwar period Japanese government regulations so sharply limited the kinds of assets and liabilities, both real and financial, that Japanese households might acquire that household savings, and household savings available for corporate sector use, rose well above what Japanese time preference might otherwise have dictated. It is in this area rather than in sectoral policy that Japanese government policy could make a difference. For much of the period since 1945, the Japanese financial system provided few inflation hedges and effectively limited Japanese household financial assets and liabilities to fixed rate savings accounts and closely related instruments offered by the Postal Savings system and commercial banks, and to residential mortgages offered on extremely poor terms. These policies left Japanese households saving mainly for residential housing, which required a large down payment, and higher education; and the price of each was inflating rapidly, with instruments yielding highly negative real rates of return. Given Japanese motives for savings, this worked to raise the savings rate.

Finale

Examination of the familiar instruments of industrial policy indicates that Japan gives less formal aid and comfort to its high technology sectors and to biotechnology in particular than do the governments of most other advanced industrialized economies. Targeting is largely reserved for agriculture. What other high profile government intervention does take place is best understood as a response to the distinctive institutions for accumulating and allocating capital and labor skills in Japan. The effective elements of industrial policy that exist in Japan are an effort to overcome the distortions that might result from the long-time absence of well-developed capital markets. Japanese industrial policy has been a substitute, and not an unfair complement, for the market allocation of capital. capital.

In the same way that industrial policy in Japan operates to ensure that the concentration of capital in Japan does not lead to a misallocation of resources, the widely discussed Japanese government-sponsored cooperative R&D projects must be understood as a substitute for what is achieved in other industrialized economies, particularly by the United States, as a by-product of well-functioning markets for experienced scientific and engineering manpower. These projects and related government policies are an effort to ensure that the barriers to informal interfirm transfer of information created by Japanese employment practices do not slow the pace of technology diffusion within Japan.

In light of this analysis it is not surprising to find that there is nothing abnormal about Japanese trade and industrial patterns. If Japanese experience is properly normalized for Japan's capital stock, labor force, geographic position, and material resource endowment, there is little left to be explained by an industrial policy that is more than a substitute for market processes, or for that matter by trade barriers. If Japan's high profile but mostly informal industrial policy is necessitated by the character of the Japanese financial system, ongoing financial deregulation in Japan may further undermine its utility even as its continued existence is a source of annoyance among Japan's more market oriented trading partners. In such circumstances total abandonment of this long-time Japanese practice could be a distinct possibility.

REFERENCES

Auten, Gerald E., and Charles T. Clotfelter. 1982. "Permanent Versus Transitory Tax Effects and the Realization of Capital Gains." *Quarterly Journal of Economics* 97(4):613-23.

Collins, Eileen. 1983. "An Early Assessment of Three R&D Tax Incentives Provided by the Economic Recovery Tax Act of 1981." *National Science Foundation Policy Research and Analysis Report* 83.7.

Deardorff, Alan V., and Robert M. Stern. 1983. "The Economic Effects of Complete Elimination of Post-Tokyo Round Tariffs on the Major Industrial and Developing Countries." In William R. Cline, ed., *Trade Policy in the 1980s*, pp. 673-710. Washington, D.C.: Institute for International Economics.

Dibner, Mark D. 1985. "Biotechnology in Pharmaceuticals: The Japanese Challenge." *Science* 229 (47.9): 1230-35.

Dixit, Avinash. 1983. "International Trade Policy for Oligopolistic Industries." *Conference Papers: Supplement to the Economic Journal* 94 (September): 1-17.

Dore, Ronald. 1973. *British Factory—Japanese Factory*. Berkeley: University of California Press.

Eisner, Robert, Steven H. Albert, and Martin A. Sullivan. 1984. "The New Incremental Tax Credit for R&D: Incentive or Disincentive?" *National Tax Journal* 37(2):171-84.

Feldstein, Martin, Joel Slemrod, and Shlomo Yitzhaki. 1984. "The Effects of Taxation on the Selling of Corporate Stock and the Realization of Capital Gains: Reply." *Quarterly Journal of Economics* 99(1):111-20.

Flavin, Marjorie. 1983. "Excess Volatility in the Financial Market: A Re-assessment of the Empirical Evidence." *Journal of Political Economy* 91(6):929-57.

Hager, Wolfgang. 1982. "Industrial Policy, Trade Policy and European Social Democracy." In John Pinder, ed., *National Industrial Strategies and the World Economy*, pp. 236-64. London: Croom Helm.

Hayes, Robert, and William Abernathy. 1980. "Managing Our Way to an Economic Decline." *Harvard Business Review* 580:98-106.

Horiuchi Akiyoshi. 1973. "Daigaku kyōiku no rieki, hiyō oyobi hōjōkin" [The economic return to tertiary education and education subsidies]. *Nihon rōdō kyōkai zasshi* [Journal of the Japan Labor Association]. 15(4):28-39.

Horiuchi Akiyoshi. 1980. *Nihon no kinyū seisaku* [Financial policy in Japan]. Tokyo: Tōyō Keizai Shimpōsha.

Hufbauer, Gary C. 1982. *U.S. International Economic Policy, 1981: A Draft Report*. Washington, D.C.: Georgetown University Law Center.

Iwata Kazumasa and Hamada Koichi. 1980. *Kinyū seisaku to ginkō hōdō* [Financial policy and bank behavior]. Tokyo: Tōyō Keizai Shimpōsha.

Jasonoff, S. 1983. "Public and Private Sector Activities in Biotechnology: The Federal Republic of Germany." Contract report prepared for the Office of Technology Assessment, U.S. Congress.

Kagaku Gijutsu Kaigi [Science and Technology Council]. 1971. *1970 nendai ni okeru sōgō-teki kagaku gijutsu seisaku no kihon ni tsuite* [The basics of a comprehensive science and technology policy for the 1970s]. Tokyo.

Kagaku Gijutsu Chō [Science and Technology Agency]. 1972. *Kagaku gijutsu hakusho 1972* [White paper on science and technology 1972]. Tokyo.

Kagaku Gijutsu Chō. 1979. *Minkan kigyō no kenkyū katsudō ni kansuru chōsa* [Survey on Japanese firm research]. Tokyo.

Kagaku Gijutsu Chō. 1984. *Kagaku gijutsu hakusho 1984* [Science and technology White Paper 1984]. Tokyo.

Keizai Kikakuchō [Economic Planning Agency]. 1981. *Keizai hakusho* [Economic White Paper]. Tokyo.

Manhattan Report on Economic Policy. 1983. Vol. 3, No. 2. "Industrial Policy: Part 2—Is a New Deal the Answer?"

Minarik, Joseph J. 1984. "The Effects of Taxation on the Selling of Corporate Stock and the Realization of Capital Gains: Comment." *Quarterly Journal of Economics* 99(1):93–110.

Mombushō [Ministry of Education]. 1979. *Gakkō kihon chōsa hōkokusho* [Report on the survey of schools]. Tokyo.

Murakami, Yasusuke. 1982. "Toward a Socioinstitutional Explanation of Japan's Economic Performance." In Kozo Yamamura, ed., *Policy and Trade Issues of the Japanese Economy*, pp. 3–46. Seattle: University of Washington Press.

National Center for Educational Statistics. 1982. *Digest of Education Statistics 1982*. Washington, D.C.

Nelson, Richard. 1982. "The Role of Knowledge in R&D Efficiency." *Quarterly Journal of Economics* 97(3):453–71.

Noguchi, Yukio. 1982. "The Government-Business Relationship in Japan: The Changing Role of Fiscal Resources." In Kozo Yamamura, ed., *Policy and Trade Issues of the Japanese Economy*, pp. 123–42. Seattle: University of Washington Press.

Ōkurashō [Ministry of Finance], Sōzei kyoku [Tax Bureau]. 1983. *Genkō sōzei tokubetsu sochi no gaiyō* [An outline of current taxation policy].

Pascale, Richard Tanner, and Anthony G. Athos. 1981. *The Art of Japanese Management*. New York: Simon and Schuster.

Rogers, E. 1981. "Technological Information Exchange in High Technology Industries in the Silicon Valley." In D. Sahal, ed., *The Transfer and Utilization of Technological Knowledge*, pp. 53–68. Lexington, Mass.: D. C. Heath.

Saxonhouse, Gary R. 1979. "Industrial Restructuring in Japan." *Journal of Japanese Studies* 5(2):273–320.

Saxonhouse, Gary R. 1983a. "The Micro-and Macroeconomics of Foreign Sales to Japan." In William Cline, ed., *Trade Policy in the 1980s*, pp. 259–304. Cambridge, Mass.: MIT Press for the Institute of International Economics.

Saxonhouse, Gary R. 1983b. "Tampering with Comparative Advantage in Japan." *Testimony Before United States International Trade Commission Hearings on Foreign Industrial Targeting and Its Effect on U.S. Industries, Phase I: Japan*.

Semiconductor Industry Association (SIA). 1983. *The Effect of Government Targeting on World Semiconductor Competition*. Cupertino: Semiconductor Industry Association.

Shiller, Robert J. 1981. "Alternative Tests of Rational Expectations Models." *Journal of Econometrics* 16(1):71–87.

Sōmuchō [Management and Coordination Agency], Tōkei kyoku [Statistics Bureau]. 1985. *Kagaku gijutsu kenkyū chōsa hokoku 1985*. [Report on the survey of research and development 1985]. Tokyo.

Susumu S. 1982. "Kanchō, kigyō gakusha no idenshi kōgaku fība" [Genetic engineering fever—Government, business and the scholar]. *Ushio* 27(3):126–27.

Tatara S. 1981. *Idenshi sangyō kakumei* [Genetic industry revolution]. Tokyo: Bungei Shunju.

Ueno, Hiroya, and Akira Goto, n.d. "Subsidy Schemes for Industry in Japan." Mimeographed.

U.S. Department of Commerce. 1977. *A Report on the U.S. Semiconductor Industry*. Washington, D.C.: U.S. Government Printing Office.

U.S. Office of Technology Assessment (USOTA). 1984. *Commercial Biotechnology: An International Analysis*. Washington, D.C.

U.S. Trade Representative. 1982. *Japanese Barriers to United States Trade and Recent Japanese Government Trade Initiatives*. Washington, D.C.

Vaquin, M. 1982a. "Biotechnology in France." Contract report prepared for the Office the Technology Assessment, U.S. Congress.

Vaquin, M. 1982b. "Biotechnology in Great Britain." Contract report prepared for the Office of Technology Assessment, U.S. Congress.

Chapter 4

Japan's Industrial Policy
for High Technology Industry

Ken-ichi Imai

Japanese industrial policy has in the past supported market-based developments in fields where success was obvious. That is not being cynical; it was a coherent, substantive policy. As to form, MITI's offical position is that "Premised upon indirect and guideline policies, Japanese industrial policy is much more soft-handed than industrial policy activities in the other industrialized democracies" (Yamanaka 1983). The key word is "soft-handed." What some of the specific policies have been for high technology industries, and an assessment of the role of industrial policy in high technology development, are the principal topics of this essay. My particular concern is how relevant past policy is to the high tech future.

What kind of government policies are effective, indeed, possible, is influenced by management style and industrial organization, and Japan and the United States have some important differences in this regard. Understanding these differences is necessary for understanding what Japanese industrial policy is and how it works. This is taken up in the first section. I then look at policies for the microelectronics, energy, and biotechnology industries, discuss technology transfer and the related "technopolis plan," and, lastly, consider the communications industry, which has been dubbed the "new media" and is MITI's current policy focal point.

Continuous, cumulative development accounts for most technological advances, and this is as true in today's seemingly fast-changing world as it was in the mid-1950s when Gunnar Myrdal talked of "cumulative causation" in industrial development (Myrdal 1957). A series of small or medium innovations collectively can produce (indeed, can be) a breakthrough. The system's learning process is what effectively builds these cumulative developments, from innovation to creation, from basics to application, from designing to testing, and from parts to assembly. How the stages are linked, and how information flows, thus influence the speed and nature of innovation, a topic we will return to.

The term "high technology industries" is generally used in Japan to indicate microelectronics, biotechnology, and new materials. This is a somewhat shorter list than is common in the United States. However, a general definition of high tech industries is not very useful, as is discussed by Patrick in chapter 1. In defining high techology for the purpose of this chapter, I use as criteria the intensity of R&D activity and the use of the technologies in a system. The latter is important because I feel high technology has become intertwined with industrial policy and is regarded by many as a new economic infrastructure; both of these relate to the systemic characteristic. In other words, the concern here is with what have been called generic technologies—those that have ramifications in production processes or as components in a variety of products, often in other industries. This is in contrast to characteristic innovation, where the effects are localized.

The simplest measure of intensity is R&D costs as a percentage of sales (table 6). The pharmaceutical industry generally ranks first in this regard, but aside from its biotechnological activities, the industry fails the second criterion because the results (specific drugs) are not systemic. On the other hand, robotics fits both criteria.

When high technology is defined and its developmental process is characterized in this way, the need for government involvement is clear. In abstract terms, R&D is simply the production of information. Who is entitled to use that information, and for what purposes? Given the

TABLE 6

Intensity of Research and Development (R&D costs as a percentage of sales) for the Top Five Japanese Industries

Industry	R&D Intensity (1981)
1. Pharmaceuticals	5.9
2. Telecommunications, electronics, electrical instrumentation	4.2
3. Electrical machinery and instrumentation	3.8
4. Precision machinery	3.5
5. Other chemicals	3.0
Manufacturing as a whole	1.9
Total industry	1.6

Source: Science and Technology Agency, General Coordination Department, Technology Research and Information Division, *Trends of Principal Indices on Research and Development Activities in Japan*, revised edition, July 1983.

public-good nature of so much of R&D, what should be the mix of private and public pursuit? These are public policy issues.

Stressing the systemic nature of high technology brings to the fore the issue of the organization creating this aggregate. The various possibilities for the structural framework cannot be classified simply into private and public sector organizations based on the fundamental or economic nature of the technology. The possibility exists for various kinds of public intervention in the R&D of private industries, and for involvement by the private sector in the bringing to fruition of development carried out in, or under the auspices of, the public sector.

The three-phase model of technological development suggested by Abernathy (1978) can be extended to provide a framework for industrial policy evolution. At the start of an industry's development, the technology (nature of the product) is still fluid and the innovations are thus centered on defining the product (what it does, how it does it, and so forth). Innovations appear from diverse sources, including universities and new firms. In phase 2, the market has been defined by the establishment of standards, either de facto ones set by a dominant producer or ones agreed to by a number of participants (users or makers). Attention then turns to carving out market niches through minor innovations and, more important, to efficiency of production (process innovations). As the industry matures, in phase 3, the product technology becomes fluid again as continued innovation allows or demands renewed product innovation. The phases are summarized in table 7.

The content of industrial policy differs according to the phase of development of the industry concerned. In phase 1 there are grounds for government fostering and intervention to avoid market failures related to uncertainty. In phase 3, government involvement can be justified to facilitate the transfer of technology between industries and regions in order to rejuvenate mature industries that have ceased to innovate because of oligopolistic stagnation or ceased to be competitive in world markets. However, in phase 2, it is difficult to find reasons for specific industrial policies, beyond promoting competition among the various firms.

TABLE 7
Phases of Industrial Development

Phase	Technology is	Innovation is in	Innovation comes from
1	fluid	products	diverse sources
2	specific	processes	competition in production processes
3	re-fluidized	systems	integration

Interpenetration of the Market and Organization

Resources can be allocated by what I call the market principle, by the organization principle, or by a combination of these. In the real world, it is usually the last, a mixture, that one encounters. I term such mixing "interpenetration," and it occurs to remedy failures of the pure principles.

I have intentionally used the word principle, because the market principle is not a pure price-driven market mechanism, and the organization principle is not simply allocation by authority. Rather, there are two aspects that define the principles: the decision rule (what one is really maximizing) and the relationships among the parties to a transaction (which constrain both the decision rule and choice of actions). These influence the extent to which market prices are "believed" to contain all the information needed for a transaction. Of course, for many transactions between firms, and particularly within them, there is no market price. Within a firm there are necessarily continuous relationships, and they involve authority. For this reason the organization principle is stronger at the firm level than it is for the economy as a whole.

What is more important to this chapter is that the patterns of interpenetration are different in Japan and the United States. These differences are important in understanding industrial policy, and this section thus seeks to provide some insight into them. (For a fuller account, see Imai and Itami 1984.)

The overall balance between the two principles is tilted more toward the organization principle in Japan than in the United States at the level of industries and definitely for the economy as a whole. A simple manifestation of this is the general perception, which I feel is correct, that Japanese firms are more likely to value stable, continuing relations with other firms than American firms are. It is well known that the price mechanism has difficulty accomodating uncertainty (which is inherent in long-run decision making) and externality. Relationships are created among firms to try to capture the externalities collectively, and to mitigate the uncertainty by coordination or by sharing consequences. For large categories of products, the buyer needs information and after-sale support (if only for spare parts and replacements). Buying in a spot market solely on the basis of acquisition price, with no allowance for ongoing costs, is not rational.

More broadly, the difference in the level of interpenetration means there is less arm's-length dealing among firms in Japan than in the United States in allocating capital and goods. The close relationship between a Japanese corporation and its lead bank is well known.

Most observers of the Japanese economic scene would agree that two of the major characteristics of Japan's industrial organization compared with the United States are (1) more organized activities among producers of the same goods, such as legalized cartels, joint R&D efforts, or coordinated behavior through governmental administrative guidance, and (2) more cooperative vertical relations between sellers and buyers of intermediate goods. In looking at the production process from raw materials to finished good, in Japan there are likely to be more companies involved than in the United States—Japanese companies are more likely to perform only a few steps. In other words, the degree of vertical integration in Japan is generally much less than in the United States (see Imai 1980). Although this means there are more market transactions for intermediate goods in Japan, as firms in the overall process sell their output as input down the line, these transactions often are not arm's-length dealings.

Joint research and antirecession cartels are Japanese practices for pooling risk. The antirecession cartels in a sense presume that all the firms will be viable in the long run if they are not drained by cutthroat competition during recessions. Figuratively, the Japanese make each firm go a little bit bankrupt when the market contracts, while in the United States some firms are driven all the way into bankruptcy. The Japanese method is like treating an infection, and the American approach is a drastic surgical excision to save the rest of the body. When there is a presumption that growth will resume for the industry , the Japanese approach can promote long-run competition. In the United States, and increasingly in Japan, for many industries such a presumption is not sustainable and allowing bankruptcies may be necessary for efficient resource allocation.

Because many innovations are the result of a combination of several pieces of information, lack of common information accumulation is undesirable. Joint research is a way of dealing with the public-good nature of information. In Japan's industrial organization, this type of interpenetration between market and organization is normal, and this is the most important aspect in a discussion of industrial policy. Saying that Japanese do not deal among themselves at arm's length as much as Americans do is not the same as saying Japanese are less competitive. It does say that there is a behavioral bias, reflected in the industrial structure and nature of contracts, for consensus forming, if not cooperation. In what has probably been a self-reinforcing process, Japanese business is attuned to responding to nonprice signals, particularly from the government or other consensus-forming organizations, and that means a government policy can be built around guidance (soft policies).

How well the Japanese pattern will work in the future is unclear, and I return to this issue later. One point is clear: the pattern is not conducive to entrepreneurial activity. Low labor mobility in Japan and limited entry into firms means an entrepreneur has a very small chance of reemployment at an established firm if he fails in a spinoff attempt. Entrepreneurs also have limited access to capital in the form of bank loans. Even more than in the United States, in Japan the uncertainty of the survivability of a small company discourages firms from giving it orders and credit.

The Information Industry

The principal focus of Japanese industrial policy, beginning in the 1970s, was the development of what is called the information industry as the strategic industry of Japan. In Japan the term "information industry" has meant computers, including such components as semiconductors, and software. With the emergence in the 1980s of new technologies in communications, this field is now also included, and I take it up in a later section. In terms of table 7, the Japanese computer and semiconductor industries are in phase 2 of their development.

Computers

In 1964, IBM introduced the System 360, and with it the concept of a family of general purpose machines. (A computer family is a series of compatible computers offering a range of prices and performance.) This can be said to represent the beginning of the computer industry as we know it today. Less than two years later, in March 1966, the Electronics Industry Inquiry Committee (formed by MITI) published a report entitled "Measures for Strengthening the International Competitiveness of the Computer Industry." This set the course for fostering the growth of Japanese producers to compete with IBM.

A policy of encouraging domestic computer manufacturers began even earlier, in 1959, when the Temporary Measure for Promotion of the Electronics Industry was enacted by the Diet. There has followed a series of other "temporary" measures designed to encourage Japanese producers of computers. (For accounts of the emergence of the Japanese computer industry, see Okimoto et al. 1984.)

The government also promoted demand for Japanese computers through its own procurement. This extended to national universities and government-affiliated institutions, and included situations where Japanese products were not the most appropriate or the least expensive. Japan is not, of course, unique in this regard, although it has perhaps gone further than most countries. To counter IBM's strength in rentals, the government created JECC (Japan Electronic Computer Corporation) in 1961 to buy computers from seven major Japanese manufacturers and lease them. During its first twenty years JECC purchased over $7 billion worth of computer equipment (see Okimoto 1984, p. 110).

Only with trade liberalization in 1971, however, when the industry was facing competition with the IBM 370 series, was a system of subsidies established. Although in effect for only a limited period, the subsidies were a powerful measure, providing 50 percent of development costs for new machines from three groups of producers. In doing this, MITI was trying to force mergers in the industry, but the companies resisted.

Perhaps equally important, with these policies went such efforts as implanting in society the concept of the increasing importance of information in the economy and the idea of an information society through reports by the Industrial Structure Council and through publicity concerning such a concept. In short, the government was actively involved in a public relations campaign. The nature of the interpenetration of market and organization in Japan contributed to the success of the campaign, and to the diffusion of computers and knowledge about them.

The subsidies were ended, in 1977, when the government felt the industry had accumulated sufficient technological and managerial resources to compete with IBM, at least in Japan and Southeast Asia. IBM's market share in Japan is half its share in the rest of the world, and three Japanese firms have 20 to 30 percent each. What Japan did was well within accepted practices for fostering infant industries. Moreover, competition from Japanese mainframe makers had undoubtedly benefited computer users worldwide.

Semiconductors

The government has recognized the importance of semiconductors as a key component of computers and a host of other products. Details of this policy are covered in Okimoto's chapter in this volume; here I will consider the context and some of the implications of the VLSI (very large scale integrated circuit) project, which lasted four years, 1976-79. The goal was the development of manufacturing technology for VLSIs, specifically, placing one megabit of memory on a chip, which was what IBM was in the process of developing at the time. Fujitsu, Hitachi, Mitsubishi, NEC, and Toshiba were invited to participate in the joint research project. These five firms, with Oki, were the same ones paired into three groups by MITI in the early 1970s; Oki was denied the opportunity to participate in the VLSI Technology Research Association.

Only about 15 percent of the research (in terms of cost) was carried out in the Joint Research Institute, which was staffed by about a hundred researchers from the five firms and MITI's Electrotechnical Laboratory. The remaining work was done by the firms in their own labs. Some 74 billion yen was spent, about 40 percent of it government money. Research ceased in 1979, when the project was deemed to have achieved its goals.

The Association continues to exist to administer some one thousand patents, the royalties from which are being used to repay the government subsidy. When repayment is complete, each patent will be assigned to the firm that developed it.

There is a strong view, especially in America, that practices that ought to be forbidden by antitrust laws are permitted in Japan, and this is a source of competitive advantage for Japanese firms. However, when the facts are carefully examined, I think such arguments can be refuted.

First, there are the issues of the nature of the practices used by firms participating in the cooperative research and the possibility of cartel-like behavior. In the VLSI case it is true the participating firms were the major suppliers of VLSIs and products using them. However, the development carried out jointly was on equipment for VLSI production and general aspects of VLSI technology, as distinguished from development of specific chips or circuits. Japan was seeking to strengthen the foundation of its semiconductor manufacturing technology. In other words, it was some distance from development of specific VLSI and VLSI-using products. Instead, each firm took the general knowledge—what is often now called generic technology—back to its own labs and built on it for specific products. There is no guarantee that collusion will not take place, but neither is collusion inherent in the joint research process. Some Americans have claimed that one purpose of the project was to make Japanese companies less dependent on U.S. manufacturers of fabricating equipment. Some U.S. firms have in fact complained about Japanese practices. The Japanese system requires cooperation between the makers of fabrication equipment and its users to make incremental innovations, and naturally having local partners makes that easier. Hence, there is a desire to develop a local (Japanese) semiconductor fabrication equipment industry.

Second, if R&D is itself considered an economic activity in the market, it might be argued that since the Association carried out R&D activities jointly, such activities clearly conflict with the intent of antitrust laws. This is not a persuasive argument. Patents—limited-time monopolies on a technology—are a compromise between considerations of the social benefits from antitrust and from invention. Cooperative R&D is analogous. In the VLSI case, the technology developed has been made public, and anyone, including non-Japanese, can use it on payment of patent use charges. On the other hand, similar American technology already existed, so social benefit could have been achieved through a policy of licensing it. Nonetheless, from the standpoint of antitrust policy, harmful effects have not occurred as a result of such cooperative R&D. Moreover, non-Japanese firms have benefited from greatly reduced prices for VLSIs in world markets.

Third, the issue of unfairness has been raised because membership in this research association was limited to five firms. Other firms wished to participate but were excluded. There are three aspects of this I will deal with here: who would have access to the results of the project, the goals of the Association, and the nature of the research process. The intention was to help all companies by making the results widely available. Although firms denied the opportunity to participate may have suffered some disadvantages by not being involved in the process, they have had access to the results. Moreover, the project was narrow in scope and limited in time. Being denied participation in one project was not the same as being cut off from open-ended, ongoing research.

The nature of the research process is an important consideration. No one benefits from an unsuccessful project, and if a research association is to succeed, there must be a coherent organization. This condition is crucial and surprisingly difficult to achieve. Simply gathering together researchers is unlikely to produce results. Because of the incremental, cumulative nature of the results being sought, the work had to be coordinated and disseminated quickly. There was thus a limit on size, as well as a need to bring together a group whose members complemented each other's skills and preferably also had cooperated before. In the VLSI case, individuals at the five firms in the Association already were engaged in the informal exchange of information through trade associations, private networks including academic circles, and the like.

The VLSI Technology Research Association is a successful example of the organization principle in a market context. It achieved its purpose and avoided anticompetitive effects.

Industrial Policy for New Energy Development

With the turning point of the 1974 oil crisis, technological development related to energy became an urgent need for Japan. New energy development and energy conservation plans were formulated under government leadership. (For an outline of these plans, see MITI 1980.) At the time of the oil crisis, the supply of energy was the most serious limiting factor in the expansion of the Japanese economy. With the possibility that it could become so again and that dependence on imports for a large proportion of energy needs makes the Japanese economy seem fragile in international terms, there are positive social reasons for the government to foster energy technology, particularly domestically produced energy.

The new energy development plan was vigorously implemented. But if we look at the resulting government expenditures, we find they were devoted overwhelmingly to atomic energy. Although the importance of the development of new energy sources such as solar and wind power was recognized, the results went no further than an acceleration of the atomic energy development already in progress. There were great expectations concerning renewable energy, but so far no great advances have been achieved.

The government's position on the development of energy technology began and ended with the administration of subsidies, leaving the impression that there was neglect of supplementary and supporting activities on the demand side. In the development of new energy sources, such as solar energy, it is advisable for the government gradually to build up its own demand, for example by using solar-powered street lights, traffic controls, hot-water heating in schools, hospitals, and so forth, and to link this with the supply side through actual production, however little, in response to such demand. Through this process, related technological improvements and decreases in cost can be expected (Imai 1982c). In the development stage of technologies, it is fundamental to include a learning process to improve technical know-how through gathering information from users while production trials are going on. On the side of the organization in charge of development, "being in motion," however slight, is necessary for the activation of the organization and in order to give the researchers incentive.

Organizations promoting new energy development have been ineffective. To remedy this, NEDO (New Energy Development Organization) was established in early 1981. This is a special-status corporation funded by governmental and nongovernmental sources and under government direction—what in Japan is called the "third sector" (similar to the "multi-sector enterprise" of Horwitch and Prahaland 1976). The formula for this third sector is to take the government's ability to plan with a broad vision and on a large scale and combine it with the private sector's vitality. Four conditions must be met simultaneously for the effective administration of this form of organization: (1) economic rationality in cost-benefit terms, (2) appropriate management techniques, (3) bureaucratic-political measures, and (4) an appropriate social and economic environment. (See Horwitch 1979 for a discussion of these points.)

Condition 4, however, has not been met, as changes in the supply and demand for oil have lowered the price of oil and thus also near-term interest in new energy sources. At the same time, MITI officials gradually shifted to the position of emphasizing economic costs in the selection of energy sources. These changed conditions eroded political and bureaucratic support, weakening condition 3. Concerning condition 2, NEDO did not have its own R&D organization; it was merely a controller of subsidies. Expenditures rose for subsidies for technologies, such as coal liquefaction, which are uneconomical even in the long term. Thus, even the first condition, economic rationality in cost-benefit terms, was not met.

It would be too strong to say that NEDO has been an organizational failure, but in an environment of stable or falling oil prices this multisector enterprise has not been fully successful. Japanese industrial policy has not produced definitely positive results in new energy development.

This is not to say that Japan did nothing about the energy problem and did not use the achievements of high technology in dealing with expensive energy. This was done by a method in which the Japanese industrial system is skilled. A large-scale reduction in energy consumption was effected through a rationalization of energy use by utilization of information technology. For example, several mechanical processes, such as plating, decreased energy use by increasing recycling and otherwise reducing waste. Implementation of these resource and energy saving technologies often involved computerized control systems. In the 1960s, a 1 percent increase in GNP involved a 1.14 percent increase in energy use; by the 1970s the elasticity of energy consumption had been reduced to 0.75.

These improvements in energy efficiency are symbolic of the characteristics of incremental innovation in present-day Japan. Explanations of the high efficiency of Japanese manufacturing generally have stressed the learning process on the production line, centering on lowering the rate of defects. But this emphasizes the results of expertise attained in using a specific technology, while overlooking the learning process of gradually improving (changing) the technology. What made Japan's energy efficiency possible was the incremental innovation in manufacturing technology. Fortunately, the period following the first oil crisis was when electronic technology was introduced across the board into the machinery industry, and feedback among machinery makers acted as a mechanism for propagating technological innovations. The interpenetration between market and organization characteristic of the Japanese industrial system was effective in paving the way for the information exchange between the machinery makers and users and in the accumulation of technological improvements for energy saving.

Industrial Policy for Biotechnology

In terms of the direction of research and prospects for production, biotechnology in Japan is in a totally fluid state. In this, Japan faces a new situation. It is new not only because Japan does not have the option of utilizing imported current technology, but also because Japanese firms have some long-standing, significant technological expertise. There are areas, such as fermentation, where Japanese companies are beginning not just on a par but ahead of non-Japanese competitors. There is a need for

critical policy decisions in the next few years, the most immediately
important of which is how to deliver what I call the "initial kick"—that
is, how to create the mechanism for initiating the cumulative process of
development.

Currently in Japan, basic research in life science and plans for fostering
biotechnology industries are being shaped independently by several agencies
and ministries. The Science and Technology Agency is promoting goal-
oriented basic research in such areas as bioreactors, mainly at the Institute
of Physical and Chemical Research, while the Ministry of Agriculture,
Forestry, and Fisheries and the Ministry of Health and Welfare are
preparing the foundation for application-oriented R&D related to their
respective spheres of control in the food and pharmaceutical industries.
These efforts, however, amounted in 1982 (fiscal year) to a mere 100 million
yen, only enough for a trial and much less than the amount required for
the initial kick. It is only one-tenth the amount the U.S. government
budgeted for life science R&D the same year. Among the Japanese efforts,
MITI's policy for promoting biotechnology has some distinguishing
features.

In biotechnology, industrial organization is at the stage of a few small
firms with specific technologies and R&D by large corporations in the
pharmaceutical, chemical, food, and synthetic fiber industries. The latter
are still at the groping stage, and there has not been any investment in
full-blown R&D. Among such efforts, Mitsubishi Chemical's Life Science
Research Laboratory is the largest in scale. This organization lies
somewhere between a university research facility and a corporation. At
present it is like a university laboratory in the freedom of its research
structure. It appears to lack the direction-oriented nature of a company
research facility.

Most of the innovations in biotechnology, as in the chemical industry,
are science based, relying on breakthroughs achieved through basic research
and large-scale experimentation rather than through a learning process
based on the accumulation of know-how. Unlike electronics and machine-
related technologies, in which innovation is made possible by the
combination of various technologies, the main manufacturing technology
is in a self-contained form generally protected as a proprietary process
or by patents. Hence it tends to be a narrow learning system tying a certain
large corporation to a specific research group in a university, and not a
broadly based learning system. In this type of sphere, the Japanese system
is at a disadvantage compared with the systems of the major corporations
of the world.

MITI's "system for research and development for basic industrial
technology for the next generation" is the policy response being formulated
and implemented to deal with this type of situation. It attempts to form

an R&D association to supplement R&D in the field of chemistry, an area in which Japan does not have a competitive edge in basic research or in industrial technology. By 1984 twelve associations had been formed in the areas of biotechnology, new materials, and new functional elements, with participation by forty-nine major corporations (see table 8). Three associations have been established to deal with biotechnology: for use of recombinant DNA, for mass cell culture, and for bioreactors.

But the expectations are too high for such R&D associations. In order for meaningful joint research to be accomplished among competitive corporations and for it not to have the negative effect of limiting competition, appropriate research subjects must be selected which will result in general input for each corporation, as was the case with the VLSI project. In many of the new R&D associations, the main feature is the aim of comprehensive research in medical, agricultural, scientific, and engineering fields by researchers specializing in engineering as well as by biologists. In order for this kind of research to be promoted effectively, conditions similar to those needed for the success of the multisector enterprise discussed in relation to the new energy development system must be satisfied.

Since the R&D associations have only recently been established for the next generation's industrial base, it is too early for evaluation. In terms of this chapter's inquiry into organizational analysis, it would appear to be ill-advised to expect too much. Other countries are keeping a close watch on Japan's industrial policy concerning biotechnology, and they tend to overreact and overestimate the results.

If Japanese industry is to achieve results in biotechnology, it will be in a sphere in which the Japanese industrial system already has a competitive advantage. Japanese firms possess the most advanced technology in the field of fermentation, which is applicable to food processing. If this technology is linked to biotechnology, for example in cell fusion, there is the possibility of innovations in the food industry. Biomass is another area of expertise. This is a field where work is done mostly with a combination of existing technologies, which makes it well suited to Japan's present system of R&D.

Biotechnology is expected to revolutionize agriculture and food processing, just as microelectronics has revolutionized industrial processes. The diffusion of technology throughout its economy, both in adapting the advances of one sector to improving efficiency and quality in another and in moving all firms in an industry toward the best technology, has been a major element in Japan's growth since the nineteenth century. There is reason to believe that Japanese firms and policy makers will, through the interpenetration of market and organization, be able to achieve significant results, although it will require more modification of past

TABLE 8

Research and Development Projects of Basic Technology for New Industries in Japan

Project	Private Research Association	Public Laboratory	Budget (fiscal year; million yen) 1981	1982	1983
New Materials			1,360	2,600	3,460
Performance ceramics	Engineering Research Association for High Performance Ceramics	Government Industrial Research Institute, Nagoya and Osaka; Mechanical Engineering Laboratory; National Institute for Research in Inorganic Materials			
Synthetic membranes for new separation technology	Research Association for Basic Polymer Technology	National Chemical Laboratory for Industry; Industrial Products Research Institute; Research Institute for Polymer and Textiles			
Synthetic metals	"	Electrotechnical Laboratory; Research Institute for Polymer and Textiles			
High performance plastics	"	Research Institute for Polymer and Textiles			
Advanced alloys with control crystalline structures	Research and Development Institute of Metals and Composites for Future Industries	Mechanical Engineering Laboratory; Government Industrial Research Institute, Nagoya; National Research Institute for Metals			

Advanced composite metals	"	Industrial Products Research Institute; Mechanical Engineering Laboratory; Research Institute for Polymer and Textiles; Government Industrial Research Institute, Osaka	680	1,040	1,290
Biotechnology					
Bioreactors	Research Association for Biotechnology	Fermentation Research Institute; Research Institute for Polymer and Textiles; National Chemical Laboratories for Industry			
Utilization of recombinant DNA	"	"			
Large-scale cell cultivation	"				
Future Electronic Devices					
Super lattice devices	Research and Development Association for Future Electron Devices	Electrotechnical Laboratory	670	1,130	1,570
Three-dimensional ICs	"	"			
Fortified ICs for extreme conditions	"	"			

Source: Science and Technology Agency, MITI.

methods than has been necessary in other industries and circumstances. The technopolis policy discussed next gives great hopes for such possibilities.

Technology Transfer Policy

Government policy is aimed at encouraging the creation of new technologies and the spread of those already in existence. In this section I take up the transfer of technology (the flow of technology in a directed manner), which is distinguished from merely allowing the technology to diffuse (spread in a more or less spontaneous manner).

Once the nature (purpose) of a product has been settled on, companies focus on improving it (making it easier to use, better looking, etc.) and decreasing the cost. Doing this means drawing on their experience in making and selling the product, a process called moving along the learning curve. It requires feedback from suppliers, the production line, and customers. The process in general, and the approach of Japanese firms in particular, is the subject of a large literature, so I will not dwell on it here. (For a summary see Imai et al. 1985.)

Suffice it to say that if one accepts rapid movement along the learning curve as being of decisive importance in a company's success with a technology, cumulative production is crucial in the initial stage of the competitive process. The experience a firm has with a product—the more it has produced—and the speed with which the experience is acquired are crucial factors in gaining and sustaining market share and profits.

In the case of a technology related to the production process, the emergence and refinement of the technology can be considered the first of a two-stage process. The second stage is to broaden the technology's application. This has two aspects. The first is to spread the technology within the industry for which it was developed; the second is to apply it in other areas. Within an industry, large corporations will transfer new technology to their subsidiaries and affiliates. Each new user is a source of potential improvement, and through feedback these enhancements will diffuse or be transferred. Japanese as individuals and as members of firms are very aware of the importance of technology, and there is a widespread grass roots basis supporting the spread and development of new and better ways of doing things. This is one part of the "accumulation of small innovations" for which Japanese firms are renowned.

Current technological innovation can be seen as the cumulative process of a network producing innovation through the integration of the knowledge and know-how developed in the system. Hence, the expansion of the scale of a network means the possibility of increases in innovation through new combinations with other technologies.

Since Joseph Schumpeter, the appropriate scale of enterprises has been a point of dispute in discussions concerning the efficiency of technological innovation. However, it is also—if not more—important to consider the roles of the size of the network of related companies, researchers, and users of the product, and the efficiency of the diffusion and transfer of knowledge and information within this network.

If Japanese companies are to produce relatively favorable results in innovation centering on high technology, they must rely on widespread and speedy transfer of knowledge and information and on the efficiency of the learning system. In creating such an industrial system, it must be noted that MITI's soft industrial policy has played a vital role. MITI's policy stimulated market activity and strengthened the industrial base for technological development by the gradual mobilization of diverse strategies such as policies for technological development, for technology transfer, for regional development, and for small and medium firms. Political pressure has resulted in policies for small and medium firms that include subsidies and support cartels. However, the current policy of a gradual process encouraging self-help reflects a transformation to a new industrial policy.

Technopolis Policy

The technopolis plan is a new type of industrial policy that gives coherence to technology diffusion policies. In more concrete terms, it is a plan to form new cities integrating industry, education, and housing near existing focal cities and utilizing the surrounding social resources to create regional centers for industrial development focusing on high technology.

At present, Japanese industry needs the following two types of R&D: (1) manufacturing-oriented R&D that aims at incremental improvements in existing production systems by using high technology (this type of R&D takes the form of close contact with the production site and strengthening of research divisions attached to factories); (2) knowledge-oriented R&D with the goal of designing a new paradigm or making breakthroughs in existing systems (this requires a science park linking research organs of various industries, joint research associations, universities, and so forth).

The goals of the technopolis policy are to promote the first type of R&D through technology transfer and to establish locations where type 2 R&D will be undertaken. To realize these goals a new organizational structure is being considered that would link industries, universities, and the government.

Legislation concerning the technopolis policy was passed in 1983 and large-scale implementation is still to come. Although it is thus too early to evaluate the policy, implementation of type 1 R&D appears to be progressing at a steady pace. Plans of the candidate regions are shown in table 9. During the last ten years, from even before the technopolis approach, the transfer of technology in the electronics and other fields has been substantial. Several groups, although not formed directly as a result of the technopolis policy, have been organized to exchange technology across different industries in particular localities, and have achieved results. These include the H technological R&D group in Himeji (12 firms), the K Industrial Information Center in Kyoto (120 firms), the T Development Center in Tokyo (40 firms), and the S R&D Enterprise Research Group in Shizuoka (31 firms) (MITI 1983, p. 323).

Based on this learning process, if the government sets up regional technological development centers in which private enterprises, university or national research institutes, and regional experimental research agencies participate, the goal of transferring electronics technology to industries, localities, and various small and medium firms will be accomplished. According to organizational theory, it is sufficient to form a loose organizational linkage as described above for the diffusion of technology.

To implement type 2 policy—the creation of large-scale science parks for R&D of new materials—no plan of action has been settled on, and there is no prospect for one. This is not just a problem of technology transfer. Since cooperative research must be actively pursued, a loose organizational linkage is inappropriate. Instead, a strong organizational framework is needed, as it was in the VLSI case, and there is little likelihood such an organization will be formed among competitive firms. As with biotechnology, too great an expectation has been placed on the many joint research associations that have been established with the goal of laying the foundation for industry in future generations. Nor have preparatory conditions needed to implement the technopolis plan been studied adequately. It is of greater importance to form linkages with international R&D networks in such fields, and this is what many Japanese firms have been doing.

The foregoing discussion suggests that it is appropriate to consider recent technopolis plans in Japan as a method of technology transfer in general. This is my evaluation, however, and some comments are required.

The idea of technopolis was formulated in order to create a high technology area like Silicon Valley or the North Carolina Research Triangle. Japan already had the Tsukuba research park, and Tokyo itself has been a true technopolis with its huge conglomeration of technological and production facilities as well as universities. In the initial phase of discussions concerning technopolis, the main theme was the building of another Tsukuba or miniature conglomerations based on Tokyo as the model in a few selected regions. But when this idea was made public by MITI, it provoked the unwonted attention of planners in Japan's provincial areas. MITI responded by utilizing this energy to promote voluntary planning in each region. At first, local governments welcomed the policy as a new way of obtaining subsidies for building local factories, without any particular concern for R&D. In this process, however, strong competition occurred among candidate regions, and MITI decreed that without concrete R&D planning a region could not be accepted as a technopolis region. This strongly encouraged independent effort by local governments to design new organizations for R&D—organizations that naturally had the character of type 1 R&D, aimed at the transfer of high technology to local industries.

How synergism among such R&D institutions, local industries, and universities could be created was quite unknown, and neither the local governments nor MITI had any specific policy instrument to promote it. In fact, it would be overoptimistic to expect new technological breakthroughs from these projects. However, if the technopolis is adopted as a method of technology transfer, the resulting raising of the technological level of the least-productive firms toward current best practice will raise Japan's overall industrial capabilities. This is a reasonable expectation.

The New Media Policy

The current focal point of MITI's information industry policy is the formulation of a policy for the "new media." Each year MITI announces the policies it considers of high priority, and new media policy was given top billing for 1984. Here the term "new media" is used to indicate all the communication media that use recent telecommunications and informational innovations. MITI is investigating how to promote new media such as CATV (cable television), teletext, and VANs (value-added networks); the form to be taken in the institutionalization and deregulation of the telecommunications industry; and beyond this, the use of these media to create a new information network for Japanese industry.

These issues have been addressed directly by the New Media Committee, which I chaired, formed by MITI's Industrial Structure Council and the Information Industry Committee. The report of the committee is published as "How New Media Should Develop: Toward an Affluent 21st Century" (MITI, Industrial Structure Council 1983).

Three major reasons can be given for focusing industrial policy on new media. (1) In Japanese industrial circles, restrictions on data communications have led to strong dissatisfaction with the Ministry of Posts and Telecommunications (MPT) and NTT (Nippon Telegraph and Telephone, until 1985 the government-run telecommunications monopoly). Protest has taken the form of demands for the liberalization of data

TABLE 9

Features of the Technopolis Development Plans

Prefecture	Name of Region	Technopolis Region Principal Universities	Targeted Industrial Sectors
Hokkaido	Hakodate	Hokkaido University	Marine-related industries and those making use of natural resources (electronics, mechatronics, biotechnology, etc.)
Akita	Akita	Akita University	Electronics, mechatronics, new materials, natural resources, energy, biotechnology
Niigata	Nagaoka	Nagaoka College of Science and Technology	Higher systems industries, urban industries (design, fashion), industries using local natural resources
Tochigi	Utsunomiya	Utsunomiya University	Electronics, mechatronics, fine chemicals, new materials, software
Shizuoka	Hamamatsu	Shizuoka University Hamamatsu College of Medicine	Optoelectronics industries, advanced mechatronics, home sound culture (electronic musical instruments), etc.
Toyama	Toyama	Toyama University Toyama College of Medicine and Pharmacology Others	Mechatronics, new materials, biotechnology (medical, etc.), information industries

Okayama	Kibikogen	Okayama University	Biotechnology, electronics, mechatronics (medical and pharmaceutical industries), etc.
Hiroshima	Hiroshima Chuo	Okayama College of Science Hiroshima University	Electronics, mechatronics, new materials, biotechnology, etc.
Yamaguchi	Ube	Yamaguchi University	Electronics, mechatronics, new materials, ocean development, biotechnology, etc.
Fukuoka-Saga	Kurume-Tosu	Kurume College of Engineering Kurume University	Mechatronics, fine chemicals, fashion, next generation (bio) industries, etc.
Oita	Kenhoku-Kunizaki	Oita University Oita College of Medicine Others	Electronics, mechatronics, bioindustry, software
Kumamota	Kumamota	Kumamoto University Kumamoto College of Engineering Others	Applied machinery industry, biotechnology, electronic equipment, information systems industry
Miyazaki	Miyazaki	Miyazaki University Miyazaki College of Medicine	Local-oriented (bio), introduction-oriented (electronics, etc.), and urban-oriented (urban systems) industries
Kagoshima	Kokubu-Hayato	Kagoshima University Kyushu Gakuin University	Electronics, mechatronics, new materials, biotechnology, etc.

Source: MITI, "The Technopolis Plan: Recent Developments," *MITI News* NR-289 (84-5), March 6, 1984.

communications. Deregulation has become a focal point of policy, strongly supported by MITI, promoting industrial development in the information and telecommunications sectors. This debate is taking place as computer and telecommunications technologies are fusing.

This fusion leads to reason (2): The information industry as a whole is entering a new stage, with broad infiltration of its technology into industry generally. Hence, it has become necessary to grasp the effects of this change in comprehensive terms. Finally, (3) new media provide a tool for opening new markets, while at the same time there is hope that demand for hardware and software related to new media will shape the frontier of domestic demand in Japan. The encouragement of domestic demand has been an important policy in order to get around the international friction accompanying the high level of Japanese exports.

I have discussed elsewhere the issue of deregulation in the telecommunications industry (Imai 1982b). NTT, formerly the government-owned telecommunications monopoly, was finally "privatized"—meaning telecommunications is being deregulated and NTT exposed to competition. This formally occurred in the spring of 1985 and the process of adjustment within NTT and within the industry will take some time. A number of issues remain open regarding deregulation, and they relate to new media policy. An essential point is that historically regulation of the telecommunications industry by the MPT has been extraordinarily restrictive, and I feel complete freedom of entry should be allowed except for basic telephone service (dial tone).

It is impressive that MITI has set a course for near-complete liberalization of the telecommunications industry, including deregulation of foreign investment. MITI's posture of strongly demanding deregulation from the MPT is a complete about-face for the "notorious" MITI. The issues usually discussed as part of Japanese industrial policy, such as governmental protection and administrative guidance, are no longer MITI's concern and have been clearly transferred to the MPT and the Ministry of Transport.

Three scenarios can be written concerning policy for new media. These are my own way of explanation, but the views of other commentators and government officals are roughly summarized. First is the "technology driven scenario," focusing on realization of technological possibilities for the system as a whole. The structure of INS (information network system) of NTT is close to this. (For descriptions of INS see Kitahara 1982 and Myers 1985.) Second is the "market driven scenario," placing importance on competition in the market, with Japan's new media shaped by various combinations of supply and demand. Third is the "policy driven scenario," which adds policies to correct government-perceived defects in the other two scenarios but otherwise envisions development along those lines. Table 10 presents the basic characteristics of each.

TABLE 10

Alternative Scenarios for New Media Development in Japan

	Technology Driven Scenario	Market Driven Scenario	Policy Driven Scenario
1. Pattern of development	Constant rate of increase	S-shaped curve with a rapid increase in development around 1990, tailing off around 1995	Relatively slow development followed by take-off around 1990
2. Type of network	National network (type 1)	Diversified local networks (type 2)	Coexistence of types 1 and 2
3. Characteristics of technology	Large system-oriented technology	Market-oriented know-how and niche technology	Supplement basic R&D
4. Characteristics of market	Oriented toward large firms and groups of firms	Diffusion into small firms and households	Develop quasi-public markets (social welfare and education-related)
5. Enterprises	NTT Small number of VAN and CATV firms	NTT Diversified VAN and CATV firms	NTT Electric utilities federation of CATVs
6. Corporate strategy	System strategy	Multiple use of managerial resources	Network formation
7. Competitive strategy	Oligopolistic competition	Excess competition	Multilevel competition
8. Impact on industry	Focused on specific industries such as distribution and finance	Industries in general	Includes impacts on social system industries
9. Impact on society	Efficiency-oriented	Includes impacts on journalism, etc.	Includes impacts on regional communities
10. Problems	High-cost	Lack of standardization	Conflicts among administrative ministries
11. Policy agenda	Market penetration to the household sector	Standardization of communications protocol	Design of administration

Technology Driven Scenario

The main features of the technology driven scenario are the emphasis put on the technological uniformity of telecommunications as a system—particularly the importance placed on the standardization of telecommunications regulations—and the concern with the quality of the devices used with the system. This scenario encourages the development of new media with large-scale networks of major industrial enterprises acting as the driving force. (In an American context one would think of small companies being involved in the innovations and some emerging as major players; such would not be the case in Japan.)

NTT will serve as the center of the new media, with select VAN and CATV firms grouped around it. In each market segment there will be a dominant firm (I use the singular, although there may be more than one) facing competition from other firms (which may be dominant in other niches). In this scenario, competitive performance is conditional on the behavior of the dominant firm. Where the dominant firm is actually two or three companies forming an oligopolistic core, there could be something close to the competitive price. When there is only one dominant firm, however, the high cost of entry into a market segment may lead to monopoly pricing.

The dominant firm in every niche will not necessarily be NTT, but the probability is small that private VAN or CATV firms can develop to the point where they will dominate a market segment in competition with NTT. (This would be not unlike the situation in the U.S. computer industry, where IBM has so far been able to dominate every niche in which it has chosen to compete, even when there were established players at the time IBM entered it.) Foreign firms would be allowed only a limited role because of regulations on standards and compatibility. (Current restrictions—to the point of specifying colors of containers and other rules completely unrelated to the function and quality of the devices—are a sore point in U.S.-Japanese trade relations. This scenario would retain that source of friction.)

As one can quickly infer, this scenario uses the claim of concern with the technological integrity of the system to preserve as much of the status quo ante as possible. Even without the trade issues, the scenario has problems, foremost of which is the lack of incentive to lower prices. For telecommunication services of all types the prices in Japan are substantially higher than those in the United States, and the service in Japan is often of lower quality. Just as pricing was an issue in the AT&T case, so has it been in the decision to privatize NTT, and it is thus doubtful that business and MITI will allow the technology driven scenario in anything like its pure form.

Market Driven Scenario

This scenario places the driving force of the development of new media on the market. The entrepreneurs best suited to fulfilling the demands of the market supply them in a competitive manner even if there may be some duplication of development effort and excess capacity. In this scenario, when demand for new media goes beyond a critical threshold because of a lowering of price by a pioneering entrepreneur, there follows a phase of rapid increase in product development. During this stage, a reshuffling of firms and industries occurs. When that phase is over, the vigor of the movement dies down, forcing a stage marked by gradual decrease in progess. This decrease is due to the negative aspect of the disorder of diversity, one of this scenario's characteristics. It is also due to a lack of investment in R&D in one phase to create the vitality for the next phase.

Although the position of NTT as the dominant firm in basic communications will not change, VAN and CATV firms will not remain on the fringes, but will enter markets along with large-scale firms. Even small firms will find market niches in the competitive process.

The problems in this scenario are the usual excesses of competition in an area that is in many respects a natural monopoly, or at least a set of natural monopolies. Lack of compatibility is a likely by-product of the diversity of service providers. Other disadvantages include the decline of incentives for future-oriented large-scale R&D and the lack of overall direction and planning.

Policy Driven Scenario

This scenario compensates for the disadvantages of the other two and proposes a policy for their coexistence. This is the direction I propose for Japan's new media. This scenario basically envisions a multiple-track policy. It takes into account the rivalry between public and private systems in the areas of basic telecommunications, value-added communications, and content (the data and services provided by teletext, the programming on cable networks, etc.). In an information-oriented society, it is dangerous to focus on only one delivery system or to move in just one direction. A policy of multiple tracking or pluralism must be followed in order to control the tendency for high cost found in the technology driven scenario and the disorder due to diversity in the market driven scenario.

In concrete terms, the CATV (cable) network would be formed as the multiple track opposite the NTT affiliated system. It is likely that CATV will develop in diverse forms in Japan. As to the future prospects of CATV, there is a difference of opinion. The possibility exists for a system consisting of scattered partial networks varying in technological quality and size. (Partial here refers to breadth of services.) A federation of such partial systems would be difficult without policy support. The policy driven scenario is designed to promote this type of policy. (It is important to keep in mind that CATV, while originally an acronym for "community antenna television" has come to refer to a whole range of services that can parallel the telephone network. Although still used almost entirely for one-way delivery of television programs, some of the systems being built in the United States, and what is envisioned for Japan, include two-way data communications capability and other features.)

NTT would be the responsible body for the entire system. It would take the leadership role in promoting the interoperability of the telecommunications system and allow free linkages with other partial systems. If necessary, it would be responsible for linking CATV systems. NTT would be allowed to pursue VAN type undertakings; at the same time, VANs would be totally liberalized. Should NTT take advantage of its superior position to exclude privately run VANs, antitrust action would be taken.

Through the guided policy of regional development, or the technopolis policy, user systems of large-scale nationwide networks and small-scale clublike or regionally based public service networks would coexist. The former would be a public utility type of network for travel reservations, banking, credit cards, medical information, and so forth. Since economies of scale are in operation here, it can be anticipated that this will develop naturally and be offered by large corporations. Clublike networks within industrial circles are also likely to become widespread along the lines of the market driven scenario. For the regionally based networks, however, there is some need for special policy efforts. Examples of such programming are broadcasts of children's track and field days, other school-related programs, city council meetings, and shopping information. A main selling point of the development structure embodied in the technopolis plan is the local broadcast information system. It is hoped that appropriate fostering of local content is linked to that system.

Recognizing the public-good nature of information, the services offered by, and the content of, new media must be fostered by policies. It is especially necessary to establish and promote actively a public data bank and to form a system of diverse informational offerings accessible to anyone at low cost. Since Japan is particularly behind in the formulation of policies in this area, there is strong need for policy reinforcement.

In terms of new media policy, I strongly urge the adoption of the liberalization policy advocated by MITI, the securing of freedom of entry, freedom of activity, and freedom of use. In the case of telecommunications, however, in order to guarantee such freedoms in concrete terms, it is necessary to devise systemic plans allowing for free linkages among networks. Even if NTT takes the leadership role in the process of determining how parts of the system are connected to each other, there must be plenty of opportunity for other enterprises and equipment makers to state their views. The ability of parts of the system to link is what I have termed "interoperability," and it should be a key goal of new media policy.

The Need for Policy

I have gone into detail about new media policy because it can be seen as symbolizing Japan's recent industrial policy concerning high technology. As I have repeatedly discussed, the characteristics of the Japanese industrial system are well suited for broad development of information- and communication-related high technology and for the penetration of this technology into the industrial sector. There is a great possibility that new media could be effective in the promotion of production and distribution networks, the regulation of the energy system, the maintenance of security in society, and the systematization of such fields as medicine. For the promotion of this in policy terms, quasi-public efforts at offering a system of information for daily life tied to certain localities are needed. It seems that a multisector enterprise composed of public and private sectors could be effective in this effort. The technopolis plan holds strong possibilities for success in this regard.

It should be stressed that the promotion of new media policies along such lines would satisfy the greatest policy concerns in Japan today by assimilating and increasing domestic demand for high technology. The promotion of industrial policy in relation to the widening of domestic demand for high technology contributes to the positive solution of international friction concerning trade.

The government, however, does not have any direct measures to promote such a policy. Available policy measures are all indirect ones: promoting public data banks, establishing guidelines for interoperability among different telecommunications systems, and so on. Even though technopolis is a new industrial policy for the assimilation of high technology into society, MITI has only moderate government funds for its promotion. Everything depends on local governmental efforts and the activation of the private sector by the impact of the technopolis policy. Japan's industrial policy is becoming more and more direct and therefore, to use MITI's term, "soft."

But this does not mean these policies are worthless, or simply decorative. In my view, a key issue in our industrial society is how to assimilate high technology into our economic and social life, and how to create new

demands for high tech products. We do not know what kind of policy
will be successful for such purposes. Trial and error is the only way we
can discover workable policy instruments, and we must be prepared to
accept the costs of errors. In the case of new media, we may end up with
both high costs and disorder in markets even if the policy driven scenario
is adopted. It is difficult to develop and administer effective policy in such
a new field. But it is also clear to me that the market mechanism is not
sufficient for the allocation of resources in the information economy. Some
new types of policy must be formulated. The new media policy discussed
above is a trial for such a purpose in my view, even though governmental
officials do not acknowledge this explicitly.

Conclusions

In each of the high technology industries examined in this essay, while
the Japanese government has provided only relatively small subsidies,
overall involvement has been extensive and pervasive. The information
industry can be considered the most successful of MITI's high technology
undertakings. Its success can in part be attributed to successful public
relations, and MITI participated in the promotion. This is part of what
MITI means in calling its policies "soft"—the creation of an environment
that encourages firms to move in certain directions. Broad agreement on
the directions to be taken has been attained through intense information
exchanges among related firms.

MITI's approach to high technology has been to select a field high in
innovative potential and economic impact. The overall criteria for doing
this are formulated taking into account the opinions of specialists having
"strong knowledge" (Nelson 1982). In addition, detailed survey work and
scenario plotting are done by mobilizing the staffs of firms in the tentatively
chosen and related industries. The results appear in reports of advisory
councils. From this, a decision is made as to whether or not the industry
should be targeted. If it is, a pump-priming subsidy is given, usually for
generic research. This initial kick is intended to intensify R&D by firms
and the industry. Ideally, as the intensity of R&D increases, the potential
for technological development is further enhanced. This reinforces the
firms' expectations, inducing even more investment, and thus the dynamic
development of the industry.

In other words, a mechanism for technological development was shaped
from the accumulation of small innovations, cumulative learning, and wide
diffusion and transfer of technology. This last included, for the information industry, the promotion of the use of computerized equipment by
firms throughout the economy.

What has made this mechanism possible was the nature of the

interpenetration of the market and organization that characterizes Japanese industrial organization. The interpenetration can lead to harmful effects, specifically in the form of cartels. Moreover, it is not a sufficient condition for success.

What has made the mechanism so successful is that, particularly through the 1970s, Japanese industrial policy can be said to have supported market-based development in fields where success or benefits were obvious. It is less clear that the mechanism will work on the cutting edge of technological development or with declining industries. Interest in new energy sources faded quickly both within and outside government when energy prices stablized, even as a society-wide effort to apply technology to decrease energy use (something clearly in each firm's interest) achieved incredible success.

In software, new materials, biotechnology, and chemicals, MITI's traditional policies have not functioned well. These are areas where different mechanisms are needed, but they have not yet been found. Whether the technopolis plan and new media policy, which at least acknowledge the need to find new approaches, work is problematic. There is still a tendency to adopt the formulas that worked in information-related fields, so the possibilities for failure are great.

In contrast to areas that will develop on their own once they are given the initial kick, industries that are in decline can quickly find themselves in a vicious spiral where redirection toward growth is not only difficult but probably a misallocation of resources. Nonetheless, because industrial policy can be seen as measures to supplement the market mechanism, many think it should nurture weak or dying industries rather than fostering growing ones. Clearly, the effective direction for policy to take is the cultivation of sectors capable of developing and absorbing those in the sectors heading for stagnation. Japan should not be faulted for fostering its growth industries.

Japan cannot, however, promote the growth of all its industries, and the Japanese should totally abandon the notion. In areas where Japan does not have a relative advantage, including biotechnology, chemicals, and software, Japan should forgo subsidies to domestic firms and rely more on an international division of labor. Japan is at the point where a new industrial policy, based on an international liberalization, needs to be constructed. This requires the formulation of an organizational theory appropriate to the international division of labor and cooperation in technological development. Table 11 shows the policy priorities of MITI for 1979-84. In 1984 the first priority was the "new media policy" and the second was "contribution to the harmony and continuous development of the world economy." The latter should be the first priority from now on, and Japan's agenda to put this idea into action.

TABLE 11

Policy Priorities of MITI (1979–1984)

Year	First Priority	Second Priority	Third Priority	Fourth Priority	Fifth Priority
1979	Policies in the vision of MITI policies in 1980s	Formations of cooperative external relations; active contribution to the world economy	Steady economic recovery; new development of industrial policy	Encouragement of policies for small and medium enterprises	Strong promotion of a comprehensive energy policy
1980	Energy security	Active contribution to the world economy	Development of industrial policy for the future; promotion of technological development	Fostering vital small and medium enterprises	Balanced regional development and human life enrichment
1981	Energy security and preparation for the post-oil age	Toward a technology-based nation	External policies in the age of interdependence	Development of industrial policy for creativity	Enlivening small and medium enterprises with originality and individuality

Year					
1982	Steady development of comprehensive energy policy	Formation of cooperative external relations; active contribution to the world economy	Development of industrial policy for vitality and promotion of technological development	Activating policies for small and medium enterprises fit for the new age	Construction of attractive regional economies; qualitative leveling up of national standard of living
1983	Vitalization of industry and promotion of technological development based on medium- to long-term prediction	Development of comprehensive natural resource and energy policy	Active contribution to revitalization of world economy; formation of cooperative external relations	Policies for small and medium enterprises adaptable to diversified needs of society	"
1984	Construction of new infrastructure for creative development (e.g., new media policy)	Contribution to the harmony and continuous development of the world economy	Steady promotion of natural resource and energy policy from the long-term standpoint	New development of policies for small and medium enterprises	Construction of attractive regional economies; fulfillment of foundation for diversified national living with high quality

Source: MITI.

168   *Ken-ichi Imai*

REFERENCES

Abernathy, William J. 1978. *The Productivity Dilemma: Roadblock to Innovation in the Automobile Industry*. Baltimore: Johns Hopkins University Press.

Horwitch, M. 1979. "Designing and Managing Large-Scale, Public-Private Technological Enterprises: A State of the Art Review." *Technology in Society* 1:179–92.

Horwitch, M., and C. K. Prahaland. 1976. "Managing Technological Innovation: Three Ideal Models." *Sloan Management Review* 17(2):77–89.

Imai, Ken-ichi. 1980. "Japan's Industrial Organization." In Kazuo Sato, ed., *Industry and Business in Japan*, pp. 74–135. White Plains, N.Y.: M. E. Sharpe, Inc.

Imai, Ken-ichi. 1982a. "Japan's Changing Industrial Structure and United States-Japan Industrial Relations." In Kozo Yamamura, ed., *Policy and Trade Issues of the Japanese Economy*, pp. 47–75. Seattle: University of Washington Press.

Imai, Ken-ichi. 1982b. "Some Proposals Concerning Japan's Telecommunications Policy." *Hitotsubashi Journal of Commerce and Management* 17(1):1–24.

Imai, Ken-ichi. 1982c. "Strategy and Organization for New Energy Development." [Shin Enerugi Kaihatsu no Senryaku to Sōshikiron]. Tokyo: Institute of Business Research, Hitotsubashi University. Discussion Paper 103.

Imai, Ken-ichi. 1983. *Japan's Industrial Society: The Process of Its Evolutionary Change* [Nihon no Sangyō Shakai—Shinka to Henkaku no Dōtei]. Tokyo: Chikuma Shobō.

Imai, Ken-ichi, and H. Itami. 1984. "Interpenetration of Organization and Market: Japan's Firm and Market in Comparison with the U.S." *International Journal of Industrial Organization* 2:285–310.

Imai, Ken-ichi, and A. Sakuma. 1983. "An Industrial Organization Analysis of the Semiconductor Industry: A U.S.-Japanese Comparison." Tokyo: Institute of Business Research, Hitotsubashi University.

Imai, Ken-ichi, Ikujiro Nonaka, and Hirotaka Takeuchi. 1985. "Managing the New Product Development Process: How Japanese Companies Learn and Unlearn." In Kim B. Clark, Robert H. Hayes, and Christopher Lorenz, eds., *The Uneasy Alliance: Managing the Productivity-Technology Dilemma*, pp. 337–75. Boston: Harvard Business School Press.

Kitahara, Yasusada. 1982. "Information Network System: Foundation of Tomorrow's Telecommunications World." *Telephony* 203(22):42–53.

Ministry of International Trade and Industry (MITI). 1980. "The Vision of MITI Policies in the 1980s." *MITI News* NR-226 (80-7).

Ministry of International Trade and Industry. 1983. "White Paper on Small and Medium Firms" [Chūshō Kigyō Hakusho]. Tokyo: Ōkurashō Insatsu Kyoku.

Ministry of International Trade and Industry. 1983. Industrial Structure Council. "How New Media Should Develop: Toward An Affluent 21st Century. Interim Report No. 1.

Myers, Del. 1985. "Japan's INS System Probes the Present for Clues to Future Services." *Telephony* 208(4):64–68.

Myrdal, Gunnar. 1957. *Economic Theory and Under-Developed Regions*. London: Gerald Duckworth and Co., Ltd.

Nelson, Richard R. 1982. "The Role of Knowledge in R&D Efficiency." *Quarterly Journal of Economics* 47(3):453–70.

Okimoto, Daniel I. 1983. *Pioneer and Pursuer: The Role of the State in the Evolution of the Japanese and American Semiconductor Industries*. Stanford: Occasional Paper of the Northeast Asia-United States Forum on International Policy, Stanford University.

Okimoto, Daniel I., Takuo Sugano, and Franklin B. Weinstein, eds. 1984. *Competitive Edge: The Semiconductor Industry in the U.S. and Japan*. Stanford: Stanford University Press.

Yamanaka, Sadanori. 1983. Remarks by Minister of International Trade and Industry Sadanori Yamanaka on Japanese Industrial Policy. MITI Press Release, April 18, 1983.

Chapter 5

Joint Research and Antitrust: Japanese vs. American Strategies

Kozo Yamamura

In the current American debate on policies for "revitalizing" the American economy, Japanese "industrial policy," especially MITI-led joint *research* projects among firms in high technology industries, occupies an important place. Seeing the rapidly increasing international competitiveness of such Japanese high technology industries as semiconductors, telecommunications, computers, robotics, biotechnology, and the like, Americans cannot avoid the question whether or not, or to what extent, joint basic research among the firms in high technology industries—those industries that many expect to occupy an increasingly important role in the economy in the coming decades—should be permitted or encouraged. This question is difficult for Americans because it asks, in effect, to what extent, if at all, they should emulate Japanese policies and practices that differ in fundamental ways from their own. Is emulation necessary for Americans to withstand the mounting Japanese challenge that, many argue, endangers the future vitality of American high technology industries?

The issue has been seriously clouded by the fact that one's view (or ideology) of the proper role for government to play and how an economy functions invariably affects one's view on industrial policy in general and on the desirability of promoting joint research in particular. An added difficulty is that much of the work on Japanese practices presented by those advocating or opposing joint research is self-serving. All too often the analyses are based on biased evidence.

Drawing on an examination of the large number of descriptions now available, both in Japanese and English, on government-sponsored research projects, and based on my discussion and interviews in Japan, at least two important distinctions appear. One is that Japanese policies and practices are designed to be amenable to the requirements of the firms in the high technology industries rather than, for instance, meeting the needs of national defense or attaining energy self-sufficiency. The other is that in Japan, antitrust concerns are ignored and joint research ventures encouraged in high technology industries, most of which are already oligopolistic. In this essay, my analysis is focused on the second distinction as it best highlights the basic differences in the policies adopted, in government-business relations, and in the antitrust philosophies of the two nations. These differences have, I believe, a major influence on competition in the domestic markets of these industries as well as on their competitiveness in international markets. (Among the numerous Japanese sources, one finds books and articles with titles like "the vision for trade and industrial policy in the 1980s," "the computer industry: strategy and responses in the 1980s," and "the frontiers of the technology war in the world." Good examples of Japanese descriptions and analyses useful in understanding the reasons for, and the characteristics of, the MITI-led joint research projects are MITI 1980, Nihon Kōgyō Shimbunsha 1981, Nakagawa 1981, Nihon Keizai Shimbunsha 1977, Kakuma 1982, Tsuruta 1982, and Imai 1983. Sources in English are given later in the chapter.)

This essay offers an assessment of the U.S. antitrust structure (defined below) restricting joint research; descriptions of the intent and practice of Japanese government policy promoting joint research and of Japanese antitrust; an analysis of the benefits and costs of joint R&D; and some reflections on the continuing debate about joint R&D.

The American Structure

The reluctance of American firms to engage in joint research is not limited to antitrust concerns. One can, however, be certain that these concerns are a principal reason for the extremely limited attempts made by the large firms to cooperate in R&D. Although there has been discussion recently of a changed antitrust climate (Baxter 1984), antitrust lawyers are fully aware that precedent weighs far more heavily in the minds of judges than does any current politico-economic atmosphere or new legal or economic analytic insight. To analyze the legal reality of antitrust issues involving joint research, this section first examines the basic antitrust structure and then analyzes recent changes, especially the spate of bills to legalize joint R&D now circulating in Congress.

By "basic antitrust structure," I mean the broadly accepted basic scope and characteristics of the antitrust statutes determining the nature and extent of their enforcement that has been built upon both the deeply ingrained politico-legal and economic history of the nation and the strength of a large number of precedents. Sections I and II of the Sherman Antitrust Act, Section 7 of the Clayton Act, and the patent law (or the precedent that has emerged from attempts to resolve the conflicts between patent and antitrust law) can be regarded as the four principal pillars of U.S. antitrust structure.

The Sherman Act, Section I

As under all laws discussed in this section, no case directly involving joint basic research among large oligopolist firms has been litigated under Section I of the Sherman Antitrust Act, which prohibits "every contract, combination, . . . or conspiracy, in restraint of trade or commerce among several States." But by studying relevant precedent and "learned opinions" involving Section I, the areas of legal concern for would-be joint basic research ventures among large firms can be anticipated. It is reasonable to assume that courts will be most sensitive to the four basic categories of anticompetitive, or socially detrimental, effects of joint research. (The summaries are based on a study of scores of relevant cases and on an examination of the following articles and documents: Ginsburg 1979, Priest 1977, and Editors, *George Washington Law Review* 1981. A list of the cases is available to interested readers.)

1. As a result of joint basic research ventures engaged in by some large firms within a market or industry, other firms (smaller firms as well as large firms not participating in the joint research) are likely to be discouraged from engaging in independent research efforts (thus significantly reducing or even eliminating competitive research within a market or industry). Such a result would be regarded as particularly harmful to those industries greatly dependent on R&D for growth and international competition.

2. When companies cooperate in research, the likelihood of their engaging in subtle and indirect collusive conduct in the marketplace is substantially increased. When a firm enters a joint research venture, its research team must maintain contact—which can be especially close in the high technology industries—with its production and marketing divisions. The marketing division's input to the research team must reflect the parent firm's assessment of demand characteristics and the division's current and future pricing policies. The input of the production division, made jointly with the marketing division, is likely to include various suggestions and requirements concerning the design, characteristics, and functions of the product. Furthermore, this behavior will be common to all firms participating in the joint research venture. This is to say that in the R&D stage, conditions causing cooperation in research to "spill over" into cooperation in the marketplace may be fostered (Keysen and Turner 1959, p. 138).

3. A related but somewhat different concern of the courts will be the decreased likelihood of unrestrained market competition among firms that jointly develop essential technological aspects of a product. Each firm sharing the new technology will be much more familiar with the technological capabilities, cost conditions, and other pertinent technological and economic constraints and characteristics involved in the production of the new product than would be the case if competing firms had developed the technology or product independently. The larger the amount of scientific, production, and other information exchanged or pooled during the the stage of joint R&D activities, the higher the risk of such constrained competition.

4. The anticompetitive risks of joint research development increase with the total market share of participants and the duration of the research. That is, in any industry, the larger or more numerous the firms that jointly develop, patent, and exploit newly developed technology or products, the more the character of competition differs from that expected among firms developing technology independently.

The insight of economists, especially in recent analyses of international and dynamic implications of innovating oligopolistic firms' market power on their market behavior, can be used to mitigate some Section I concerns that are likely to be raised by the courts. But much of the new insight has analytic limitations and has not been accepted by a majority of economists, let alone by the courts.

The validity of this observation is demonstrated in a recent Section I case—*Berkey Photo, Inc.* v. *Eastman Kodak Co.*—in which the Supreme Court observed that "where a participant's market share is large . . . , we believe joint development projects have sufficient anticompetitive potential to invite inquiry" and that the Court's decision in such a case will be made considering "the size of the joint venturers; their share of their respective markets; the contributions of each party to the venture and the benefits derived; the likelihood that, in the absence of the joint effort, one or both parties would undertake a similar project, either alone or with a smaller firm in the market; the nature of the ancillary restraints imposed on the reasonableness of their relationship to the purposes of the venture." See 603 F21 263, 302; Cert. denied, 444 U.S. 1093 (1980).

The Sherman Act, Section II

For large firms contemplating a joint research venture, Section II of the Sherman Act is of more direct and real concern. Although there has not been a Section II case explicitly involving basic joint research among large or oligopolist firms, hundreds of Section II cases dealing with closely related issues can help us ascertain the likely judicial reactions to joint basic research ventures.

In *American Tobacco Co.* v. *U.S.*, the Supreme Court stated that "an attempt to monopolize" a relevant product market is "the employment of methods, means, and practices, which would, if successful, accomplish monopolization, and which, though falling short, nevertheless approach so close to create a dangerous probability of it." See 328 U.S. 781, 785 (1946). In other cases, the courts have ruled that (1) such an attempt to monopolize requires a specific intent to exclude competitors, but collaboration among competitors that collectively possess a large portion of the relevant product market could imply the existence of the requisite intent to monopolize, (2) a large number of patents obtained by a joint venture which could enable the collaborating firms to develop products superior to those currently marketed would furnish evidence supporting the existence of an intent to monopolize, and (3) a refusal to license patents or highly restrictive licensing agreements would also demonstrate an intent to exclude competitors.

From this, it is evident that large firms assume a substantial legal risk under Section II should they proceed with a joint research venture. The editors of a law review were sufficiently pessimistic to conclude, in 1971, that "participation alone in a joint research venture might possibly be considered an *attempt* to monopolize the relevant product market" (Editors, *George Washington Law Review*, 1971, p. 1125).

The Clayton Act, Section 7

The Sherman Act, however, is only part of the legal hurdle. American firms planning a joint research venture must also be concerned with Section 7 of the Clayton Act, which prohibits firms from acquiring "the whole or any part of the assets of another corporation engaged also in commerce, where in any line of commerce in any section of the country, the effect of such acquisition may be substantially to lessen competition, or tend to create a monopoly." Section 7 can impose even more restrictions on joint research ventures because it requires only "a reasonable probability of a substantial lessening of competition or tendency towards monopoly," while the Sherman Act requires "actual restraint" or a "high probability" of such restraint.

Originally enacted to prohibit anticompetitive mergers, Section 7 has been held applicable to joint manufacturing ventures. Of the cases tried under this section with significant implications to joint basic research ventures, the best known is *U.S.* v. *Penn-Olin Chemical Co.* See 378 U.S. 158 (1964). In this case, which involved a joint venture (Penn-Olin) created by Pennsalt Chemical and Olin Mattieson (now Olin Corp.) to produce and sell sodium chlorinate, the Supreme Court ruled a Section 7 violation existed if the reasonable probability of one firm entering the market with the other firm remaining a significant potential competitor could be shown. The Court listed several criteria in determining the probability of a substantial lessening of competition: the number and the market power of competitors in the relevant market; the market power of the joint venturers; the competition existing among firms in the joint venture; the reasons for and the necessity of creating a joint venture; the potential market power of the joint venture in the relevant market; the effect on competition in the relevant market if a member of the joint venture had entered alone; and the effect, in the event of this occurrence, of the other parent firm's potential competitive ability.

These comprehensive criteria are likely to be adopted (or adapted) in determining the anticompetitive potential of joint research ventures, even for basic research. Thus, the legality of joint basic research ventures will be examined against the criteria of (1) the ability and willingness of the parent firms (members of a joint basic research venture) to conduct research independently, (2) the economies of scale or other demonstrable cost-saving advantages in research should a joint effort be permitted, (3) the amount of actual and potential competition in relevant product and research markets, (4) the number and significance of patents likely to be involved, and (5) the scientific nature of research conducted.

Section 7 of the Clayton Act was amended in 1950 to broaden its purview to include merger cases to "cope with monopolistic tendencies in their incipiency and well before they have attained such effects as would justify a Sherman Act proceeding" (Ch. 1185, 64 Stat. 1125). Thus, unlike Sherman Act cases, Section 7 cases against joint research ventures can be initiated at the inception of the joint research venture. But joint R&D between small firms was specifically exempted from the purview of all of these antitrust statutes by the Small Business Act of 1964. See 15 U.S.C. Chapter 638 (1964).

Relation to Patent Law

The precedent evolving out of the courts' efforts to solve conflicts between antitrust statutes and patent laws will also be important in determining the scope and characteristics of permissible joint basic research. There is no direct precedent from adjudication involving patents emerging out of joint basic research ventures, but there are numerous analytically similar precedents. Stated simply, joint research ventures, which by definition involve collaboration among member firms, have a greater opportunity to violate antitrust statutes by abusing their rights under the patent law than an individual firm holding patents. As the findings of numerous cases attest, it is likely that participants in a joint research venture involving large and oligopolistic firms will be inclined to use the patents in a pool, which can be highly conducive to supressing competition in various ways, including such per se violations as territorial divisions and most forms of "tie-in" agreements.

An examination of patent-antitrust cases reveals that issues involved in these cases are often extremely complex. But it is possible to summarize several categories of conduct that courts, based on precedent, are likely to prohibit among firms in a joint research venture:

1. A "combining of patent owners" with an intent to "dominate" or monopolize an industry by pooling, cross-licensing, or accumulation of patents is likely to be prohibited (though cross-licensing as such is not a per se violation). To be illegal, the intent to dominate an industry need not be communicated explicitly among the firms involved. Even if such an intent is "tacit" or affected "by aid of acquiescence," it will be illegal (*U.S.* v. *The Singer Mfg. Co.*, 795 O.G. Pat. Off. 523: 1963).

2. The combining of a number of patents by one person or entity, not for the purpose of exploitation but of preventing uses by others, is likely to be judged illegal (*Steward-Warner Corp.* v. *Staley*, D.C. Pa., 42 F. Supp. 140; and others).

3. Restriction of both membership in a pooling or cross-licensing group of firms and patent rights allowed to each member participating in the group, if this is seen to be used as a "lever" by which the group is attempting to control the market, is likely to be prohibited (*U.S.* v. *United Shoe Machine Corp.*, 110 F. Supp. 295, 333; D. Mass., 1953; *Transparent Wrap Machine Corp.* v. *Stokes and Smith Co.*, 329 U.S. 646-47, 1947; *U.S.* v. *Singer Mfg. Co.*, 795 O.G. Pat. Off. 523: 1963).

4. If the combination of patents is intended to, or *results* in, maintaining price, dividing markets, or suppressing all but a dominant patent, a judgment of illegality is likely (*U.S.* v. *National Lead Co.*, D.C. N.Y., 63 F. Supp. 513, Aff'd 332 U.S. 319, 1947; *U.S.* v. *Masonite Corp.*, 316 U.S. 265; and others).

5. Joining a patent pool, which was organized with the intent to monopolize or restrain trade, as a latecomer is likely to be judged illegal (*U.S.* v. *Masonite Corp.*, 316 U.S. 265, and others).

6. Crafting patent combination agreements so as to restrain improvement or suppress valuable patents is likely to be judged illegal (*Blount Mfg. Co.* v. *Yale and Towne Mfg. Co.*, 166 Fed. 55, C.C. Mass., 1909).

7. Making licensing agreements requiring lessees or buyers of patent products to use, in exploitation of the patent leased, only the nonpatented products supplied by the licensor is likely to be prohibited (*U.S.* v. *Masonite Corp.*, 316 U.S. 265).

Many more refinements can be made in the list above and a technically more comprehensive list of those most likely to be judged illegal can indeed be a long one. For further discussion of these issues, see Bowman 1973, Goller 1968, Landiorio 1964, Woodbridge 1972, Kitch 1977, Gallo 1966, and Martin 1974.

Other Factors

In assessing the legal barrier to cooperative research, two important facts need to be borne in mind. One is that although the Antitrust Division has a review procedure whereby companies interested in forming joint ventures can get a decision before committing themselves to a project, this provides scant comfort. Only the incumbent administration is bound by the decision. A well-known example of this is the Cooperative Automotive Research Program, which was initiated under the Carter administration to conduct research into pollution-control devices for the major automotive manufacturers. In a not entirely unexpected fashion, given the structure of the domestic automotive industry, the venture was later suspected of actually impeding the progress of research, and the firms involved were sued by the government under the Reagan administration. The process also requires early disclosure of a firm's intentions (Congressional Budget Office 1983, p. 45).

In addition, American firms are in constant danger of being hit with a private suit. These can be filed even against a venture that has successfully satisfied the Antitrust Division's review procedure, and are costly and time-consuming to fight. The triple-damage provision in American antitrust law exacerbates the problem.

Thus, legal barriers to cooperative research in the United States are well entrenched, embodied in several different statutes, and present formidable hurdles to companies contemplating cooperative research.

Proposed Changes

Over the last dozen years, the American political climate concerning antitrust issues has changed perceptibly. In the early 1970s, Congress considered a law to specify the market share for a firm that would constitute a per se offense under Section II (attempt to monopolize) of the Sherman Act, and the Justice Department viewed virtually all horizontal mergers and many conglomerate mergers as basically anticompetitive and worthy of judicial scrutiny. In the 1980s, after thirteen years, the Section II case against IBM was dropped as being "without merit," and Congress has enacted several laws restricting antitrust enforcement and is debating a score of bills that will substantially restrict antitrust enforcement (H.R.

4043, 3393, 3975, and S. 1561). Although Section I of the Clayton Act and FTC Section 5 are mentioned in several of the bills currently circulating in Congress, they are not discussed here.

These front-page changes have brought another important change: both economists and lawyers have begun to ask new questions and offer new analyses. More economists are examining antitrust and trade issues from an international perspective. Analytic works by economists in the past decade have yielded many insights into vertical price restraints, "tying" arrangements, and the effects of cartels and mergers which challenge some of the once widely accepted views. (A useful summary of these theoretical works is Schmalensee 1982. On the issues raised in this chapter, useful articles include, among others, Dixit 1982, Koenker and Perry 1981, Schmalensee 1976 and 1979, White 1981, and Spence 1981. A paper containing a theoretical insight especially pertinent in analyzing the Japanese economy—in which many large firms enter into new product lines by creating new divisions or separate fully owned entities—is Schwartz and Thompson 1983. For nonspecialists, Scherer 1980 is useful, since it provides good discussion on many issues dealt with in this chapter and contains several insightful comments on "new" versus "old" views. On the relation between technological change and antitrust issues, recent analytic efforts by economists include Stiglitz 1981, Von Weizsacker 1980, Kamien and Schwartz 1975, and Dasgupta and Stiglitz 1980.)

Members of the legal profession, more directly involved in the changing legal and economic environment of the past decade than economists, have also been made more aware of the international implications of antitrust and other decisions of American courts. Their research and briefs on international trade and antitrust issues have significantly changed during the past decade.

Aware both of the essential characteristics of the antitrust structure just sketched, which constrains joint research ventures, and of the increasingly evident need to stimulate "the development of innovation," President Carter directed the Justice Department in 1979 to "clarify its position on collaboration among firms in research to make certain that the antitrust laws are not mistakenly understood to prevent cooperative activity, even in circumstances where it would foster innovation without harming competition." The result was *The Antitrust Guide Concerning Research Joint Ventures* of November 1980. (The directive is quoted from the *Guide's* preface. Quotations in what follows are also from the *Guide*.)

In examining the *Guide*, my assessment is that it provides little substantive guidance to would-be participants of a joint research venture among large firms. The most that can be said for the *Guide* is that the Justice Department, given an extremely difficult task, valiantly attempted to offer, in 104 pages, a "clarification" of its position. The result, even with the discussion of realistic cases which the Department appended to the *Guide*, is not likely to induce many large firms to engage in joint research ventures.

The *Guide* begins by noting the basic dilemma of joint research ventures. Such ventures can contribute to innovation, which is "a key to productivity and competitiveness," and there are "many sensible reasons such as the large size, scope or risk of a project, or the complementary nature of the cooperating firms" to undertake joint research. *But* these research activities can raise substantial antitrust issues "because joint research many involve or create market-dominating technology, may be conducted by competitors or potential competitors, or may involve restrictive agreements concerning the use of the research" (p. 1).

Attributes of a project which affect its permissibility are: "the closer the joint activity is to the basic research end of the research spectrum— i.e., the further removed it is from substantial market effects and developmental issues—the more likely it is to be acceptable under the antitrust laws. Also, the greater the number of actual and potential competitors in an industry, the more likely that a joint research project will not unreasonably restrain competition. And, the narrower the field of joint activity and the more limited the collateral restraints involved, the greater the chances that the project will not offend the antitrust laws" (p. 3). However, the *Guide* quickly adds that the determination of what constitutes a lessening of competition will "involve application of Section I of the Sherman Act and Section 7 of the Clayton Act" with the latter stressing "probabilities not certainties" of anticompetitive effects.

More specifically, what the Justice Department considers anticompetitive behavior includes: agreements by participants to forgo independent research in competition with the joint venture (p. 4); sharing of information about costs and similar matter (p. 18); and collective denial of access or of licenses, particularly by major competitors in regard to actual or potential competitors, with resultant significant injury to competition in a relevant market, which can raise serious problems under Sherman Act, Section I (p. 23).

In reference to actual cases used as examples, the *Guide* states that while foreign competition will be taken into account in assessing the relative market power of a research combination, no anticompetitive conduct is permissible even if it would "defend or improve the position of the U.S. firms vis-a-vis foreign competitors" (p. 45). For government-assisted basic research, immunity is available only when exemption is "clearly articulated and affirmatively expressed as state policy" (p. 61), and "no statute empowers [the funding agency] specifically to immunize conduct of the Program from the antitrust laws" (p. 62).

Although it is quite possible some specialists in antitrust and patent law can find passages indicating a changed enforcement criteria, in reading the *Guide* and its appendixes as a whole, most readers are unlikely to find any substantive discussion or analysis that cannot be readily deduced from relevant legal precedent. Moreover, the politico-economic climate that produced this *Guide* can change quickly, compounding the uncertainty faced by a large firm contemplating a joint research venture.

To dispel this uncertainty, no fewer than twelve bills are now circulating in Congress. Their contents vary from a simple removal of the trebling of damages sought in suits involving joint research (H.R. 3641, 1983) to legalizing nonexclusive ventures, with the attorney general's investigation required only for those involving firms controlling more than 50 percent of the world market (or, involving a firm that controls 25 percent) (H.R. 1952 and S. 737, 1983). Two bills propose no change in the basic laws, allowing the attorney general to issue a Certificate of Review ensuring antitrust immunity only if the venture is "unlikely to violate antitrust laws (H.R. 108 and S. 1383, 1983). Most allow effective exemption from antitrust prosecution to ventures that do not unduly restrict member firms, publicly release all results after three to six years, register with the attorney general, and meet other criteria. All the bills except J.R. 3641 (a no-triple-damage bill) seek exemption for joint ventures from all pertinent statutes. Only Senator Paul Tsongas's bill specifically mentions Sections 1 and 2 of the Sherman Act and 7 and 16 of the Clayton Act as the laws from which immunity is sought. But the other bills' intended breadth of immunity is no less broad, as they refer to " 'antitrust law' as defined in Clayton Section 1," which lists the Sherman Act, the Clayton Act, and others; immunity under FTC Section 5 per "unfair methods of competition" is also sought.

The "qualifications" specified in the bill (S. 568) proposed by Senator Tsongas of Massachusetts include: (1) that participation in the joint research and development venture is open to all firms; (2) that any firm can obtain on reasonable and nondiscriminatory terms the results of the research and development within six years after the venture receives title to such results; (3) that restraints associated with a participant's involvement in the venture are not part of an overall pattern of restrictive agreements that restrain competition; and (4) that the venture places no restrictions on the participants' individual research nor obligations to provide the venture with the results of the participants' individual previous or future research.

One set of bills would amend the Clayton Act to make agreement to convey patents, copyrights, and other intellectual property no longer per se violations and would amend the patent laws to relax significantly codes intended to prevent suppression of competition through patents, and to allow patenting of process innovations.

And, as a deterrent to costly private suits, almost all the bills would disallow treble damages and would assess defendant's attorney fees against an unsuccessful claimant (S. 1841 and H.R. 3878, 1983). The Reagan administration has proposed disallowing treble damage civil suits and an increase in patent protection (Congressional Budget Office 1983, p. 46).

In this changing administrative atmosphere, two joint research ventures have been launched—the Microelectronics and Computer Technology Corporation and the Semiconductor Research Corporation. In addition, the Small Business Act of 1964 has been brought forth to justify the formation of the Small Business Technology Group (Congressional Budget Office 1983, p. 46).

Despite these changes, it would be a serious error of judgment to believe that American antitrust enforcement in regard to joint research has or will undergo a sudden and fundamental transformation. The American antitrust legal structure is a well-established edifice not readily transformed. New analytic insight and a new international economic reality can only change the structure one stone at a time. The point can be made even more tellingly when we ask: Even in today's politico-economic climate, how readily will seasoned antitrust lawyers advise large corporate clients to engage in joint basic research? Or, why are so few joint research ventures being formed among large American firms in high technology industries when similar joint research is being conducted among firms in other industrial nations that are now seriously challenging the U.S. leadership in these industries?

I believe it is accurate to conclude that despite recent changes in the legal, political, and theoretical atmosphere, the American antitrust structure continues to stand as a formidable barrier to large firms contemplating joint research.

The Japanese Structure

The political, economic, and legal environment for joint basic research among large Japanese high technology firms differs significantly and substantively from the U.S. environment. This section will describe that environment and then offer an overview of joint research undertaken with frequent and substantive government involvement by the large Japanese high technology firms. Lastly I will outline the pertinent sections of Japanese antitrust law.

The involvement of the Japanese government in the postwar economic growth continues to be considerable more extensive than that of the U.S. government in its economy. During the 1950s and 1960s, the basic goal of economic policy, adopted to promote the rapid growth of output and increase productivity in major industries, was to encourage large and usually oligopolistic firms to adopt increasingly large and more efficient scales of production. To achieve this goal, the capital market was effectively to allocate capital preferentially to large innovating firms, and the risks involved in rapid expansion of capacities were substantially reduced by means of "administrative guidance" and various laws that de facto freed the firms from virtually all antitrust concerns. That is, as I have elaborated elsewhere (1982), large innovating firms in major industries were able to engage in market-share-maximizing competition, rapidly expanding total productive capacity (thus productive efficiency and international competitive ability) under implicit and explicit governmental assurance that the firms or industry as a whole could "administer" (or even fix) prices or limit output as they faced temporary excess capacity (due to a recession or too rapid an expansion of productive capacity). The debate among specialists is not whether these progrowth policies were adopted to aid the postwar Japanese industries, but how many industries took advantage of the policies, and the extent of the effectiveness of these policies. (On the role of the government in the postwar Japanese economy, see Murakami 1982, Yamamura 1982, Patrick and Rosovsky 1976, and Yamamura 1967.)

By the late 1960s, more and more Japanese industries had caught up or were rapidly catching up with the Western level of productive efficiency, and the postwar policy to aid large firms in adopting new technology had achieved its goal. There was far less new technology in the West for Japan to borrow, and the rate of investment slackened, causing the growth rate of the economy to decelerate visibly. Put differently, the end had come to the rapid growth period during which a policy enabling large firms to realize efficiency gains (achievable by borrowing Western technology) could be justified. The oil crisis of 1973 only made this turning more pronounced and dramatic.

Against this background, the government (i.e., MITI) began to place major policy emphasis on the promotion of high technology industries as a means of sustaining economic performance. MITI chose to focus its attention on high technology industries because they are the industries able to increase their efficiency and international competitive ability by rapidly increasing their productive capacities. Like major industries in the 1960s, high technology industries now are amenable to MITI's progrowth "guidance" and policy, along with de facto exemption from all antitrust concerns (see Yamamura 1982).

Thus, MITI is again pursuing, with some variations to be noted below, the familiar policy that includes MITI "guidance," government subsidies, and de facto total exemption from the antitrust concerns that can arise from cooperation among large oligopolistic firms. As was usually the case between MITI and such rapidly growing industries as steel and chemical in the 1950s and 1960s, it again appears that little difficulty is encountered in maintaining close and effective cooperative efforts between MITI and the high technology industries. And again, MITI policy toward high technology industries is being justified in the name of maintaining Japanese economic performance.

There were two additional impetuses to this development. One was the fact that, by the early 1970s, Japan could no longer rely, to the extent it had in the preceding decade, on import restrictions as a means to aid the growth of its industries. MITI was, in a sense, in search of a new policy to take the place of import restriction. The second impetus was the fact that by the late 1960s, MITI was facing the mounting difficulties its past policy had helped create: seemingly chronic excess capacity in a number of growth industries of the 1960s (industries that are declining and becoming increasingly critical of MITI policy to reduce capacity) and "export drives," engaged in by some industries, that tend to intensify trade conflicts. Thus, to maintain and possibly increase the bureaucratic power and prestige it had begun to lose, MITI needed major new progrowth program that would be highly visible and welcomed by industries. This is one reason MITI is demonstrating a strong sense of mission and more than its usual zeal in administering the joint basic research programs for high technology industries.

Given the political reality of postwar Japan, the ruling, conservative Liberal Democratic Party (LDP) could ill afford not to give full support to MITI policy by providing the necessary wherewithal for the high technology industries. These industries promise to aid the continuing economic performance of Japan and thus the continuing success of the LDP at the polls.

An explicit observation must be made of the reasons for the virtual absence of discussion concerning antitrust implications of the MITI-initiated joint research ventures among the high technology firms. The reason, I submit, is the openly advocated and widely supported view that having rapid growing and internationally competitive high technology industries, even at the cost of courting anticompetitive behavior, is preferable to slowly growing and international noncompetitive high technology industries. This view is challenged, both in scholarly publications and in mass media, by only a small minority of Japanese.

It is in such an environment that the current joint basic research projects in high technology are actively promoted by MITI. What follows is a highly abbreviated summary of these joint research projects and a brief description and discussion of the specific language of Japanese antitrust laws and the current state of the Japanese antitrust structure pertaining to joint research ventures. (The most important antitrust and economic analytic issues raised are discussed from a comparative perspective in the conclusion.)

Two government agencies—the Ministry of International Trade and Industry (MITI) and Nippon Telegraph and Telephone Public Corporation (NTT)—are actively involved in large-scale joint research in high technology fields. We will first describe the MITI-directed projects.

MITI Projects

Two major projects of significant interest for the purpose of this essay have already been completed. The super-high-performance computer project, begun in 1972 and concluded in 1976, involved six firms organized by MITI into three teams—Fujitsu-Hitachi, NEC-Toshiba, and Mitsubishi-Oki. The total government subsidy for the project amounted to 160 billion yen (or about $700 million) (MITI 1982, pp. 400-403), not including ancillary grants relating to the development of semiconductors, preferential loans from the Japan Development Bank, and vital assistance rendered through the partly government-funded Japan Electronic Computer Corporation (JECC) (Okimoto, Sugano, and Weinstein 1984, pp. 109-10, and MITI 1982, pp. 400-403). The second was the VLSI project, involving very large scale integration of semiconductor circuits.

Omitting descriptions of about two dozen lesser projects, both completed and ongoing, table 12 is a list of completed major projects and current long-term and medium-term projects. Some of the listed projects are, in effect, multiple projects appearing under one broad heading.

Although projects can be and undoubtedly are at times put forward by firms themselves (the firms informally request the Ministry to initiate MITI-led joint projects), I believe it is accurate to say that in most cases MITI exerts strong leadership. We know, for example, that MITI attempted to merge the six largest computer companies into one firm in order to compete effectively with IBM. (In this instance, MITI failed to achieve its goal, but succeeded in 1971 in pairing the six firms into three collaborative teams developing the super-high-performance computer project.)

The most important among the modi operandi of MITI (and its research agencies) is the close relations it maintains with industry leaders. In virtually all of its programs, the Ministry selects a varying but relatively small number (usually around five or six, though in rare instances up to around twenty) of large, typically oligopolistic firms with a demonstrated capacity to conduct research relevant to the program. To select the firms, MITI consults extensively with the trade association (existing or created *de novo* for specific projects), the top managerial and research representatives of all large firms in the relevant industry, and leading scientists. But the final judgment on which firms have adequate research capabilities, and are

TABLE 12

MITI-led High Technology R&D Projects

Major projects completed
1. The super-high performance computer (1972–76) discussed in the text
2. VLSI (1976–79) discussed in the text
3. Pattern information (computer) processing system (1971–80)
4. High-speed computer for scientific and technical uses (1966–71)
5. Multichannel biotechnical analyzers (1976–81)
6. Jet engines for aircraft (1971–75, 1976–81)

Current long-term major projects
1. Ten-year basic R&D projects for the Next Generation industries
    (a) "New" elements (fine ceramics, separation diaphragms, crystalline macro molecules, conductive macro molecules, lightweight high strength alloys, and high and composite polymers for various uses)—six projects
    (b) Biotechnology (bioreactors, accelerated cell cultures, and genetic recombinatory engineering)—three projects
    (c) Semiconductor-related new molecular element (super lattice elements, stacked ICs, and environment-resistant elements)—three projects
2. The Fifth Generation "intelligent" computers

Current projects with a three- to five-year planning period for which budget allocation was made in 1981 and 1982 (out of the MITI budget), and for which MITI requested funding for fiscal 1983
1. Composite production system for applied uses of super-high capacity laser
2. Optic-IC measurement and control system
3. Production of basic chemical products using monocarbon
4. High-speed computer for scientific and technical uses (can be seen as a partial continuation of completed project 4 above)
5. Automatic (computer) sewing system
6. Basic ancillary technology relating to the Next Generation computers
7. Health-care related high technology projects
8. Information processing technologies (software)
9. Development projects for YX and YXX commerical jet aircraft (can be seen as a continuation of completed project 6 above)
10. Commerical aircraft jet engine (XJB) development (can be seen as a continuation of completed project 6 above)

Note: About thirty-five projects relating to space, nuclear energy, energy uses (the so-called Sunshine and Moonlight projects for energy source development and promotion of more efficient uses of energy sources), and uses of ocean resources, are not listed even though they are included in the MITI budget. Although some projects had substantial high technology parts (even defining high technology narrowly as was done in preparing this table), they are not included here because their antitrust implications are either limited or nonexistent.

Sources: Two pamphlets published by the Science and Technology Agency, MITI: one is entitled Ōgata projekuto (Large-scale projects) (1982) and the other is Jisedai sangyō kiban gijutsu kenkyū seido (A system for the basic R&D projects of the Next Generation industries) (1982). And a monthly, Kōgyō gijutsu (Industrial technology), also published by the Agency, 24 (1983):11–16.

"large" enough (to be able to "match" research support given by MITI and to make "effective" use of the fruits of the joint research), is made by MITI officers.

To gain insight into selection procedures, let us focus on the computer and semiconductor-related projects. Table 13 shows there were eleven major projects in this area. One was designed to promote software, involving no large firms; and the names of participants in another are unavailable. The participants in the nine other projects form a surprisingly small group: almost all are Japan's largest, most important electronics firms with considerable importance as exporters (table 14). Several of these firms control their own extensive distribution channels, which in the 1960s were closely scrutinized by Japan's Fair Trade Commission for their roles in price-fixing (Yamamura 1975, p. 86).

MITI seems to be inviting most major firms to join its research projects, and in the past few years few large firms appear to have declined the invitation. It is apparent that even today's technological leaders believe the costs of compromising their current technological superiority are less than those of nonparticipation, which is viewed as detrimental to their future competitive position in relation to firms that participated. This also means a disproportionately large share of government funds flow into a relatively small number of major firms that work in close cooperation with MITI and its agencies and that collectively enjoy a substantial share of the Japanese high technology market. This is not to say that one can readily find evidence that these firms are engaging in the socially undesirable conduct often associated with oligopolistic firms.

It should be stressed that in initiating and implementing these projects, MITI officials—usually senior officials having close knowledge of the affected industry and the necessary technological expertise—often exert leadership openly. This clearly reflects MITI's desire to ensure that effective and full research cooperation will take place among the scientific personnel of the participating firms, which understandably tend to be more eager to absorb new knowledge than to share what they know. MITI also exerts leadership in more subtle, but no less definite, ways. It selects the scientists and industry representatives who are consulted, and assumes a major role in the selection of specific research agendas for the joint programs. MITI officials are playing a no less visible and important role today than in the 1950s and 1960s in promoting the technological capabilities of major industries.

Sufficiently detailed case studies, supporting many of the preceding observations and assessments, have been made available in English during the past few years by the Office of Technology Assessment of Congress, the International Trade Commission, and other agencies of the U.S. government as well as by several scholars. Let me present several quotations

TABLE 13

Major MITI Projects in Computers and Semiconductors, 1966–80

Project Area	Time Schedule	Funding*	Companies Involved
Third, Fifth Generation computers	1972–76	160,000	Fujitsu Hitachi Mitsubishi Electric NEC, Oki, Toshiba
VLSI project, Fourth Generation	1976–79	30,000	Fujitsu Hitachi Mitsubishi Electric NEC, Toshiba
Development of basic software and related periphery, Fourth Generation	1979–83	47,000	Fujitsu Hitachi Matsushita Electric Mitsubishi Electric NEC, Oki, Sharp Toshiba
Pattern information processing system (PIPS)	1971–80	22,073	Hitachi Fujitsu Matsushita Mitsubishi NEC, Oki, Sanyo Electric, Toshiba Hoya Glass

Project	Period	Amount*	Participating firms
High speed scientific computer	1981–89	22,073	Fujitsu, Toshiba NEC, Mitsubishi Electric Sanyo, Matsushita Konishiroku, Hoya Glass
Flexible manufacturing system using lasers	1977 to present	13,000	N/A
Software automation	1976–81	6,600	Over 100 software firms
Development of Fifth Generation computers	1979–91	11,375	Fujitsu, Hitachi Mitsubishi, NEC Oki, Toshiba
Supergrid components (ICs)	1981–90	8,000	Fujitsu Hitachi Sumitomo Denko
Three-dimensional components (ICs)	1981–90	9,000	NEC, Oki, Toshiba Mitsubishi Electric Sanyo Electric Matsushita Electric Sharp
Elements with increased resistance to the environment (ICs)	1981–88	8,000	Toshiba Hitachi Mitsubishi Electric

*Million yen.

Source: Compiled from U.S. International Trade Commission, *Foreign Industrial Targeting and Its Effects on U.S. Industries, Phase I: Japan*, USITC Publication 1437 (October 1983), appendix G, table G-2.

TABLE 14

Japan's Major Computer and Electronics Manufacturers

Company	Total Sales 1981 (billion yen)	% of Output Exported	National Ranking: Top 30 Exporters of all Commodities*	MITI Projects Participated In	NTT "Family" Member?
Matsushita	2,346	30	4	4	no
Hitachi	1,947	12	9	7	yes
Toshiba	1,547	24	14	8	no
Mitsubishi Electric	1,253	20	25	8	no
NEC	892	33	23	7	yes
Sony	780	71	10	0	no
Sanyo	752	55	not ranked	3	no
Fujitsu	581	15	not ranked	7	yes
Sharp	501	59	16	2	no
Sumitomo Electric	428	21	not ranked	1	no
Oki	186	15	not ranked	5	yes

*Excludes overseas sales of offshore production. This understates Sony's, and to a lesser extent Matsushita's, non-Japanese sales, since both have extensive offshore production.

Source: Compiled from U.S. International Trade Commission, *Foreign Industrial Targeting and Its Effects on U.S. Industries, Phase I: Japan*, USITC Publication 1437 (Octuber 1983), appendixes H and G, table H-1, table 37, p. 152.

from Japanese sources. With the exception of the first source (a MITI pamphlet) the quotations are direct observations of MITI-led joint research projects by "disinterested" Japanese (i.e., not MITI or industry officials). These are precisely the observations, I believe, that can provide us with a more direct understanding of the modus operandi of these projects, an understanding we must have in discussing the costs and benefits of adopting an American "industrial policy" à la Japanese. (Good English-language sources include Okimoto 1984, USITC 1983, Dore 1983, Controller General of the United States 1982, Borrus, Millstein, and Zysman 1983, Schacht 1980, and a collection of three articles in the July-August 1983 issue of *Journal of Japanese Trade and Industry,* by Tanaka, Konaga, and Reich.)

A pamphlet published in February 1982 by the Industrial Science and Technology Agency is useful as an indicator of the "mission" MITI has set for itself. It succinctly summarizes, for example, the goals and reasons for MITI's Next Generation basic technology research development inaugurated in 1981 (see table 12). That is, for Japan to become "a nation based on technology" (*gijutsu-rikkoku*), it "must promote technological progress in such industries as aerospace, space, information processing, new energy, and biotechnology that are expected to make significant progress during the 1990s and that also are essential for industries of the coming generation" (p. 5).

The importance of promoting the technology in these industries is "obvious," the pamphlet goes on to argue, because they are behind those in the West by five to ten years and because they have "a strong potential for rapid progress" and "wideranging effects." And it goes on to note that in promoting these technologies, "the role of MITI is to devise an appropriate policy and a planned and effective development method that can make the most positive use of the potential of the private sector." It also notes that the need for MITI's active participation cannot be questioned because these projects "involve high risk" for private firms to undertake and require "about ten years and a large amount of research expenditure to develop." In short, the intention of MITI is to see to it that these technologies will be developed from "seedlings" to "young trees" under its leadership during the next decades (p. 6).

MITI's new role is clearly evident in the actions it has taken to induce cooperation among large firms, even when the firms must be "guided" to cooperate. Understandably, the technological leaders in the field are inclined to be reluctant to share knowledge, while the smallest firms strongly resent exclusion from the projects, fearing they will be further disadvantaged in, or even excluded from, competing with the favored firms. The Ministry's active involvement in bringing the reluctant firms together is clear in the following excerpt from *Asahi* (a major daily newspaper):

To challenge IBM, the VLSI research and development was begun, uniting government and the private sector. To carry out the research, the VLSI Technology Research Association was formed in April 1976.

Initially, given the differing ideas concerning VLSI development among the member firms, decisions on the extent and nature of the joint research and which firm was to be responsible for which aspects of development, were extremely difficult to make. Interests of the member firms conflicted. And, even after the research topics were settled, there were numerous problems to be expected in such a joint venture. Thus, six research rooms were created, each headed by a leader from one of the five member firms and one headed by a person from the Electronics Research Institute. During the first year, the walls between these rooms were thick. Participants tried to prevent others from finding out the progress being made in each room. "In extreme cases, the entrance was barricaded to prevent other researchers from coming in," recalls Nebashi [of MITI], who headed the joint research institute.

Nebashi did his best to eliminate the egoism of the member firms and to create the harmony among researchers necessary for joint research. In the evenings he went to the rooms and listened to the researchers' opinions and any dissatisfactions they had. At times, he drank sake with the researchers.

The monthly meetings, attended by senior officers of the member firms, were intentionally held at the joint research institute... . The purpose was to let these officers become familiar with the projects and boost the morale of the researchers. In time, tennis and golf clubs were organized among the researchers ... and the walls of secrecy dividing the research rooms were gradually removed. [June 22, 1981, p. 9]

Concerning the optic laser project, *Asahi* had this crucial observation concerning the role of MITI in the motivation of the participating firms:

It was not easy to create the new institute. According to Jun'ichi Shimoda, the head of the Electronics Research Institute who coordinated the creation on behalf of MITI and the participating members, "it was nothing but a daily struggle against the arguments advanced by profit-making firms." It was not easy to bring joint research under one roof with researchers from nine companies that were competing in the marketplace and had different levels of technology. . . .

The common desire of the member firms seemed to have been to have a "not too large" joint institute. And, the two firms that already were receiving research subsidies from MITI were obviously reluctant to join. The remaining three largest firms were initially opposed, assuming that they could also receive some research subsidies. But, when they found that they could not obtain any research assistance, they suddenly became eager to establish and join in the new institute. [October 5, 1981, p. 9]

Also, the clamor from small firms seeking to join these projects strongly suggests that joint research projects contribute to the strength of the major firms, leaving excluded companies at a disadvantage. For example, on the VLSI project, a team of reporters—"a techno-science" team—from *Chūō Kōron* (a major monthly) had the following revealing observation:

> An executive of an IC producer in Kansai complains that "not having
> been able to join the VLSI project was a severe blow. Our company
> asked to be allowed to participate, but we were denied on the grounds
> that VLSI was for computers. We are doing our utmost, but we have
> not caught up with those who were selected to participate in the joint
> program." Oki Electric, which also expressed a strong desire to
> participate but was rejected, must also be extremely resentful of not
> having been selected. All the firms in the industry know full well the
> merits of participating in the government-private joint research projects.
> [Fall 1981, p. 120]

More broadly, on the seemingly increased desire of both large and small
high technology firms to participate in the MITI-initiated projects, the
same *Chūō Kōron* writers offered the following general assessment:

> The number of firms which hope to increase their technological
> capabilities by joining public-private joint research will undoubedly
> increase. As of now, about 100 firms have expressed their wish to join
> the fine ceramic project and approximately 50 firms are eager to join
> the biotechnology project, both part of MITI's Basic Technology
> Development Projects for the Next Generation. [Fall 1981, p. 121]

And the same team reported on one of the ongoing major projects, the
optic laser project referred to earlier:

> The reasons why these public-private joint research ventures became so
> popular is not limited to the fact that participating firms could receive
> research grants. Some point out the equal importance of such joint
> research in enabling "exchange of technical information," in
> "stimulating researchers competitively," and in encouraging the member
> firms "to undertake better research." . . . In the new institute,
> researchers of rival firms will be carrying out research in the same room.
> [Fall 1981, p. 120]

Although I am able to present here only a small fraction of the
observations found in Japanese sources, they clearly indicate the essential
character of MITI-led joint research projects. In pursuing its declared goal
of strengthening Japan's high technology capabilities, MITI not only has
shown little concern for the substantial antitrust issues that are, I believe,
raised by joint research projects and especially by the way they are carried
out, but also has chosen to take an active and leading role in advocating
the national necessity to engage in these joint research projects.

NTT

Nippon Telegraph and Telephone is Japan's government-owned
telephone monopoly and heads the country's large and growing
telecommunications industry. NTT assists or "sponsors" the research

activities of many of the same firms helped by MITI. Four firms—NEC, Oki, Fujitsu, and Hitachi—enjoy a long history of close dealings with NTT and are the "big brothers" in the so-called NTT family, consisting of nearly three hundred large and small firms. NTT has no production facilities. Thus, after doing preliminary work in its own lab, NTT has further research (and production) done under contract, primarily by its member firms. Although NTT cooperates closely with MITI, as exemplified by the VLSI project involving highly coordinated efforts by both organizations, the research done for NTT is oriented to products to be purchased by NTT, rather than basic R&D or the commercialization of products initiated by a firm. But few would deny that the technology developed under NTT contract has been extremely valuable, involving products such as optical fibers, electrical exchange systems, telecommunications hardware and software, microwave equipment, and integrated circuits.

What is to be stressed in making the above observation is that NTT-funded research is generally carried out in the supplying company's labs; NTT assigns and coordinates tasks. The researchers meet on a regular basis, comparing results and exchanging information. NTT holds all resulting patents but each participating company has the right to use them. (The observations made regarding NTT in the preceding paragraphs were obtained from Kato and Sando 1983, Yayama 1982, and numerous other sources available on NTT.)

One consequence of such family-oriented research has been the difficulty of nonfamily members (both Japanese and foreign) in supplying products to NTT. Although few Japanese have discussed the antitrust implications on family-oriented research and its effect of the ability of nonfamily firms to supply NTT, many outside of Japan have been vocal in criticizing procurement practices that have long effectively excluded foreign suppliers. The United States has been the strongest critic of the NTT procurement policy partly because Japan's telecommunications industry is today the world's largest exporter of telecommunications equipment (in 1983, Japan's world market share was 27 percent) and because the United States is the market for 31 percent of Japan's total export of telecommunications equipment (UNCTAD 1983, p. 214, and USITC 1983, appendix I, p. 5).

Japan's Antimonopoly Law

Antimonopoly law in postwar Japan is modeled on American statutes. In 1948, the Antimonopoly Act and the Fair Trade Commission, the agency charged with enforcing the statute, were established. The sections of the act most pertinent in the context of this chapter are as follows (see Iyori and Uesugi 1983 for the complete text in English).

Chapter II, Section 3 prohibits "private monopolization," which is defined as "such business activities by which an entrepreneur, individually or by combination or consipiring with other entrepreneurs, or in any other manner, *excludes* or *controls* the business activities of other entrepreneurs, thereby causing, *contrary to the public interest, a substantial restraint of competition* in any particular field of trade" (emphasis added). Chapter IV, Section 10, analogous to Section 7 of the Clayton Act, reads: "no company shall acquire or hold stock of a company or companies in Japan where the effect of such acquisition or holding of stock may be substantially to restrain competition in any particular field of trade, or shall acquire or hold stock of such company through unfair business practices."

Important also in considering joint research activities are Chapter III, Section 8 of the act and *The Guidelines Concerning Activities of Trade Associations Under the Antimonopoly Act*, issued by the FTC in 1979. Chapter III, Section 8 prohibits trade associations from engaging in such acts as (1) substantially restricting competition in any particular field of trade, (2) entering into an international agreement or an international contract involving unreasonable restraint of trade or unfair business practices, (3) limiting the present or future number of entrepreneurs in any particular field of business, (4) unduly restricting the functions or activities of members of associations, and (5) causing entrepreneurs to do acts which constitute unfair business practices.

Some of the specific prohibitions listed in the *Guidelines*, based on the provisions of Chapter III, Section 8 include: exchange of information among members that may affect future prices and the timing and amount of price change; restrictions on the development and use of technology; collecting and providing "information on matters normally kept secret (such as details of dealing among members, names of clients, selling prices, rebates, etc.)" in order to "compete effectively as individual" firms; and restriction of the number of trade association members "by means of obstruction or discouragement of the opening of new businesses."

Some Japanese would undoubtedly argue that Japanese antitrust "law" has been strengthened by the 1977 amendments to the Antimonopoly Act, the 1980 decision by the Tokyo High Court in the "Oil Cartel" case, and the seemingly increased vigor of the FTC in enforcing the amended act and in conducting an increasing number of studies on enterprise groups, distribution channels, and other topics. However, as is evident in the preceding description of MITI-led joint research projects in high technology, it is no less naïve to believe that the Japanese antitrust "structure" has undergone a substantive change in the past few years than to argue that the American antitrust structure has recently been transformed. Even the developments described in the preceding paragraph, when examined closely, cannot serve as evidence signaling the beginning of a fundamental change—a strengthening—in the Japanese antitrust structure.

For example, while the 1977 amendments to the Antimonopoly Act enable the FTC to prosecute more effectively such per se offenses as price fixing, the act remains far less effective in prosecuting offenses dealt with under Sections I and II of the Sherman Act in the United States. As described by a leading Japanese scholar of the Antimonopoly Act and a former commissioner of the FTC, the conditions that must be met before "monopolistic situations" (as defined in Chapter I, Section 2-7) can be prosecuted are:

> the value of the total annual supply of a particular field of business's goods or services of the same kind exceeds fifty billion yen,... the market share of one entrepreneur in the field of business exceeds fifty percent, or the combined share of the two largest entrepreneurs exceeds seventy-five percent; entry into the field of business is extremely difficult; price increases in field of business have been extremely large or price decreases extremely small relevant to supply and demand fluctuations in the field; and profits, selling expenses, or general administrative expenses of the entrepreneurs in question are excessive. . . . [And furthermore,] upon deciding that a monopolistic situation exists, the FTC may order measures, including a transfer of part of the business of the company or companies involved, for the purpose of restoring competition to the industry concerned. However, before ordering such measures the FTC must first notify the minister having jurisdiction over the industry concerned (very often the Minister of International Trade and Industry), thereby providing the minister a chance to present his views. The FTC must also hold a public hearing to obtain the views of the general public. Then after once again consulting with the appropriate minister, the FTC may open a formal adjudicative procedure on the case. [Ariga 1967, pp. I-18-19]

This observation is not quite complete, since even after overcoming all the hurdles described above, including the politically formidable one likely to be mounted by MITI, the FTC *cannot* act if the divestiture in question would "cause a loss of international competitiveness" of the affected firm (Matsushita 1967, p. II-13). The difficulty in proving all the conditions enumerated above is the reason the FTC chooses to focus its enforcement efforts almost exclusively on blatant cases of price-fixing cartels and why it has demonstrated reluctance to bring suit against "monopolistic conditions." And, in discussing the difficulties of challenging collusive conduct and monopolization, we must be reminded that private suits are extremely rare in Japan, partly because Japanese legal proceedings tend to be more time consuming even than in the United States and no treble damages are allowed, and partly because the courts rarely recognize the legal "standing" of the public—consumers as individuals or groups—to bring such challenges.

Despite the ruling against price-fixing among major oil refiners, the 1980 decision of the Tokyo High Court in the widely publicized "Oil Cartel" case cannot be seen as evidence of the beginning of substantial change in the Japanese antitrust structure. Instead, the significance of the decision is that the court chose not to rule against "administrative guidance" as such, even if substantial anticompetitive effects of the "guidance," evident in this case, could be demonstrated:

> The case shows the concepts of "administrative guidance" to be of no help in evaluating administrative activity. The Tokyo High Court tells us that administrative guidance is sometimes lawful and sometimes it isn't; sometimes private parties who follow administrative guidance will be protected from subsequent prosecution and sometimes they won't. In each case where a public official requests some action by a private party the request can only be usefully evaluated in light of the surrounding circumstances and the particular statute under which the official derives his power. The label "administrative guidance" tells one nothing more than that the administrative activity in question is not expressly authorized by the statute. [Repeta 1982, p. 44]

One can add several more observations further demonstrating that the oft-cited recent changes hardly constitute evidence of a significant strengthening of the Japanese antitrust structure in the making. For example, surprising though it may seem, given the numerous mergers among the largest firms during the past decades, there have been only two cases tried (in 1957 and 1973) under Chapter IV, Section 10 of the Antimonopoly Act (Iyori and Uesugi 1983, pp. 85-86). The 1979 *Guidelines Concerning Activities of Trade Associations*, which Smith and Haley (1979, p. 118) characterized as "representing one of the most ambitious attempts thus far by the Japanese FTC to detail publicly the parameters" of the Antimonopoly Act, have yet to be invoked against trade associations that "have been blatant in their disregard of antitrust concerns."

Noteworthy also is the fact that in sharp contrast to the United States, in postwar Japan there have been only four cases involving conflicts between the Antimonopoly Act and patent law. As a result, scholarship on the issues related to the conflicts of these two statutes is still extremely limited. One important reason for the small number of cases is that until recently large Japanese firms have been borrowers of technology from abroad (often under MITI guidance). Another no less important and obvious reason is the limited enforcement of the Antimonopoly Act against the "monopolistic situations" of large firms which are the major holders and users of patent rights (Iyori and Uesugi 1983, pp. 13-40).

Thus, despite the 1977 amendments and the valiant efforts made by the understaffed and underfunded FTC, one must conclude that Japanese antitrust structure has not undergone a significant change during the past several years and is not likely to be changed in the near future. In other words, although Japanese antitrust laws are an important legacy of the American occupation, the basic intent is respected only as long as it does not stand in the way of Japan's industrial policy, especially the activities of the largest firms that are viewed by the LDP, MITI, the large firms themselves, and by many Japanese as being essential in increasing the productivity and international competitive abilities of Japanese industries. MITI's joint research projects, along with NTT's family-oriented research programs, are overt evidence that the Antimonopoly Act occupies such a position in Japan.

Analysis and Reflections

The preceeding observations and discussion clearly demonstrate, above all, that the antitrust structures of the United States and Japan differ fundamentally even though one served as the model for the other. The American structure effectively restricts joint research among large firms while the Japanese structure does not. The differing legal systems and government policies have had a definite effect on the structures of high technology industries in the two countries, as have differences in capital markets and technological base. This section presents an overview of American and Japanese industries, analyzes the strengths and weaknesses of a Japanese-style structure, and offers some reflections on the current debate.

Because of the heterogeneity of high technology products—the label includes aerospace, computers, telecommunications, semiconductors, biotechnology, and robotics—there is no readily delineable "high-tech industry" as such. But certain structural features of the American industry are clear. With few exceptions, such as the aerospace industry and the superlarge computer mainframes industry which are highly concentrated and enjoy at least one half of world market share, many Americans high technology industries are less concentrated and have more fluid market structures including several distinct types of firms. That is, in most industries, one finds small, innovative producers capable of quick adaption and often at the leading technological edge; large, integrated companies, such as Texas Instruments, Motorola, and National Semiconductor; systems manufacturers, such as RCA and Hewlett-Packard; and the two dominant, vertically integrated giants—IBM and AT&T. IBM alone supplied 61.9 percent of the U.S. computer market (large mainframes) in 1978 and holds a similar share of the global market, except in Japan, where its share is approximately 30 percent.

While the strength of the American venture capital market (particularly in relation to the very weak Japanese one), the high mobility of technical personnel, and liberal licensing by pioneering firms are important determinants of this structure, antitrust policy has also had a major impact. Antitrust constraints on IBM and AT&T entry into the open market for semiconductors in particular forced these R&D giants to sell the rights to results of much of their research, greatly aiding the diffusion of technological advances through the industry (Borrus et al. 1983, p. 151). In conjunction with the structural features, as well as NASA and Defense Department procurement practices, American antitrust policies have fostered an industry dynamism encouraging the entry of numerous small firms and focusing competition on innovation. The semiconductor industry from 1966 to 1972 has been described as "a shining example of two venerated features of competitive capitalism: the success of entrepreneurship backed by venture capital, and the triumph of the technological innovativeness of the small firm" (Borrus et al. 1983, p. 152).

In the last ten years, while small companies have continued to find market niches, particularly in software and custom chips, the major movement had been toward consolidation through cross-licensing, acquisitions, technology-development contracts from large manufacturing concerns such as General Motors, and importantly, vertical integration (Borrus et al. 1983, pp. 222-34). The role that joint R&D ventures could play seems significant in this atmosphere.

Overall, the American industry's major strength is its diverse structure, giving rise to a wide variety of strategies, rapid diffusion of technology, ease of entry, high mobility of personnel (especially into independent entrepreneurial activity), and forward momentum based and focused on competition in innovation. American antitrust policy has been important in shaping this growth, just as the very different policies of the Japanese government have formed that industry structure.

The behavior patterns and structure of Japanese firms differ significantly from those found in the United States. In robotics, an area in which Japan has distinguished itself, R&D is dispersed among the many large Japanese producers of, for instance, cars, machinery, and ships, and financed from their general operations. In biotechnology as well, R&D is generally carried out by a section of a large diversified manufacturer who is the final user of the product.

Another difference, as seen in Japan's telecommunications, computers, and semiconductors—the heart of high technology—is that there are about ten very large, diversified firms that dominate the industry. These are the firms listed in table 14. Although there are smaller companies, they are in most cases at a disadvantage to the giants, which can spread the risk of venturing into new R&D and new markets and achieve other gains resulting from their size and diversity of activities. Although the large consumer electronics arms (often de facto divisions, though legally organized as independent firms) of many of these firms—particularly Matsushita, Sony, Sanyo, and Sharp—place them in a somewhat differentiated group, and Fujitsu is heavily involved in computers, all the firms are broadly based (see USITC 1983, appendix H).

Yet another important distinguishing feature is the well-known high debt-equity ratios—ranging from 150 to 400 percent—of most large Japanese firms (Flaherty and Itami 1984, pp. 144-46). Despite the more recently observed increasing variance in the ratios among the largest firms, this feature is significant because it reflects the fact that large Japanese firms, this feature is significant because it reflects the fact that large Japanese firms can avail themselves of dependable lines of bank credit. That is, these firms rarely face, as do U.S. firms, difficulties in obtaining investment funds when profits falter, even in the short run. (U.S. firms typically have debt-equity ratios of 5 to 25 percent.)

Taking into account these ratios and interest rate differentials, the capital costs for large Japanese firms enjoying dependable access to funds are said to be 20 percent lower than those in the United States (Imai and Sakuma 1983, p. 16). This favorable position, however, does not apply to most small and medium-size Japanese companies, which face substantial difficulty in obtaining capital. In short, an American strength has been the innovative small company started on readily available venture capital, while the Japanese strength has been the ability of its large oligopolistic firms to fund major long-term projects that allow the large-scale mass production of their products. One result has been a debilitating weakness in innovative small software firms; Japan is said to be at least several years behind the United States in software capabilities. (For the oligopolistic market structure of most of the products of high technology industries, see Senō 1983 and USITC 1983, p. 135.)

It is essential to emphasize the recognized consequences of the dual structure of the Japanese capital market: (1) the difficulty of obtaining venture capital by small firms is not conducive to innovation-led competition such as that seen among American semiconductor producers; and (2) the competition among large firms is production-led—that is, oriented toward high volume, standardized (low unit cost) products. The latter explains why the American product markets that Japanese have been able to penetrate deeply—memory chips (RAMs) in particular—are often the markets of mass-produced products and the competition was in production capability and cost, not in technological superiority. This, in addition to the limited mobility of the labor force, has been an important reason why some Japanese argue for government involvement in joint research. That is, the government must create centers of innovative activity and disseminate the fruit of that activity in order to assist those tasks that are performed in the United States by the industry's dynamic character.

Japanese methods have not proven as creative in new and uncharted areas as American methods have. Or, generally seen in an international perspective, it is accurate to observe that Japanese methods have been effective in mass production that boosts export rapidly while American methods have demonstrated their strength in innovating and producing advanced custom designs. This difference has been one reason why some Americans are expressing the fear that the strength of Japanese high-volume production could displace small American firms in commodity markets, particularly merchant semiconductor producers, and deny them the profit margins needed to underwrite dynamic, innovation-led growth.

Some American scholars and political leaders advocate "targeting" high technology industries in the United States, and several are proposing basically the Japanese method or a policy quite similar to it. Unfortunately, however, we have only a limited amount of scholarly analysis directly useful for discussion of such proposals. Much of the accumulated research on competition is irrelevant because it focuses on American firms in the domestic market; it typically does not consider the competitiveness of U.S. firms in relation to foreign firms. To make matters even more difficult, economic theoretical analyses of the relationships between market structure, technological change, and the effects of the enforcement of U.S. antitrust and patent laws are in an early speculative stage and do not yield unequivocal theoretical findings. Economists usually specialize in either "industrial organization" (in industrial economies, antitrust issues, and related problems) or "international economics" (international trade theory and institutions)—the former dealing with the industrial organization of a nation (or of nations from a comparative perspective) and the latter examining trade issues. As a result, few economists have analyzed the relationships between the industrial organization (and antitrust policy) of an economy and its effects on the international trade performance of the economy and on those of its trading partners.

The preliminary nature of the scholarly analysis reflects the fact that what must be examined is an analytically new type of interfirm collaboration. These new collaborative activities in R&D could benefit their members through strategy coordination and cost reduction. Whether the gains to members would also mean gains to society as a whole depends on the relative magnitude of what these collaborative R&D activities provide to society balanced against the costs their activities impose on society, both in the short and long run, because of the necessarily market-power enhancing effect these collaborative activities will have.

The benefits of joint R&D to member firms and society—that is, those advantages most frequently discussed by many Japanese and American supporters of joint R&D—include (1) saving on overlapping R&D costs (more invention per dollar is possible through coordination benefiting both firms and society), (2) reducing the risk that a competitor will produce a similar innovation first, by conducting R&D in coordination with that competitor, (3) reducing the risk a competitor will "reverse-engineer" and produce a similar but legally different product soon after the introduction of the original, in effect free riding on R&D expenditures, by coopting that competitor into the original R&D, and (4) preventing "squeeze out" of smaller American firms by Japanese joint projects. Put differently, benefits 2 and 3 argue that joint projects increase the total amount spent on research for the benefit of both society and firms involved, since the firms can be surer of appropriating a significant share of the value of the innovation; and benefit 4, along with 2 and 3, claims, in effect, that if the Japanese are going to do it that way, then we must also, simply for competitive reasons.

On the other hand, one can readily enumerate serious disadvantages, especially the potential high social costs, that must be expected of joint research among large firms as it is practiced in Japan. That is, the Japanese method, including joint research projects led by MITI, clearly benefits selected large firms and has already contributed significantly to increasing their market power in several high technology industries that benefited from MITI's projects. There is no doubt that these projects will continue to have the same effect in other markets, thereby increasing the difficulties faced by both domestic and foreign would-be entrants into various high technology markets. The smaller the number of firms participating in joint research projects, the longer the duration of the projects, and the more successful the joint efforts, the increasingly more significant the entry-deterring effects. The manifestation of the anticompetitive consequences of limited entry on market behavior cannot long be prevented, and these consequences will become increasingly significant as the industry involved matures. By seriously discouraging or even suppressing the R&D activities of small firms, the overall pace of innovation would decline.

The entry-forestalling effect of the Japanese method would increasingly restrain competition among the participants in the joint projects in many subtle (and not so subtle) ways. Despite its claims to the contrary, when MITI aided large firms in the major industries during Japan's rapid growth period, the following occurred: as the industries matured, competition in their markets became significantly compromised, as attested by considerable evidence of various forms of collusive conduct by the large firms in the steel, home electronics, chemical, and other industries in the 1960s. To believe that similar anticompetitive behavior will not be repeated by the large firms in the high technology industries as they mature is to ignore the lessons of postwar Japanese antitrust history.

Even more important, the Japanese experience of the 1970s should warn us that MITI-led joint research among large firms makes it impossible for MITI to dissociate itself from the various problems (possible excess capacities, strong foreign competition, sudden changes in technology, etc.) that may occur in the high technology industries in the future. That is, since MITI is playing an important role in the growth of these industries, it will be "obligated" to help the industries cope with problems as they arise. This happened in several industries MITI promoted during the rapid growth period, resulting in the MITI-sponsored laws of 1978 and 1983 to aid the "structurally depressed" industries. Despite foreign criticism, these laws provided the industries with public funds and the ability to engage in legal cartels and raise prices (Saxonhouse 1979). Thus, political "dependence," once acquired, is not easily stripped away just because it has become inconvenient and counterproductive. And government involvement, once begun, has a way of increasing. In recalling what was described in preceding sections, readers can easily add several other costs, likely to be high, of the Japanese method, such as the risk of reducing the probability of breakthroughs which actually occur in presumed "wasteful" duplicative research, picking wrong winners, and the like.

This, however, is not to say that Americans should not engage in a broad-based search for an American policy promoting efficient technological progress and the international competitiveness of their high technology industries. A case in point is the current debate concerning the conditional exemption from American antitrust statutes of joint research ventures among firms in high technology industries.

It is evident that discussion of exemption must proceed with extreme caution in view of the analysis presented in the preceding sections and the assessment of the Japanese method just offered. But the usefulness of the discussion, I believe, cannot be questioned even if it is only to force a debate of the validity of the American antitrust structure and to reexamine thoroughly the reasons why our international competitiveness has eroded and why we have come to seek refuge in the trigger price mechanism, "voluntary" import restrictions, International Trade Commission proceedings under Section 201 of the Trade Act of 1974, and the like.

Therefore, with as much openness of mind as we can muster, we must debate the nearly one dozen bills now pending in Congress that, if enacted, would exempt some privately organized joint research ventures among high technology firms from antitrust statutes. There are several crucial questions. Are the limitations on the ventures required in the bills sufficient in minimizing the anticompetitive consequences of joint research ventures? (Should not the bills contain some explicit mechanism to prevent ventures between very large firms from commanding a specified significant market share? Should not these bills offer more explicit guidance to be useful in differentiating basic research from product-oriented research in order to stringently minimize potential risks of anticompetitive effects of close cooperative product commercialization?) Above all, in terms of total research activities, are these "qualified" joint research ventures likely to provide a net gain to the economy?

What we must undergo in our effort to resolve these issues is the difficult process of consensus building among those Americans advocating differing views and between a large majority of Japanese and Americans who hold fundamentally conflicting views. What I offer in the remainder of this section are some reflections which I hope will be useful in the continuing debate on American policy toward joint research as an important part of our "industrial policy" and in the bilateral attempts being made to reduce the economic conflict now marring relations between the United States and Japan.

While the preceding analyses of the impact of antitrust law and industrial structure on innovation are useful in illuminating options, we must recognize that the view one holds regarding which antitrust structure is preferable and how best to promote high technology industries depends, in the final analysis, largely on personal judgment reflecting knowledgeable but nonetheless subjective views of the relative magnitude of the roles government and market are to play in economic activities. For this reason, there is an obvious need for both American and Japanese to reexamine as analytically and objectively as possible their antitrust structures and their policies affecting the economic well-being of both nations. Each needs to understand the other's economic policy and the political, economic, and even historical reasons for the policies. In this spirit, let me summarize what I believe are the reasons why American and Japanese chose, as evidenced by their revealed preferences, their respective antitrust structures and policies toward high technology industries.

It is reasonable to infer that the majority of Americans, in principle, continue to hold that the market power possesed by large firms does tend to exceed socially desirable limits. In addition, the social costs of having such large firms is considered sufficiently high to require an antitrust structure capable of limiting, or preventing the exercise of, their market power. Thus, as a matter of principle, a quite highly competitive market structure needs to be preserved, and no public policy should be adopted if its direct or potential consequence is to bring about a market structure conducive to restricting competition.

Americans are not inclined to support a public policy intended primarily to promote the technological capabilities of large firms. The large majority of Americans—specialists analyzing such issues and laymen alike—justify this policy inclination on their belief that a competitive and unconstrained market is better able to predict and pick future technological winners than government officials administrating a public policy intended to achieve the same goal.

A necessary corollary is that even if private innovative activities result in duplicative efforts, no one wishing to engage in them should be enticed away or deterred in any manner from doing so as a direct or indirect result of public policy which may use various forms of economic incentives (including subsidies, as in Japan) to achieve its goal. The principal reason for this American view is that even seemingly wasteful duplicative research has been a source of major breakthroughs.

In contrast, most Japanese implicitly accept the view that the contributions made to society by large productive firms are evident in the performance of the postwar Japanese economy and these contributions more than compensate for the social costs the large firms might impose as a result of their anticompetitive practices. For most Japanese, the oligopolistic market structure and even various indications of collusive conduct that appear are not viewed with widespread concern. The existing market structure is seen basically as a necessary consequence of scale economies to be realized, and the indication of collusive conduct is accepted as an inevitable side effect of maintaining the highest possible economic performance.

Because of this view, held with little variation for over a century of Japanese industrialization, the various forms of government involvement in aiding efforts of large firms to increase their productive efficiency widely accepted as socially necessary and are not regarded as an undesirable intrusion in market activities. The favored status that is accorded large firms by public policy, therefore, is not, as a rule, challenged.

Many Japanese are inclined to support a public policy whose goals and effective results promote virtually exclusively the technological capabilities of the large firms. Questions are rarely raised regarding the potential risks involved in nonmarket, MITI-led selection of future winners. In short, the Japanese have little doubt that their large firms can engage successfully in expensive, long-term, and risky joint research because of their method of active government participation. They also believe that their method is more effective than the American method of relying on market-determined innovative activity.

If these summaries of the dominant views in the United States and Japan are accurate, the difference between them is indeed substantial. But this wide gap between the perceptions these countries have of the roles government is to play in the economy compels them to reexamine their respective antitrust structures in relation to the social desirability of joint research ventures among large firms. This reexamination will be extremely difficult because it is no less than an attempt to determine the net welfare effects of a policy whose complex consequences affect not only the domestic economy but also the economies of trading partners. As world leaders in high technology, Japan and the United States have a special obligation not to be tempted to adopt policies that promote their own high technology industries to the detriment of the other. Perhaps even more important, the policy course chosen upon this reexamination should not restrict or hamper the growth of the high technology industries of European allies and the newly industrializing countries.

REFERENCES

Ariga, Michiko. 1967. "Antimonopoly Regulations in General." In Robert J. Ballon, ed., *Doing Business in Japan*, chapter 1. Tokyo: Sophia University Press.

Baxter, William F. 1983. "Antitrust Law and the Stimulation of Technological Invention and Innovation." Discussion paper for the Preparatory Conference on Government Organization and Operation and the Role of Government in the Economy. July.

Borrus, Michael, James E. Millstein, and John Zysman. 1983. "Trade and Development in the Semiconductor Industry: Japanese Challenge and American Response." In John Zysman and Laura Tyson, eds., *American Industry in International Competition: Government Policies and Corporate Strategies*, pp. 142–248. Ithaca and London: Cornell University Press.

Bowman, Ward S., Jr. 1973. *Patent and Antitrust Law: A Legal and Economic Appraisal*. Chicago and London: University of Chicago Press.

Congressional Budget Office. 1983. "Alternative Industrial Strategies." In *The Industrial Policy Debate*. Washington, D.C.: Congressional Budget Office.

Controller General of the United States. 1982. *Industrial Policy: Japan's Flexible Approach*. Washington, D.C.: U.S. Government Printing Office.

Dasgupta, Partha, and Joseph Stiglitz. 1980. "Uncertainty, Industrial Structure, and the Speed of R&D." *Bell Journal of Economics* 11 (Spring): 1–28.

Department of Justice. 1980. *The Antitrust Guide Concerning Research Joint Ventures*. Washington, D.C.

Dixit, Avinash K. 1982. "Recent Developments in the Theory of Imperfect Competition." *American Economic Review Proceedings* 72 (May): 12–17.

Dore, Ronald. 1983. *Flexible Rigidities: Industrial Policy and Structural Adjustment in the Japanese Economy, 1970–80*. Geneva: ILO.

Editors, *George Washington Law Review*. 1971. Editorial Notes on "Joint Research Ventures under Antitrust Laws." *George Washington Law Review* 30(5):1112–40.

Feigenbaum, Edward A., and Pamela McCorduck. 1983. *The Fifth Generation: Artificial Intelligence and Japan's Computer Challenge to the World*. Reading, Mass. and Menlo Park, Calif.: Addison-Wesley.

Flaherty, M. Therese, and Hiroyuki Itami. 1984. "Finance." In Daniel I. Okimoto, Takuo Sugano, and Franklin B. Weinstein, eds., *Competitive Edge: The Semiconductor Industry in the U.S. and Japan*, pp. 134–76. Stanford: Stanford University Press.

Gallo, Nicholas A. 1966. "Patent Interchanges: An Analysis of Their Effects on Competition." *Journal of the Patent Office Society* 48(11):669–88.

Ginsburg, Douglas H. 1979. "Antitrust, Uncertainty, and Technological Innovation." *Antitrust Bulletin* 24(4):635–86.
Goller, Gilbert. 1968. "Competing, Complementary, and Blocking Patents: Their Role in Determining Antitrust Violations in the Areas of Cross-Licensing, Patent Pooling, and Package Licensing." *Journal of the Patent Office Society* 50(11):723–53.
Imai Ken-ichi. 1983. *Nihon no sangyō shakai* [Japan's industrial society]. Tokyo: Chikuma Shobō.
Imai, Ken-ichi, and Akimitsu Sakuma. 1983. "An Analysis of Japan–U.S. Semiconductor Friction." *Economic Eye* 4(2):13–18.
Iyori, Hiroshi, and Akinori Uesugi. 1983. *The Antimonopoly Laws of Japan*. Washington, D.C.: Federal Legal Publications, Inc.
Kakuma Takashi. 1982. *Sekai gijutsu-sensō saizensen* [The frontier of the world's technology war]. Tokyo: Green Arrow Publishing.
Kamien, Morton I., and Nancy L. Schwartz. 1975. "Market Structure and Innovation: A Survey." *Journal of Economic Literature* 13:1–37.
Kantrow, Alan M. 1983. "The Political Realities of Industrial Policy." *Harvard Business Review* 61(5):79–86.
Kato Hiroshi and Sando Yōichi. 1983. *Kokuden, Denden to Senbai: Zeisei no kōzu* [Japan National Railway, NTT and government monopolies: The patterns of the tax system]. Tokyo: Tōyō Keizai Shuppansha.
Keysen, Karl, and Donald F. Turner. 1959. *Antitrust Policy: An Economic and Legal Analysis*. Cambridge, Mass.: Harvard University Press.
Kitch, Edmund W. 1977. "The Nature and Function of the Patent System." *Journal of Law and Economics* 20(2):265–90.
Koenker, Roger W., and Martin K. Perry. 1981. "Product Differentiation, Monopolistic Competition, and Public Policy." *Bell Journal of Economics* 12 (Spring): 217–31.
Konaga, Keiichi. 1983. "Industrial Policy: The Japanese Version of a Universal Trend." *Journal of Japanese Trade and Industry* 2(4):23–27.
Landiorio, Joseph S. 1964. "Patent Pools and the Antitrust Laws." *Journal of the Patent Office Society* 46(10):712–45.
Martin, John R. 1974. "Patent Licensing—Antitrust Interface." *The Patent Law Annual*, pp. 143–70.
Matsushita, Mitsuo. 1967. "Private Monopolization and Monopolistic Situations." In Robert J. Ballon, ed., *Doing Business in Japan*, chapter 2. Tokyo: Sophia University Press.
Ministry of International Trade and Industry (MITI). 1980. *80-nendai no tsūsan seisaku vision* [MITI's policy vision in the 1980s]. Tokyo: MITI.
Ministry of International Trade and Industry (MITI). 1982. *JECC Kompūtā nōto* [Japan Electronic Computer Corporation Computer notes]. Tokyo: MITI.
MITI, Industrial Technology Agency, 1982. *Kōgyō gijutsu-in shōkai* [An introduction to industrial technology]. Toyko: MITI.
Murakami, Yasusuke. 1982. "Toward a Socioinstitutional Explanation of Japan's Economic Performance." In Kozo Yamamura, ed., *Policy and Trade Issues of the Japanese Economy: American and Japanese Perspectives*, pp. 3–46. Seattle: University of Washington Press.
Murakami, Yasusuke, and Kozo Yamamura. 1982. "A Technical Note on Japanese Firm Behavior and Economic Policy." In Kozo Yamamura, ed., *Policy and Trade Issues of the Japanese Economy: American and Japanese Perspectives*, pp. 113–21. Seattle: Univeristy of Washington Press.

208 *Kozo Yamamura*

Nakagawa Yasuzo. 1981. *Nihon no handō-tai kaihatsu* [Development of semiconductors in Japan]. Tokyo: Diamond Publishing Co.

Nihon Keizai Shimbunsha, ed. 1977. *Kompūtā sangyō: 80-nendai eno senryaku to taiō* [The computer industry: Strategy and response in the 1980s]. Tokyo: Nihon Keizai Shimbunsha.

Nihon Kōgyō Shimbunsha, ed. 1981. *Sentan gijutsu ni kakeru kigō* [The companies betting on the technological frontier]. Tokyo: Nihon Kōgyō Shimbunsha.

Noguchi, Yukio. 1982. "The Government–Business Relationship in Japan: The Changing Role of Fiscal Resources." In Kozo Yamamura, ed., *Policy and Trade Issues of the Japanese Economy: American and Japanese Perspectives*, pp. 123–42. Seattle: University of Washington Press.

Okimoto, Daniel I. 1984. "Political Context." In Daniel I. Okimoto, Takuo Sugano, and Franklin B. Weinstein, eds., *Competitive Edge: The Semiconductor Industry in the U.S. and Japan*, pp. 78–133. Stanford: Stanford University Press.

Patrick, Hugh, and Henry Rosovsky, eds. 1976. *Asia's New Giant: How the Japanese Economy Works*. Washington, D.C.: Brookings Institution.

Priest, George L. 1977. "Cartels and Patent License Arrangements." *Journal of Law and Economics* 20(2):309–77.

Reich, Robert. 1983. "High Tech Industrial Policy: Comparing the U.S. with Other Advanced Industrial Nations." *Journal of Japanese Trade and Industry* 2(4):28–33.

Repeta, Larry. 1982. "Notes on the Limits of Administrative Authority in Japan: A Report on the Petroleum Cartel Decisions and the Reaction of MITI and the Fair Trade Commission." *Law in Japan: An Annual* 15:24–56.

Sameth, James, and John O. Haley. 1979. "Guidelines Concerning the Activities of Trade Associations under the Antimonopoly Law." *Law in Japan: An Annual* 12:118–52.

Saxonhouse, Gary R. 1979. "Industrial Restructuring in Japan." *Journal of Japanese Studies* 5(2):304–16.

Schacht, Wendy H. 1980. "Industrial Innovation and High Technology Development." Issue Brief No. 11380005, Library of Congress, Congressional Research Service, Major Issues System.

Scherer, F. M. 1980. *Industrial Market Structure and Economic Performance*. 2nd edition. Chicago: Rand McNally.

Schmalensee, Richard. 1976. "Is More Competition Necessarily Good?" *Industrial Organization Review* 4(2):120–21.

Schmalensee, Richard. 1979. "On the Use of Economic Models in Antitrust: The ReaLemon Case." *University of Pennsylvania Law Review* 127 (April): 994–1050.

Schmalensee, Richard. 1982. "Antitrust and the New Industrial Economics." *American Economic Review* 72(2):25–28.

Schwartz, Marius, and Earl A. Thompson. 1983. "Entry Patterns under Decreasing Cost Conditions." Department of Justice, Antitrust Division.

Senō Akira. 1983. *Gendai Nihon no sangyō shūchū* [Industrial concentration in contemporary Japan]. Tokyo: Nihon Keizai Shimbunsha.

Spence, Michael A. 1981. "Competition, Entry, and Antitrust Policy." In Steven C. Scalop, ed., *Strategy, Predation, and Antitrust Analysis*, pp. 137–59. Washington, D.C.: U.S. Federal Trade Commission.

Stiglitz, Joseph E. 1981. "Potential Competition May Reduce Welfare." *American Economic Review* 71(2):184–89.

Tanaka, Toshio. 1983. "Setting the Record Straight on Semiconductors." *Journal of Japanese Trade and Industry* 2(4):18–22.

Techno-science team. 1981. "Gijutsu kaihatsu rengō no jidai" [An era of technological development]. *Chūō kōron* Fall:110–21.

Thurow, Lester. 1980. *The Zero-Sum Society*. New York: Basic Books, Inc.

Tsuruta Toshimasa. 1982. *Sengo Nihon no sangyō seisaku* [Industrial policy in postwar Japan]. Tokyo: Nihon Keizai Shimbunsha.

United Nations Conference on Trade and Development (UNCTAD). 1983. *Handbook of International Trade and Development Statistics, 1983*. New York: United Nations.

U.S. International Trade Commission. 1983. *Foreign Industrial Targeting and Its Effects on U.S. Industries, Phase I: Japan*. USITC Publication 1437. Washington, D.C.: U.S. Government Printing Office.

von Weizsacker, C. C. 1980. "A Welfare Analysis of Barriers to Entry." *Bell Journal of Economics* 11 (Autumn): 399–420.

White, Lawrence J. 1981. "Vertical Restraints in Antitrust Law: A Coherent Model." *Antitrust Bulletin*, Summer: 327–45.

Woodbridge, Richard C. 1972. "Recent Trends in Technology Interchanges: The Case For and Against Pooling." *Journal of the Patent Office Society* 54(8):507–37.

Yamamura, Kozo. 1967. *Postwar Economic Policy of Japan: Growth vs. Economic Democracy*. Berkeley: University of California Press.

Yamamura, Kozo. 1975. "Structure Is Behavior." In Isaiah Frank, ed., *The Japanese Economy in International Perspective*, pp. 67–100. Baltimore: Johns Hopkins University Press.

Yamamura, Kozo. 1982. "Success that Soured: Administrative Guidance and Cartels in Japan." In Kozo Yamamura, ed., *Policy and Trade Issues of the Japanese Economy: American and Japanese Perspectives*, pp. 77–112. Seattle: University of Washington Press.

Yayama Taro. 1982. *Buttaku! Nihon no byōgen* [Destroy! The sources of ills in Japan]. Tokyo: Taiyō Shuppansha.

Chapter 6

Technology in Transition:
Two Perspectives on Industrial Policy

Yasusuke Murakami

Industrial policy is broadly defined as a spectrum of policies that change, directly or indirectly, resource allocation within an economy from what would have resulted had unconstrained markets been allowed to function. Narrowly, the term covers specific policies that directly affect the performance and conduct of "targeted" firms or industries. Whatever definition one uses—broad, narrow, or somewhere in between—few disagree with the observation that Japan's industrial policy differs in significant ways from that of Western industrial nations, especially the United States. Indeed, this difference has produced a large body of literature. In this chapter I intend to offer two broadly conceived perspectives I believe are useful in the continuing discussion of industrial policy.

The first perspective views the current maleficent manifestations of the slower economic growth faced by advanced industrial nations—the principal reason for the industrial policy debate—as a result of the ending of what I term the twentieth-century system of an industrial technological paradigm (defined below). The second perspective views the process of industrialization not as a basically homogeneous process approximating "Westernization" but as a process that reflects various indigenous characteristics, and that therefore can have a range of relationships between the political and economic spheres of a society that differ in character from one industrial nation to another. I conclude this chapter with reflections on the current discussion of industrial policy—especially on Japanese industrial policy in a comparative context—from these two perspectives.

Century-to-Century Model

Terms and Concepts

To present the first perspective, I begin by asserting that industrial civilization can be divided into three historical stages representing three technological paradigms, each roughly corresponding to a century: the nineteenth-century system, covering the beginning of the Industrial Revolution to the 1870s; the twentieth-century system, extending from the 1880s to the 1970s; and the twenty-first-century, which began in 1973, the year of the first oil crisis. The last, of course, is a speculative designation.

Before proceeding, I must define "technological paradigm" and "system" and offer a brief discussion of the phases of a technological paradigm. An analysis based on these phases is essential for understanding the nature of the technological change, and is thus an important part of the first perspective.

By "technological paradigm" I mean a broadly identifiable body of knowledge that most persons can readily recognize, at least conceptually, as determining the essential characteristics of the economy in which they live. Following Thomas Kuhn (1970), a historian of science who first used the term "paradigm" for the analysis of history, each paradigm is considered unique and able to solve some problems more effectively than others. A new technological paradigm has first to get through the stage of "revolution," which is in many ways comparable to Kuhn's "scientific revolution." In this incipient stage, not all innovations characterizing the new paradigm are immediately appliable to industrial activity or necessarily bring about increases in productivity (see, e.g., Abernathy 1978 and Utterback and Abernathy 1975). Rather, it is even possible that the total productivity of an economy as a whole may decline. But once a paradigm is established, it readily finds solutions to those problems it is best adapted to solve. Each established paradigm gives birth to a body of technological innovations that occur to solve the problems being posed by the paradigm—that is, innovations that might be called "normal" in the sense following Kuhn. These "normal" innovations result in a consistent rise in productivity, demonstrating that the paradigm is now fully established. The meaning of technological paradigm will be further delineated in describing the specific character of each of the paradigms we examine. (For a good example of use of a technological paradigm in a similar way, see Dosi 1983.)

"System" refers to the ways in which the relations between man and his environment as well as among men are determined. In determining the character of these relations, we assert that technology, as a collection of knowledge used to control the environment for the benefit of man, plays the principal role. This is not to say that technology has been the most crucial determinant of all systems to the same degree or extent throughout the course of human history. Thus, only in an industrial civilization, one in which man exerts extensive control over his environment, is it justified to argue that technology is the decisive factor that molds and determine the course of change in man's existence.

I believe it is possible to identify two phases in each technological paradigm of both the nineteenth- and twentieth-century systems. In the first, "breakthrough" phase, an initial and often partial breakthrough occurs; that is, new technology breaks through the existing paradigm typically in those industries offering the least resistance because future demand is assured and because the existing organization and technology in these industries more readily accommodates new technology. Once a breakthrough takes place, technological innovation soon occurs elsewhere in the economy, ultimately involving numerous industries.

As more industries adopt and make successful use of innovations, the character of the paradigm becomes defined and, in this sense, the paradigm reaches the second, "maturation," phase. Like the "breakthrough" phase, this too is a shorthand expression for a phase in which industries are undergoing varied experiences. Some industries exploiting mature technology may still be enjoying the most expansive and profitable periods. A larger number of industries, however, will sooner or later find that they have reached their respective peaks and diminishing returns to their technology have set in. Thus the economy as a whole awaits innovations—a revolution and then new normal innovations—which can revitalize its industries; in short; it is ready for a new breakthrough.

In the nineteenth-century system, the breakthrough phase appeared as innovations in the cotton textile and closely related industries, and the maturation phase was a broad range of technologies that enabled the rapid growth of rail transportation. In the twentieth-century system, the breakthrough phase began with innovation giving rise to the electrical and chemical industries, as well as the automobile industry (Rosenberg 1976), and the maturation phase arrived with a wide spectrum of technology that enabled the economy to produce numerous types of consumer durables following the example of automobiles.

These four phases—the alternation of breakthrough and maturation over two centuries—correspond roughly to four Kondratiev long waves. Kondratiev accounted for his cycle (about half a century in average duration) in terms of four factors: war or revolution, technological innovation, gold production, and agricultural production. But, like Schumpeter, I stress the technological factor. The change from the cotton textile wave to the railway wave was technologically continuous, so it is viewed only as the transition from the breakthrough phase to that of maturation within one technological paradigm. On the other hand, the change from the second wave to the third—electricity, chemistry, and automobile—wave was much more fundamental, indicating that these waves belong to different technological paradigms.

Each half-century Kondratiev wave consisted of an upswing and a downswing in the economy of about a quarter-century each. As Kondratiev first pointed out, downswings are characterized by increases in the rate of discovery and invention—a surge in technological creativity—while upswings feature large-scale applications of the innovations of the preceding downswing. The last quarter of the nineteenth-century was clearly a period of major innovation, as was the second quarter of the twentieth century. If this pattern persists, the last quarter of the twentieth century will be another period of technological creation, but a downswing in the economy.

The first perspective can thus be seen as a stage analysis in which technological changes are the motivating force. But it is both more and less than a stage analysis, because while I feel free to elaborate on political and social changes (including those changes in a nation possessing hegemonic power that occurred as a result of the rise and fall of the systems), I am aware that the analysis is, to borrow a phrase from economic historians, an explanation sketch that is specific to the two centuries in question, for which I claim no universal applicability. (There is an analytic similarity with the approaches of such political scientists as Gilpin 1981, Modelski 1978, and Kurth 1979. Some parts of my analysis benefited from their work.)

The Nineteenth-Century System

Stated broadly, the first technology to appear in the industrial civilization of the nineteenth-century system was, in essence, large-scale use of steam energy (Levy 1966). Steam energy was familiar, as was the iron used in machines harnessing and conveying steam power. The machines were also an extension of what had been familiar, in that they simulated human actions. Even spinning, carding, and weaving machines, blast furnaces, lathes, wheeled vehicles, and ships had familiar antecedents.

Aided by these developments, the cotton textile industry blazed the trail for the Industrial Revolution. The machinery, iron, and coal industries quickly followed, and the railroad and transoceanic shipping industries, needed to transport cotton and coal, also grew rapidly. The breakthrough phase of the nineteenth-century paradigm first appeared in England; the cotton textile revolution and a dominance in naval power enabled England by the end of the Napoleonic War to capture one-third of total world trade and to establish itself as *the* world power. International adjustments in the nineteenth-century system were completed relatively quickly.

Responding to the impetus for growth generated within the breakthrough phase by the increasing output of the cotton textile industry, the railroad industry soon began to grow, and, as it gathered momentum, it began to stimulate other industries. The total length of railroads in England grew at a remarkable annual rate of 15 percent during the 1830-60 period, and, even more surprisingly, the growth rate of railroads for the world as a whole approximated 10 percent during the 1840-80 period. Industrial cities of several hundred thousand mushroomed, a development made possible by the rail network capable of transporting huge quantities of raw materials, coal, and food. This network—the first infrastructure of industrial civilization—rapidly transformed society.

The importance of the rapid growth of the railroad should be stressed. Built mostly by English and European capital, the railroad played a crucial role in the economic expansion and growth of North America, Russia, Argentina, and other regions in the nineteenth century. This new means of transportation, seemingly insatiable for more cargo, linked European and American cities with distant fertile plains. It transformed the network of world trade, providing an unprecedented impetus for agriculture to adopt new methods and to plant new crops. Waves of immigrants—another hallmark of the nineteenth-century—was also an important by-product of the rapid expansion of the railroad. It was indeed the iron horse that changed the face of the nineteenth century.

The third quarter of the century saw the maturation of the nineteenth-century system, with the growth of the railroad being the principal element. And, no less important, to meet the needs of the continuing expansion of railroads as well as of overall economic growth, the technologies relating to railroads and other industries underwent significant changes beginning in the 1870s. The most salient among these was the appearance of a large-scale and economically attractive means of producing steel. Its effect was widespread and fundamental: dependence on steel for various uses rose in the railroad, shipbuilding, construction, machinery, and other industries. Steel made possible machines with much higher precision and speeds of operation, thereby linking nineteenth-century technology with that of the twentieth century.

These technological innovations supported economic growth and brought an observable rise in the standard of living. Although debate continues on the magnitude of change in real wages during the second half of the century, and conditions varied among the industrializing nations, it is clear that the 1850-70 period was prosperous, resembling in many ways the worldwide prosperity enjoyed during the 1945-73 period.

The economic growth achieved in the nineteenth century was not without problems. One was the time it took to complete domestic adjustments—the restructuring of the sociopolitical fabric of society needed to cope with a wide range of problems created by the industrial character of economic growth. For example, as symbolized by the fateful year 1848, the middle decades of the century were fraught with social turmoil and even civil war, and part and parcel of the turmoil were urban problems—a dark blot on industrial civilization. The "coke cities" of Dickens, the inevitable result of densely concentrated large factories, were corrupt to a degree unprecedented in human memory. These hardships, if not outright miseries, were suffered by urban wage earners deprived of the traditional support agricultural communities and guilds had once given them. These social costs transformed the social order from an agrarian society that had lasted nearly ten millennia to a new industrial society, and in historical perspective, the transformation, however painful to many individuals, was rapid.

The Twentieth-Century System

The twentieth–century system differed substantively from its predecessor. This system—the second of industrial civilization—saw the appearance of quasi-artificial energy, artificial (man-made) materials, and the use of new combinations of technologies that opened unanticipated horizons for industrial progress.

Above all, however, what became the *force majeure* in the technology of the twentieth-century system was electricity. Not existing in nature in a form that can be harnessed, electricity had to be created to be readily controlled, transmitted, and used. In short, it had to be produced as a quasi-artificial energy. The machinery that made the twentieth-century system possible depended on this quasi-artificial energy. Besides this energy source, the twentieth-century system made use of gas, petroleum, and then nuclear energy. Although I do not downplay the importance of petroleum, I believe electricity was more crucial in characterizing the twentieth-century system.

This also was a century of artificial materials. The list begins with cement, glass, and rubber, and continues on to artificial dyes, ammonia, nylon, polyethylene, and the like. The list increased further after World War II as a result of the waves of scientific progress that enabled us to make extensive use of newly acquired knowledge concerning various properties of molecules and the crystallization process.

The beginning date of the technological basis of the twentieth-century system can be set as either 1879, when Thomas Edison brought the incandescent lamp to practical use, or 1882, when electric-generating plants were built in London and New York. This system can be divided into four segments. The first was two or three decades beginning with the 1880s, a period of preparation and experimental research before the arrival of the final breakthrough. Some people even call it the Second Industrial

Revolution, because it was a period rich in discoveries: the rubber, gas, electric, cement, chemical, paper, printing, automobile, and other industries began, from the 1890s onward, to make their presence felt in the industrial economies. Despite the momentum for growth generated by these industries, this was also a period of frequent panics, and the real wage levels of urban workers showed little sign of rising as the productivity level of society as a whole failed to increase. What occurred in these decades demonstrated that innovation does not inherently lead to increased productivity (see Abernathy 1978 and Utterback and Abernathy 1975).

These also were the years during which Britain's leadership in the world began to erode. In steel output, the United States surpassed England in 1890. Germany also overtook England in 1893 and led all other nations in such new industries as chemicals, electrical machinery, and internal combustion engines. Germany and the United States were about to overtake England as the leading industrial powers. England, however, still wielded more power than any other nation, including Germany or the United States, in shaping the economic order of the world. Its wealth allowed it to make half of the total investments abroad and its naval supremacy deterred challenges to British interests around the globe. The position of London as the center of world finance remained unquestioned. Pax Britannica, despite a few clouds on the horizon, prevailed. In both technological and politicoeconomic senses, this first segment was a period of transition and preparation for what was about to dawn.

The second segment, also about a quarter-century, extended into the 1920s. This was basically a period of industrial vigor and prosperity, although this feature was in many ways blurred and distorted by World War I. As a matter of fact, preparation for war at least partly brought about industrial development in Europe in this period. But war or preparation for it is not a stable way for a society to create demand for its industries. Thus the most significant development during this segment was the automobile revolution which began in the United States following successful implementation in 1913 of assembly line production of the Ford Model T, the first machine ever made for mass consumption. By the mid-1920s, automobiles dominated manufacturing, benefiting from contributions of the steel, electric, rubber, combustion engine, petroleum-refining, and other industries, and a breakthrough phase was thereby ushered in.

The third segment was a downswing including the bitter experience of the Great Depression. The second segment foreshadowed this phase. During World War I, the German economy became exhausted and the European economy as a whole lost much of its vigor. The whole world economy changed its structure, and the emergence of the U.S. economy as the world's largest during the 1920s only aggravated this structural instability. Although still enjoying remnants of past glory, Britain was eclipsed. Far away in the Pacific, Japan, its economy unscathed by World War I and having reaped large gains from the war boom, emerged as an industrial power; its increasing export of cotton textiles during the 1920s was a challenge Britain could well do without.

An integral part of the twentieth-century system, an organizational revolution, also occurred during this period. The revolution was typified by the appearance of the Taylor system and by the innovative organizational changes adopted to meet the needs of evolving strategy, a point stressed by Chandler (1977). This revolution continued in the third segment and in fact forced all industrial economies to undergo further adjustments. Cartels and trusts became prevalent in Europe as well as in Japan during the interwar period, even while stringent antitrust measures were adopted in the United States. Business organization continued to be reexamined and revised.

In respect to the structure of the world economy, international adjustment was also lagging. One could assert that the post-World War I United States as the dominant economic power was less than fully aware of the roles a world leader needed to play to maintain the international political and economic order. Perhaps the responsibility came too rapidly. As a wealthy world power, the United States did little more than exhibit generosity in proposing the Dawes (1924) and Young (1929) plans. The huge trade surplus that accumulated during World War I was not invested abroad, thereby leaving a large portion of the world money supply (gold) in the United States. Monetary policy was conceived solely as a domestic policy. An inevitable result was that the gold standard system became, in effect, the dollar standard, causing U.S. domestic monetary policy to dictate, in substantial ways, the changes in the world money supply and the course of world trade.

A significant reason why the world economy was unable to free itself from instability and stagnation during the interwar years was this manifest unwillingness or inability of the United States to exercise its economic power in a way that benefited the world at large. Franklin Roosevelt's telegram instructing the American delegation attending the London economic conference in 1933—"look homeward angel"—was a pithy characterization of the United States in these decades.

The fourth segment of the twentieth-century system, the most prosperous in industrial civilization, began with the Bretton Woods Agreement of 1944 and ended in the oil crisis of 1973. One reason for these three decades of unprecedented prosperity was that the United States finally asserted itself as world leader, by acting as the catalyst and banker for an unprecedented integration of the world's economy. Under the Bretton Woods Agreement, the principle of free trade based on a fixed exchange rate system was created, establishing what came to be known as the IMF-

GATT system. The United States, with its unchallenged economic power, consistently had large trade surpluses well into the early 1970s, which were exported as investments outside the United States. The result was a stable world economic order and rapid growth in international trade.

The second reason for prosperity was the emergence, with gusto, as it were, of the maturation phase in the United States, characterized by the rapid growth of consumer durables, including automobiles, radios, refrigerators, televisions, and air conditioners. Given the high living standard in post–World War II America, the rate and technological vigor of growth of industries producing these products sharply differed, qualitatively and quantitatively, from those achieved by the same American industries during the mid-1920s. And, of course, the American life-style and industrial structure, along with the technology and organization know-how that made them possible, were successfully emulated by other advanced industrial nations.

This prosperity, to the extent it depended on demand for consumer durables, was possible because of the steady increase in real income and security of employment enjoyed by many people. Rising income and continuing high employment in time satisfied most needs for food, clothing, housing, and consumer durables; the peoples of the advanced industrial nations became satisfied and felt prosperous. These prosperous consumers understandably grew increasingly desirous of protecting the world and society they now enjoyed. Also, along with this conservatism in their world view, they were becoming, if only latently, doubtful or even critical of such traditional values as industriousness, thriftiness, and respect for the sanctity of marriage and family—all the basic ethical values of industrial civilization. This group—"the new middle mass"—is a large majority in the advanced industrial societies (Murakami 1982a). An esentially pro-status quo population, they occupy a broad middle layer of society and by the 1960s had become crucial in determining the political, social, and economic character of advanced industrial nations and of industrial civilization.

The technological paradigm of consumer durables continues to evolve. It is growing increasingly sophisticated and, in most intances, even larger in scale of production. But the pace of such a normal technological innovation could not but falter, sooner or later. The demand for consumer durables is not limitless. By some standards, it has been satisfied for large segments of the population of advanced countries. And, this in turn has contributed to the quickening of the erosion of the ethical values of industrial civilization. A result has been a decline in productivity growth. No advanced industrial economy has been able to avert these developments. The United States was the first to encounter such problems because it is the richest. European nations and then Japan followed. This development signals the fact that the technological paradigm of the twentieth-century system had been exhausted.

The United States, by the end of the 1960s, was visibly losing the ability to achieve a trade surplus. As a consequence, the IMF-GATT system, so dependent on American economic dominance, could no longer be maintained. What followed was Nixon's New Economic Policy of 1971 and the flexible exchange rate regime that began in 1973. The world is still groping for stability in its international economic order.

The Twenty-First-Century System

We are now entering the twenty-first-century system. This system is one of so-called high technology, which, in its fundamental technological characteristics, differs qualitatively from the paradigm for maturation of the twentieth-century system. In brief, the new technology is distinct because it makes use of and depends crucially on the degree of precision measured in millionths of seconds or millimeters, on digital analytic constructs that have no visualizable analogues, and on multifaceted and complex scientific discoveries that are understood only by a small number of specialists. The new technology uses less energy than its predecessors, but requires many novel skills and new behavior patterns. This means that is requires new specialists (scientists, technicians, operators, and production workers) as well as unfamiliar infrastructures, including huge data bases and probably a new educational system. The difference between the old and new technologies has many more dimensions, including those affecting modes and distribution of labor forces, definitions of products and markets, concepts of private property, and the like.

What is taking place in the first years of the twenty-first-century system is not a normal evolution within a technological paradigm but a change in the paradigm itself. And recall that the time it takes to establish a new technological paradigm for breakthrough is measured not in years but in decades. During the 1980s and 1990s, the productivity of the economies of the advanced nations may continue to stagnate or even decline, and the risk of even greater unemployment cannot be dismissed.

Consider, for example, the robots being used increasingly by several industries, particularly the automotive industry. They increase productivity, easing the current difficulties confronting these industries. But robots in use today essentially imitate human movements, just as early spinning machinery did, and must be seen only as a primitive application of a new technology. Unless new demand for them in new industries emerges because of new technological progress that radically transforms the notion of the robot itself, their usefulness will diminish.

In the short term, we are unlikely to see rapid economic growth, based on the new technological paradigm, raising the productivity of society as a whole. The question to be asked then is, Which nations will be the first to develop the new industries capable of making use of the new technological paradigm?

And, perhaps no less important, which nation will be the first to devise an institutional paradigm capable of facilitating the changes necessary in adopting the new technological paradigm? Obviously, the new institutional paradigm will have many new dimensions we cannot anticipate. We can, however, be reasonably certain that the new dimensions will include firms whose organizational and behavioral patterns will differ significantly and in unanticipated ways from those we observe today, including new definitions of production, office work, and management, and new means of obtaining capital, new interfirm relationships, and new forms of interaction between firms and markets. There will also be new forms of educational structures, and significantly changed political and legal frameworks.

Indeed, the societal capabilities required of a new institutional paradigm can be significantly different from what we observe today. The institutional paradigm that emerges will most likely differ more substantively in character from that of our current twentieth-century system than the current system did from its nineteenth-century predecessor. The nation that first succeeds both in making use of a new technological paradigm and in devising a new set of institutional capabilities will be able to seize the leadership in the coming world economic system.

To summarize, the century-to-century model consists of four elements: technology, demand, domestic structure, and international structure. Technology is the most crucial. Each century system is composed of two phases, breakthrough and maturation. Each of these half-century phases includes an upswing based on technological application and a downswing characterized by technological creativity. This description is intended only to present our idea of the dynamics of industrial society. Table 15 summarizes the periodization and characteristics of the paradigms; the designation of each phase's timing is approximate.

Multilinearity of Modernization

Two Approaches to Modernization

Modernization can be conceptualized to occur in two principal ways. One way is to see modernization as synonymous with Westernization and encompassing the Westernization of the political, sociological, and cultural dimensions of a society. The other is to view modernization as industrialization and as primarily an economic process. Under the former,

TABLE 15
Periodization and Characterization of the Technological Paradigms

Period	Technology	Demands	Domestic Structure	International Structure
Nineteenth-Century System				
Fourth quarter, 18th century	Creation of steam and iron technology	Cotton textile	Emergence of laissez-faire capitalism including factory system	Pax Britannica: gold standard
First quarter, 19th century	Diffusion and improvement	"	"	"
Second quarter	Application to rail transport and ocean-going vessels	Railroad	Malfunction of laissez-faire capitalism: riots and revolutions	"
Third quarter	Expansion of railways (invention of steel)	"	Prosperity and relative domestic stability	"

Twentieth-Century System

Fourth quarter, 19th century	Creation of electric and chemical technology	(Urban facilities)	Emergence of organized capitalism	Decline of Britain begins
First quarter, 20th century	Application to automobiles	Automobile	"	World War I; international system in disarray; end of gold standard
Second quarter	Further electric, chemical, and electronic technology	"	Malfunction of organized capitalism: World War II	"
Third quarter	Application to consumer durables; start of computers	Consumer durables	Great prosperity and full employment	Pax Americana: fixed exchange rate system

Twenty-First-Century System

Fourth quarter, 20th century	Creation of microelectric and biological technology	(Automation of office factory)	Emergence of informational capitalism	Relative decline of United States

a modern society is conceived of as an idealized, integral whole, and the modernization-Westernization process consistently leads all societies toward an ideal, fully modern final state. In this final state, mankind, after long historical progress, becomes modernized in every aspect—social, economic, political, sociological, and cultural. The societal value orientation necessary to achieve this modernization-Westernization can be formulated in various ways. My earlier formulation (1975) included (1) individualism, (2) active humanism (oriented toward ever-increasing human control over nature, or as some might call it, anthropocentrism), and (3) instrumentalism, orientation toward instrumental rationality (or toward achievement orientation, i.e., *zweckrationalität*).

According to the Westernization approach, industrialization is merely an economic manifestation of these basic values. Particularly since individualism is a cardinal value, the principal institutional framework for industrialization is the market mechanism, and a pluralist or libertarian democracy is the only acceptable political system. Sociologically, each individual should be free from all restraints based on an ascriptive principle. Furthermore, we should stress that in this first conceptualization, societies continuing to modernize can reach an *ultimate state* which is supposedly fully and harmoniously integrated by the three basic values and what they imply in terms of economic, social, and political characteristics. Stated differently, this conceptualization is likely to give rise to a unilinear theory of evolution under which all societies reach a final state closely resembling extant Western societies.

In contrast, in the industrialization-modernization conceptualization, modernization is but a process of industrializing a society by the steadily increasing use of production technologies based on a combination of specialization of labor and use of both machines and inanimate energy, and the process inevitably causes friction and conflict within the existing social system of an agricultural society.

In this conceptualization, for industrialization to proceed, a society must possess a certain minimal social framework. It must, for example, be able to achieve specialization (of labor and production) that is required by large-scale, diversified systems of allocation of goods and services; the choices range from the market mechanism to a centrally planned system of physical allocation. A capital market or a system of central investment planning is also needed. Beyond these economic aspects, a political or sociological framework is also necessary. Finally, diffusion of certain value orientations, such as active humanism and instrumentalism, is essential in industrializing. Although it is difficult to specify definitely a minimum set of properties a social system must have to achieve industrialization, it is evident that such a set must exist. However, the fact that many non-Western nations have industrialized or are doing so today demonstrates that it is possible to industrialize with a set of societal characteristics significantly different from the set an idealized Western system is supposed to possess, so long as it gives rise to the minimal social framework we have been discussing.

The modernization-Westernization conceptualization has fallen into disrepute and no longer has the support it did in the 1950s and early 1960s. One reason for this has been a reassessment of the validity of the theoretical analysis. This partly reflected the reality of developments in the 1970s, three of which warrant mention here.

The first phenomenon compelling reconsideration of the Westernization approach was the emergence of newly industrialized countries and a visible stagnation of the old industrial nations. That is, while the West suffered from stagflation and other ills, such newly industrialized countries (NICs) as Korea, Taiwan, Hong Kong, Singapore, and Mexico were achieving rapid economic growth. Japan was an exceptional case. It was not an NIC, but in the 1970s it overcame the difficulties it encountered more successfully than other old industrialized countries.

The second development was the breakdown of the postwar world economic order that had been maintained by U.S. economic and military predominance. The replacement of the 1944 IMF-GATT fixed exchange rate regime by a flexible exchange rate regime, the precarious military balance with the USSR that resulted from a relative decline of U.S. strength, and a widening gap between the advanced economies and most of the developing economies are all aspects of this breakdown.

What some scholars called postindustrialization is the third development. In terms of the model presented here, it was a period in search of a paradigm for the twenty-first-century world system. Advanced industrial countries had achieved material affluence far beyond the level of subsistence. This affluence engendered pathological phenomena dysfunctional to industrialization, including what sociologists termed "consummatory" life-styles (all pursuits including work itself are to be enjoyable), the political militancy of minorities, and highly fluid, almost capricious mass politics. And even "active humanism" lost its original meaning in the face of environmental pollution and resource limitation.

The future of advanced industrial societies is viewed with pessimism by many. As an example, Olson (1982) finds no viable way to mitigate, let alone eliminate, what he regards as the principal problem—the deadweight imposed on the political economy by interest groups that defy integration into the general society. The problems of postindustrialization seem to have been inherent in the problems of industrialization. Industrialization itself is suspect, and this view seems to have credibility to many people. What are called postindustrial syndromes may thus occur even in countries still industrializing. (This pessimism is evident in Bell 1976, Crozier et al.

1975, Goldthorpe et al. 1969, Club of Rome 1972, and Touraine 1969.)

More fundamentally, the concept of modernization, along with its connotations of convergence, harmony, determinancy, unilinearity, and the like, has been more or less openly disclaimed by many people, including neo-Marxists. In sharp contrast to previous scholarship, particularly the neo-Marxist approach emphasizes worldwide confrontation between center and periphery as well as conflicts within specific societies. With the stress on conflict, neo-Marxists do not believe harmony can be achieved among highly differentiated subsystems within an industrial society, a view paralleling the non-Marxists' concern with integration. It is to be noted, however, that their approach almost totally disregards the effects of indigenous culture, an inevitable result of which is a failure to explain such things as the successful industrializations in East Asia. (This group includes Anderson 1974, Moore 1967, Skocpol 1979, and Wallerstein 1974 and 1980. A response to the neo-Marxist approach is found in Katzenstein 1978, Keohane and Nye 1977, and Krasner 1978).

Thus the modernization-Westernization conceptualization seems inappropriate today because its inherent optimism does not reflect the realities of the past dozen years or more. Rather than resulting in convergence to the ideal ultimate state, blessed with a well-integrated, harmonious embodiment of all idealized basic values, the postwar economic order has proved incapable of solving many problems. No comprehensive theory can offer a consistent explanation of developments in the 1970s such as the Japanese performance, the success of nearly developed countries mostly in East Asia, or the decline of old industrialized countries.

Against this background of intellectual confusion, we suggest the usefulness of viewing industrialization—and especially that of Japan for the purpose at hand—from the industrialization-modernization approach and from what we call the "politico-economic interaction approach."

A primary difference between the Westernization approach and the industrialization approach is the gap between the idealized Western social system and the "minimal" social system necessary for industrialization. Obviously, it is very difficult to obtain a consensus on what a minimally required system is. I will, however, attempt to identify the "minimum" requirements.

Politico-economic Interaction

The "minimum" social system for industrialization may tentatively be presented as follows:

1. Basic technological requirements: (*a*) Intensified specialization of labor. (*b*) Utilization of inanimate energy.

2. Economic systemic requirements: (*a*) Development of a large-scale allocation system such as a market mechanism of national (as distinct from local or interlocal) scale, or a mechanism for national planning of material mobilization. (*b*) Regular investment and development of an intertemporal allocation system such as capital markets or a mechanism for national investment planning. (*c*) Technological innovation. These three characteristics can give rise to self-sustained economic growth.

3. Noneconomic requirements: (*a*) Political integration—establishment over a defined geographical area (which is called the nation-state) of law, police, defense, transportation, communications, and so forth. These are required to maintain the large-scale allocation system. (*b*) Bureaucratization (the formation of a standing organization specialized in executing and maintaining political integration). (*c*) Organization of production units, such as capitalist or socialist firms, that combine specialized labor, machines, and inanimate energy. This means separation of production unit from consumption unit, or workplace from family. The labor force thus has to be mobilized from agriculture in which production units and consumption units are identical. (*d*) Institutionalization of education, aiming at supplying literate workers (capable of adjusting to changing technologies), administrators, and scientists or technicians responsible for technological innovation.

4. Value requirement: Diffusion of active humanism and instrumentalism, but individualism per se is not considered necessary for industrialization.

Although two of the three values listed as essential to Westernization are included in these minimum requirements, individualism is not considered a necessary requirement for industrialization. Although individualism has a wide range of definitions (Lukes 1973), there are many cases of viable industrialization that are nonindividualistic in any sense. These include the socialist planned economies, Japan, and many NICs. The essential consideration is that the minimal autonomous decision-making unit that embodies industrial technology is a *firm*. In the early phase of capitalist industrialization, firms and individuals were not always distinguishable in regard to decision making—an individual entrepreneur often exhibited both a strong urge for ever-expanding control over the external world (active humanism) and a desire for maximal efficiency (instrumentalism). But later, beginning near the end of the nineteenth century, sometimes called the period of "organized capitalism," firms became large organizations no longer identifiable with particular individuals.

Strong leadership exerted, often collectively, within a tightly organized hierarchical system can motivate employees of an industrial firm, as was the case in the early stages of the socialist economies. Even when individuals are oriented toward expansion and efficiency, it is possible they may choose to devote their primary efforts to the collective activities of some group, as do Japanese employees in ways that are often described (e.g., Iwata 1977 and Dore 1973). In short, we believe it is reasonable to assume that individualism is not an indispensable prerequisite for industrialization.

There are other assumptions. Differentiation between economy and polity is not regarded as essential. Neither do we assume the necessity of differentiation of polity from religion (or its surrogate, such as Marxism-Leninism). There is no inherent reason to expect any of the major religions to always prevent industrialization. By and large, the difference between the idealized Western system and the minimal system is that the minimal system does not require differentiations within a social system that are regarded as essential to the idealized version of the Western social system.

In short, the minimally required system is indeed minimal, leaving significant latitude for each industrializing society. Modernization is a *process* of interaction between industrialization and indigenous culture, a process of conflict between universal economic imperatives and particular cultural tradition. The Westernization approach dooms the indigenous culture to collapse in the face of the universal pattern of civilization that originated in the West, so that as industrialization continues, all that remains of an indigenous culture will be folklore, folk art, and the like. In the industrialization approach, however, indigenous culture maintains itself in more substantive ways. In some cases, the social characteristics and patterns of indigenous culture can coexist with the minimally required ingredients for industrialization, however much the two affect each other.

The process of industrialization is painful and time-consuming. In some cases, all attempts at adaptation might result in failure because of the lack of compatibility of the culture with even the minimum set of requirements, or simply because of lack of time. In other cases, attempts might succeed as societies find ways to integrate the process and their culture. In short, the process need not be unilineal; there can be diverse types of industrial societies, and the diversity depends on the compatability between industrial technology and indigenous culture. We classify levels of compatibility into the following three categories.

First is the high compatibility case. Britain, which created an industrial society out of its own indigenous culture, can be regarded as sui generis. In a somewhat modified sense, to be sure, many former British-settled colonies also belong to this case, including the United States (Bellah 1970). Other European countries, including Germany, Italy, and even France, faced more serious conflicts between industrialization and their own traditions, but these later developers nonetheless belong to the high compatibility case because they shared basic values with England. In these continental European societies, however, the traditional sectors (agriculture and traditional commerce) were much more rigidly organized and resistant to industrialization than their counterparts in Britain. In a sense, integration rather than differentiation was emphasized in these European cases, as exemplified by state-led industrial policies and social policies. The German-Franco-Italian case is closer to non-Western cases than is the Anglo-American case.

The second case is low compatibility. A culture rooted in the agricultural stage of social development cannot be compatible with industrialization unless and until wholesale adaptation is made. In certain cultures, the fundamental ideas of social organization, however consciously adapted, tend to remain contradictory to such minimum values of industrialization as instrumentalism and active humanism. Even in cases in which extensive adaptation might be workable, external conditions confronting the society may disrupt adaptation or may not allow sufficient time to achieve it.

The middle compatibility case is simply any one between the two polar cases just described, and it is the category in which most cultures fit. Non-Western societies often have traditions that are, in varying degrees, beneficial to progress in some aspect of industrialization. For example, highly developed, long-standing societies, such as the Chinese, Hindu, and Islamic, have a general and deep-rooted respect for literacy and knowledge and, to some extent, for such instrumental virtues as industriousness, frugality, and efficiency. These societies also have experience with political integration and bureaucracy. If such societies are given sufficient time and freedom, it is likely they will achieve a largely indigenous pattern of industrialization.

The pattern of industrialization is different depending on the type of civilization to which a society belongs. For example, we may distinguish the mainland China type, the China periphery type (Korea, Taiwan, Hong Kong, Singapore), the Indio-Hispanic type (Brazil, Mexico, etc.), the Islamic type (Iran), and possibly many others.

Japan was the first to succeed in the middle compatibility case. Its unique characteristic was the preindustrial basic unit of social group formation called *ie*, which had exceptional compatibility as a production unit in industrial society (Murakami 1984). The *ie* had exhibited strong capabilities for expansion, efficiency, and achievement, as well as for creating and thriving within a system of functional hierarchy. However, a basic group unit similar to the *ie* is rarely found in other agricultural societies. Therefore, I argue that the *ie* has been one of the main reasons Japan could adapt its indigenous culture to industrialization with extraordinary rapidity. This also is the reason Japan should be distinguished from other societies of the China periphery type and why in all likelihood it will remain a unique case among societies achieving industrialization.

Literally meaning "household," the initial *ie* form of social group formation—the samuri-led agro-military organizations providing a stable authority capable of guaranteeing rights to reclaimed land and defending local inhabitants—emerged in the eastern regions of Japan during the twelfth century. The *ie* gradually replaced an older form of social organization called *uji* (a stratified clan), and underwent several stages of adaptation and evolution over the subsequent centuries. However, its principal characteristics have been retained to the twentieth century. Broadly stated, these characteristics include: a membership that is functionally and broadly based (relying on an adapted form of stem linearity accompanied by adoption) rather than membership that is kinship based; an internal homogeneity of membership (that is, the samurai versus the cultivator distinction, and later the employer and employee distinction, were much less significant than their counterparts in the West); and a hierarchy that is principally functional (rather than being based on such criteria as inherited social status, ethnic origins, and the like, as was frequently seen in historical societies); and others. What is argued in this chapter is that these characteristics, which went through adaptations to meet the requirements of each historical stage, provided social organizational bases in the period of organized capitalism for the relationships and linkages that are regarded as being distinctively Japanese. These relationships include those between employer and employee, bureaucracy and industry, and intraindustry associations and firm. A fuller discussion of the *ie* and its role in Japanese industrialization is presented in Murakami (1984), which includes extensive references.

Modernization is, generally speaking, a dialectic process between two phases: differentiation and integration. The two phases interact in a variety of ways, alternating in some cases and overlapping in others. In several Western examples, most notably the British, the phase of integration—the period of absolutism—had almost been completed prior to the beginning of the phase of differentiation, which was the "Industrial Revolution" proper. Most writings through the 1970s viewed human history in terms of the upgrading of functional differentiation. But even Parsons, a leading proponent of this approach, had admitted that it is evident that any increased functional differentiation always asks for an enlarged and sophisticated integration—"comprehension" in Parsons's (1966) terms—of differentiated subsystems.

In many cases, including even such European examples as Germany, Italy, and France, integration was contemporaneous with or lagged behind the beginning of industrialization. In East European countries, including Russia, and non-Western countries, including Japan, political integration (establishment of a fully effective polity) lagged far behind the beginning of industrialization. In contrast, political integration in the lower compatibility case had to contend with not only the reintegration of increasingly differentiated subsystems in society (i.e., establishing political authority over all parts of differentiated cultural, social, and even political subsystems within a polity), but also the adaptation of the indigenous culture to industrialization.

If a society has already completed its political integration, readying itself, as it were, for economic differentiation (separation of economic activities and those involved in each of these activities by specific economic function), the separation of economy and polity can be conducive to the process of industrialization. But if political integration has not been completed, what I call interpenetration of the economy and the polity will result. In the case of late developers, the initial stage of industrialization was thus accompanied by vigorous efforts to achieve political integration, taking the forms of centralization of authority and power, bureaucratization, governmental regulation of industries, and even the introduction of economic planning. In such cases, a differentiation of economy and polity, as typified in the Anglo-American experience, was very difficult, if not impossible to achieve.

Analysis of politico-economic interpenetration can be made by several approaches. One is to determine the nature and effects of interpenetration—that is, of the possible patterns of linkage between the economy and the polity. Linkages between government and the private sector are of two types: directive interaction and cognitive interaction. Linkage can be *directive* in the sense that a polity or, more specifically, a government attempts to restrict the private sector's behavior directly in order to achieve some policy objective. A linkage is *cognitive* in the sense that government and the private sector (or its diverse components) affect each other's perception of the future state of the society, possibly reaching some consensual understanding. Cognitive interaction is a weaker linkage than directive interaction, but can be important nonetheless.

Indicative planning is one example of the attempts to make use of cognitive interaction. *Planification* in France and economic planning Japanese style (*keizai keikaku*) seem to have achieved some success, attesting to the importance of cognitive influence by government on the private sector. Such indicative planning in fact needs a basic consensual understanding of the society's current situation as well as the goals the society is prepared to pursue. For example, in postwar Japan, there was a strong national consensus for catch-up economic growth: most people shared the belief that the country should and could follow the pattern of industrial development exhibited by advanced nations. This catch-up consensus represents *the* basic cognitive interaction linking the polity and the economy during the 1950s and 1960s. In many late-developing countries, a similar consensus has often been a source of efforts to pursue the goals of political integration and economic development simultaneously.

Closely related is the economic concept of expectations (as exemplified in rational expectations theory). Any long-term economic behavior (such as investment, saving, or employment) is subject not only to current market-determined economic variables, notably the interest rate, but is also influenced crucially by each actor's expectations—by his perception of the future. If a firm or an industry expects a very favorable future environment (such as a trend of declining long-run average cost or an explosion of demand), investment will increase even with high interest rates. Obviously, the future environment is determined by policy choices or, in effect, by the society's total performance as well as by economic behavior in the narrow sense. Thus the economics of expectations provides a foundation for a theory of politico-economic linkage via indirect, cognitive channels. But a weakness in the current state of economics of expectations is its inability to specify how and why expectations differ, and how the differing expectations interact. Every economic actor—government, industry, organized labor, investors, and so forth—forms its own expectations and tries to persuade the other actors to help meet those expectations. Cognitive interactions among the differing expectations constitute the politics of expectations. But, if these expectations somehow converge, as in the case of the consensus in postwar Japan, cognitive interaction will play a crucial role in determining the course of economic development. In this sense, for the economics of expectations to be a truly comprehensive theoretical framework, it must be extended to the theory of politico-economic interpenetration.

Directive interaction consists of a broad range of government interference ranging in form from strong regulations to weak guidance. This involves the level of each of three elements: discretion, specificity, and enforceability. At one extreme, the only restriction imposed on every economic actor in an idealized market economy is based on a legal framework that is nondiscretionary, universal, and legally enforceable.

Government interference in postwar Japan, often called "administrative guidance" (*gyōsei shidō*), was *specific* to a particular issue, or more accurately, to a particular industry, and also was and is largely *not* enforceable in a strict legal sense. Administrative guidance had little legal ground on which to defend itself against an appeal to unconstitutionality, yet no major firm has ever filed a case against administrative guidance. But administrative guidance as practiced by Japanese ministries usually had a fixed-rule character—a ministry implementing guidance usually dealt with all firms in each industry equally. In other words, government interference in postwar Japan was basically indicative and nondiscretionary, while it was applied specifically to each major industry.

And, especially in the growth period, the firms or trade association in these industries generally complied with the government's guidance voluntarily (without legal sanctions). This voluntary compliance was evidently due in part to the fact that the guidance was often accompanied with various forms of economic inducements. But the degree and extent of the voluntary compliance by postwar Japanese firms could hardly be explained had it not been for the catch-up consensus for economic growth.

The administrative guidance in postwar Japan thus consisted of a network of quasi-fixed rules (such as investment coordination, extralegal recession cartels, and restrictions on entry), but it did not prevent firms from competing fiercely in each industry. The main part of the postwar Japanese politico-economic system in the rapid growth period can be characterized as a system of compartmentalized competition (Murakami 1982b). Thus, government interference Japanese style was one mode of combining two factors, regulation and competition. One result was a particular type of politico-economic interpenetration.

The Japanese pattern is only one example. Each late-developing nation with high or middle compatibility is likely to have its own mode of government interference, and insights into the industrialization process can be obtained by comparing these to each other (see, for example, Fei, Ohkawa, and Ranis 1985). The organizational tradition of each indigenous culture will influence choices involving such trade-offs as egalitarian fixed rule versus elitist discretion, guided compliance versus enforcement by sanction, and discriminatory industrial policy versus general industrial promotion. Some countries may choose to interfere by means of nationalization of certain industries. Others may rely only on tax concessions and subsidies. Adaptation of the indigenous culture to the imperatives of industrialization leads to a necessarily unique pattern.

Policies in the New Paradigm

The advanced industrial nations today face an apparent end of the maturation phase of the twentieth-century paradigm that brought postwar prosperity. At the same time, these nations are facing the dawn of a new paradigm with its new promises and uncertainties. What policies can best help fulfill the promises? We shall first summarize how Japan successfully exploited its opportunities in the maturation phase of the passing paradigm, and then offer a few reflections regarding the future now confronting the industrial nations.

Why has postwar Japanese industrial policy been able to help achieve a remarkable success? In the first place, by the 1950s, Japan's indigenous culture had fully adapted to the imperatives of industrialization, or, more specifically, to organized capitalism of the twentieth-century form, and

234 Yasusuke Murakami

this enabled Japan to create and profit from a unique pattern of politico-economic interpenetration. Second, the 1950s and 1960s were, globally speaking, the decades in which the maturation phase of the twentieth century came to full fruition. And, the convergence of these two factors enhanced the effectiveness of Japanese policies.

Until World War I, the Japanese economy was by and large in the laissez-faire mode (Lockwood 1954), showing characteristics common to the nineteenth-century system. Before World War I, interfirm labor mobility was high, and no industrial policy had been consistently adopted for the major industries. In this nineteenth-century stage of the Japanese economy, organization traditions such as the *ie* played no major role at the institutional level. To enter the twentieth-century stage, the Japanese economy had to wait for the World War I boom that spurred the growth of many heavy industries in Japan.

It was in this twentieth-century stage that the indigenous organizational tradition was gradually incorporated into the institutional framework of the Japanese economy. For example, the now-celebrated Japanese management system began to emerge in the 1920s. Also, as Johnson has stressed, the government-industry linkage, prototype of postwar Japanese industrial policy, came into being in the late 1930s and early 1940s (Johnson 1982, pp. 83–115). The interwar Japanese economy was, in effect, experimenting with ways of combining the indigenous organization tradition and the imperative of the twentieth-century organized capitalism. Although the Japanese economy was physically devastated at the end of World War II, Japan was able to resume catch-up economic growth because of its organizational know-how at the intermediate levels of the economy— in firms and industries. One major reason the economy was able to follow the path of rapid growth was thus the efforts since the prewar period to adapt Japanese organizational tradition to the task of industrialization. Postwar Japanese industrial policy was an essential component as well as a remarkable product of such efforts at adaptation.

It was indeed due to a fortuitous combination of historical circumstances that organizational tradition came to play key roles in the catch-up growth of the postwar Japanese economy. Most important, the Japanese had started their industrialization at roughly the same time the twentieth-century system had begun. The Japanese economy rushed through the nineteenth-century system in a few decades and remained free of craft-union labor practices and other costly leftovers of laissez-faire capitalism that have haunted Western economies. Under organized capitalism, the distinct organizational tradition of Japan was able to establish a particular advantage in achieving rapid growth. This could have been difficult under the laissez-faire capitalism of the nineteenth century.

The second reason for the success of Japanese industrial policy is that the global economy was in the maturation phase of the twentieth-century system. The period 1945–73 had the following features characterizing the final *upswing* phase of the twentieth-century system:

Technology: The technological paradigm of the twentieth-century system was fully established; it was a period of application rather than creation. Productivity increases were achieved because of normal innovation.

Demand: A mass demand for numerous consumer durables emerged— one could almost say mass demand was institutionalized. Accordingly, the industrial structure Japan sought to achieve was quite clear.

Domestic structure: Industrialized nations had stable patterns of organization of firms and industries. Similarly, the modes of government involvement were institutionalized, including Keynesian demand management and welfare-state redistribution. Political stability prevailed.

International structure: Because of the overwhelming political and economic strength of the United States, a free trade regime under the fixed exchange rate system, IMF-GATT, was maintained. Under the Pax Americana, world trade grew more rapidly than world production.

The combination of these features gave rise to very favorable circumstances for late-developing countries pursuing catch-up economic growth; as an early latecomer, Japan was a prominent beneficiary. It had only to import an already completed technological paradigm that could immediately raise productivity. Japan could also rely on mass demand for consumer durables, spurred by the demonstration effect provided its population by the affluent advanced societies, particularly the United States. This meant that the industries and industrial structure to be targeted by Japan and other late developers was largely determined or readily foreseeable. And, no less important, free trade created large export markets, providing opportunities to achieve rapid increases in productivity.

Japan in the postwar period succeeded because, as a latecomer, it had advantages and opportunities not open to the United States as the leader in the maturation phase of the twentieth-century system. Japan's advantage was evident, for example, in its R&D policy, adopted by both the government and private firms, that consciously gave priority to applied technology ahead of basic technology. With the United States acting as policeman for the world, and psychologically and politically averse to armament in any case, Japan spent little on military capabilities, enabling it to concentrate on consumer durables and related industries. In the 1960s and 1970s, Japan became what can be termed a new middle mass society (Murakami 1982a), in which almost all members enjoy high levels of mass consumption, mass education, and mass media. The result is a life-style with little or no class distinctions. In this sense, Japan has a purer form of the maturation phase of the twentieth-century system than does the United States.

This achievement was by no means inevitable, for many other late-developing countries did not realize similar success, or at least have not yet fully. Just as industrialization per se requires a certain minimal set of social preconditions, each phase of industrialization demands a certain minimal range of structural characteristics in the economy and the polity. If the followers are to catch up or be able to jump to the new phase, they must find a way to overcome the inertia of the previous phase. For Japan, such a way was among others its Japanese-style industrial policy that could be justified as a means to achieve the goal of catch-up development.

More generally stated, the industrial policy required to achieve this jump calls for certain conditions. The government must be aware of what kind of industrial structure the new phase will necessitate. Second, the pattern of government interference must be congruent with the imperative of the new phase. Above all, the government must be politically strong enough to execute its policies consistently by overcoming the inertia of the old phase.

Much of the credit for the success of postwar Japanese industrial policy is therefore given to the facts that the government remained under the control of one party and that bureaucrats accurately perceived the character of this new phase of the paradigm of the postwar industrial world, and adopted policies appropriate to this phase of industrialization.

Above all, however, what made this jump possible was the national consensus for rapid economic reconstruction and catch-up economic growth. Although basically a continuation of the consensus that had existed since the start of modernization, the postwar version was more widely and strongly shared because of the collective psychological reaction to the devastation and humiliation suffered in the defeat in World War II. This reinforced postwar consensus is the cognitive interaction on which the whole practice of postwar industrial policy is based. That is, this interaction, when combined with the already accumulated organizational know-how, became the foundation of postwar Japanese industrial policy.

As stated before, postwar Japanese industrial policy was a multifaceted means to create a combination of regulation and competition. It indicated in several ways the industrial structure to be created, controlled the entry (particularly foreign entry) into major industries, limited excessive investment in those designated industries, and eased recessionary pressures by introducing recession cartels. Otherwise, however, the competitive force was set free, encouraging competition in price, quality, technological progress, exports, and other areas. This competition occurred, as intended, primarily within each of the designated industries. This is why the postwar Japanese economy may be called a system of compartmentalized competition.

A crucial point in this competition system was that government interference was not legally enforceable. Industrial promotion under force of law, I believe, is self-defeating because of the time-consuming character of legal enforcement and especially because of the adverse effects it has on sound business management. Thus success of industrial policy hinges not on short-run promotional measures such as subsidies, tax concessions, and government contracts, but on the stability of long-run government-industry relations, such as those found in postwar Japan. In this sense, much of the success of Japanese industrial policy was due both to the historical experience of the pre-1945 period and to the political stability maintained after 1955 by the dominance of the Liberal Democratic Party—conditions that have no parallel elsewhere.

Japanese industrial policy, however, has its own problem: an inherent unfairness to nondesignated industries (those not selected as targets of the policy) and to various groups (particularly urban consumers) and sectors (including foreign firms and nations)—to all but what can be broadly called the industrial (or what some call neomercantilist) interests of Japan. But such unfairness is not a serious issue as long as the economy continues to grow rapidly and the gains from rapid growth are more or less equally distributed throughout the society. Neither is the unfairness to foreign firms and nations of serious concern as long as world trade is expanding and the Japanese economy remains relatively small. Once the Japanese economy stagnates and world trade ceases to expand, government-industry cooperation may become an alliance protecting narrow interests, causing domestic as well as international disharmony and instability. The success of Japanese industrial policy was limited to the period of rapid growth enjoyed by all industrial nations because of the maturation of the twentieth-century paradigm.

The preceding observations on Japan lead us to the final and most important questions. What are the consequences to all advanced industrial nations of the changes occurring in the technological paradigm? How can they best ease the pains of transition and take advantage of the promises offered by the new paradigm of the twenty-first century?

The difficulties of these questions are obvious in light of the following considerations: (1) The coming phase will be the period of technological creation rather than application—of economic downswing rather than upswing. The very nature of this transition is likely to continue to impose a heavy burden of structural unemployment for at least the next few decades. Increases in productivity and employment are far from assured as the transition to the new paradigm continues. (2) The demand structure in the new paradigm is still highly uncertain, and it is difficult to antici-pate, with any precision, what type of industrial structure should or can be promoted by public policy. (3) As the transition progresses, some economic institutions, such as firms or the government-industry linkage, may well undergo radical changes, and the course of the change is difficult to predict. (4) The world economic system will also remain in a state of constant realignment, if not confusion, for the time being as the new paradigm continues to replace the old. Any export drive mounted, or protectionism indulged in, by a major industrial country will cause serious turmoil to the detriment of the world economy. (5) The new paradigm will require, if it is to yield the promised benefits, a new set of values we are as yet unable to anticipate with confidence.

In the context of the analyses offered in this chapter, these are the most obvious reasons why confusion prevails in the debate on the policies industrial nations are to adopt. The debate becomes entangled because of the difficulties in discriminating the policies required to solve the problems of the old paradigm from those needed to cope with those created by the new. Clearly the policies successfully adopted by the late developers cannot be those of the nations entering a new paradigm.

With these difficulties in mind, it is possible to offer a few broad reflections. Policies in the transition period must be intended to remove institutional constraints bequeathed by the twentieth-century paradigm. The policy makers must be fully cognizant of the fact that the twenty-first-century paradigm is likely to be distinctly different from nineteenth-century laissez-faire capitalism or twentieth-century organized capitalism. In short, they must realize that a significant transition, discontinuous in nature, is taking place in the technological paradigm.

In this transition, a policy government can fruitfully adopt is one promoting the very basis of the economy, such as basic R&D and education that better meets the needs of the new paradigm. In so doing, the government should have little illusion that it can determine or select the course of the breakthrough phase of the new technological paradigm. Continuation of the old industrial policy is a serious strategic error.

For Japan, this is not to say that policies designed to change its organization tradition on broad fronts need to be adopted. On the contrary, we speculate that the organizational tradition can and will continue to play a substantial role in the management of Japanese firms. But the above does suggest that policies promoting changes and realignment of the existing government-industry linkage can and need to be adopted if Japan is to be able to take maximum advantage of the new paradigm. This, of course, involves the difficult task of reevaluating and transforming its politico-economic structure, and its industrial policy, deeply imbedded in the structure. Japan's industrial policy, if not reevaluated thoroughly, can cause misallocation of resources at home and intensified trade friction with its trading partners.

However difficult the task, if these changes are resisted and fail to be made, Japan will fall behind in adopting the new paradigm. Should this occur, future historians will observe that Japan failed in the new system because it was unable or unwilling to change its past politico-economic structure that was once so instrumental in achieving the catch-up economic growth in the twentieth-century system.

The observations made for Japan apply to the United States as well, with some modifications. Unless a reexamination and changes are made in the U.S. politico-economic structure (especially in the patterns of government-industry linkages established while economic dominance of the nation was unquestioned within the twentieth-century system), the United States too is not immune from committing an error similar to that Japan could make in failing to alter its politico-economic structure. When the technological paradigm is changing, past successes in the old paradigm are no guarantee for the same in the new, as the case of Britain amply demonstrates. This of course implies that, since the United States will continue to be, for the foreseeable future, the single most powerful actor in the world economic system, its future policy must be one that strengthens free trade and not one that would repeat the tragedy of the 1930s.

For these two nations and the industrial nations in Europe as well, the promise of the emerging paradigm can be realized only if the policy chosen reflects the wisdom demanded of would-be beneficiaries of the new paradigm. An important part of this wisdom must be that we are all in a transition between two paradigms. The transition will severely test each industrial society's ability to change, not only in economic policies but also in all the spheres of their respective societies that collectively determine the future of each society and that of the new system we share.

REFERENCES

Abernathy, William J. 1978. *The Productivity Dilemma: Roadblock to Innovation in the Automobile Industry*. Baltimore: Johns Hopkins University Press.

Anderson, Perry. 1974. *Lineages of the Absolutist State*. London: New Left Books.

Bell, Daniel. 1976. *The Cultural Contradictions of Capitalism*. New York: Basic Books.

Bellah, Robert N. 1970. "Kindai Nihon ni okeru kachi–ishiki to shakai henkaku." In Takeda Kiyoko, ed., *Hikaku kindaika ron*, pp. 95–163. Tokyo: Miraisha.

Chandler, Alfred D. 1977. *The Visible Hand: The Managerial Revolution in American Business*. Cambridge: Belknap Press.

Club of Rome. 1972. *The Limits to Growth*. New York: Universe Books.

Crozier, Michel, Samuel P. Huntington, and Joji Watanuki. 1975. *The Governability of Democracies*. New York: Trilateral Commission.

Dore, Ronald P. 1973. *British Factory—Japanese Factory: The Origins of National Diversity in Industrial Relations*. Berkeley: University of California Press.

Dosi, Giovanni. 1983. "Technological Paradigm and Technological Trajectories." In Christopher Freeman, ed., *Long Waves in the World Economy*, pp. 78–101. London: Butterworths.

Fei, John C. H., Kazushi Ohkawa, and Gustav Ranis. 1985. "Economic Development in Historical Perspective: Japan, Korea, and Taiwan." In Kazushi Ohkawa and Gustav Ranis, eds., *Japan and the Developing Countries*, pp. 35–64. Oxford: Basil Blackwell.

Gilpin, Robert G. 1981. *War and Change in World Politics*. Cambridge: Cambridge University Press.

Goldthorpe, J. H., David Lockwood, Frank Beckhofer, and Jennifer Platt. 1969. *The Affluent Worker: Industrial Attitudes and Behavior*. Cambridge: Cambridge University Press.

Inglehart, Ronald. 1977. *The Silent Revolution*. Princeton: Princeton University Press.

Iwata Ryushi. 1977. *Nihon-teki keiei no hensei-genri*. Tokyo: Bunshindo.

Johnson, Chalmers. 1982. *MITI and the Japanese Miracle: The Growth of Industrial Policy, 1925–1975*. Stanford: Stanford University Press.

Katzenstein, Peter, ed. 1978. *Between Power and Plenty: Foreign Economic Policies of Advanced Industrial States*. Madison: University of Wisconsin Press.

Keohane, Robert, and Joseph Nye. 1977. *Power and Interdependence*. Boston: Little, Brown.

Krasner, Stephen. 1978. *Defending the National Interests: Raw Materials Investment and U.S. Foreign Policy*. Princeton: Princeton University Press.

Kuhn, Thomas S. 1970. *The Structure of Scientific Revolutions*. 2nd edition. Chicago: University of Chicago Press.

Kurth, James R. 1979. "The Political Consequences of the Product Cycle: Industrial History and Political Outcomes." *International Organization* 33(1):1–34.

Levy, Marion J. 1966. *Modernization and the Structure of Societies*. Princeton: Princeton University Press.

Lockwood, William W. 1954. *The Economic Development of Japan: Growth and Structural Change, 1868–1938*. Princeton: Princeton University Press.

Lukes, Steven. 1973. *Individualism*. Oxford: Basil Blackwell.

✓ Modelski, George. 1978. "The Long Cycle of Global Politics and Nation States." *Comparative Studies in Society and History* 20:214–35.

Moore, Barrington, Jr. 1967. *Social Origins of Dictatorship and Democracy: Lord and Peasant in the Making of the Modern World*. Boston: Beacon Press.

Murakami Yasusuke. 1975. *Senshin koku no byōri*. Tokyo: Chūō Kōronsha.

Murakami, Yasusuke. 1982a. "The Age of New Middle Mass Politics: The Case of Japan." *Journal of Japanese Studies* 8(1):29–72.

Murakami, Yasusuke. 1982b. "Toward a Socioinstitutional Explanation of Japan's Economic Performance." In Kozo Yamamura, ed., *Policy and Trade Issues of the Japanese Economy*, pp. 3–46. Seattle: University of Washington Press.

Murakami, Yasusuke. 1984. "Ie Society as a Pattern of Civilization." *Journal of Japanese Studies* 10(2):281–363.

✓ Murakami Yasusuke, Kumon Shumpei, and Sato Seizaburo. 1979. *Bunmei to shite no ie-shakai*. Tokyo: Chūō Kōronsha.

Olson, Mancur. 1982. *The Rise and Decline of Nations: Economic Growth, Stagflation, and Social Rigidities*. New Haven: Yale University Press.

Parsons, Talcott. 1966. *Societies: Evolutionary and Comparative Perspectives*. Englewood Cliffs, N.J.: Prentice-Hall.

Rosenberg, Nathan. 1976. *Perspectives on Technology*. New York: Cambridge University Press.

Skocpol, Theda. 1979. *States and Social Revolutions: A Comparative Study of France, Russia, and China*. Cambridge: Cambridge University Press.

Touraine, Alain. 1969. *La Société Post-Industrielle*. Paris: Gontheir.

Utterback, J. M., and W. J. Abernathy. 1975. "A Dynamic Model of Process and Product Innovation." *Omega: The International Journal of Management Science* 3(6):639–56.

Wallerstein, Immanuel. 1974. *The Modern World-System*. New York: Academic Press.

Wallerstein, Immanuel. 1980. *The Modern World-System II*. New York: Academic Press.

Chapter 7

Japanese High Technology Policy:
What Lessons for the United States?

George C. Eads and Richard R. Nelson

In 1971, we published an article commenting on what seemed at the time to be a possible major new trend in U.S. government support of advanced civilian technology (Eads and Nelson 1971). Two large and extremely expensive projects—the supersonic transport and the breeder power reactor—were being funded with massive amounts of federal aid. The uniqueness of these two projects was that the products they were intended to yield were to be solely commercial. The government itself would not be a customer. To a large extent, the model for this form of assistance was taken from Europe, where such "launching aid" was commonplace. Indeed, one important rationale for the U.S. government's support of both the supersonic transport and the breeder reactor was the existence of similar European programs. If we did not match these programs, the argument went, important commercial markets would be lost to this country.

In examining the history of U.S. support for advanced civilian technology and the European examples that were serving as models, we questioned the conclusion that the European experience with "launching aid" had produced a record deserving of emulation. In fact, by and large, the projects where it had been used were commercial failures. We also suggested that there were lessons to be drawn from the U.S. experience in the fields of aviation and agriculture, where successful programs had been mounted in support of civilian technology. It was noteworthy, we argued, that the governmental R&D support in these fields had focused on the development (and, in the agriculture case, the dissemination) of generic technologies—that is, technologies not associated with particular proprietary product designs. The commercialization decisions involving specific products were left to private industry. We urged that U.S. policy makers devote more attention to how these successful domestic models might be reproduced rather than be lured into emulating the largely unsuccessful European models (Eads and Nelson 1971, pp. 425–27).

The American SST and breeder reactor projects were eventually terminated. The European technological challenge faded. While the American flirtation with product-specific support for civilian-oriented advanced technologies largely ended with their demise, substantially increased federal support for activities of the sort we had recommended did not follow.

In recent years, discussion of the appropriate role of the U.S. government in industrial R&D has heated up again, piqued by the perception of a new challenge and a new model. Now the challenge is seen as Japan. The model is the role the Japanese government, particularly MITI, is perceived as playing in helping Japanese firms.

This chapter examines the Japanese government's role in supporting its high technology industries and attempts to distill lessons that this experience may hold for the United States. As a subsidiary question we ask whether, having now become aware of the "Japanese model" (a model that both we and the world were largely unaware of when we wrote our 1971 paper), we have any cause to change our earlier conclusions.

Japanese Policies in Support of High Technology Industry

Many government policies contribute to the climate in which industry can grow and prosper. Does it make sense to single out policies explicitly aimed at fostering the commercial competence of high technology industries? If so, how does one identify those policies? How does one distinguish them from a wide range of traditional policies that stimulate and support high technology industries?

All governments support education (including the training of scientists and engineers); they fund basic and even applied research in many fields; they establish tax policies that reward (or punish) saving, investment, and entrepreneurship; and they encourage or discourage the development of open and highly liquid capital markets. Some governments—those with large defense establishments or with large nationalized sectors—are significant purchasers of high technology products and, in this role, fund product-specific research and development. Some, as the U.S. government did with respect to agriculture, recognize the "public goods" aspect of certain forms of technology and support its development and dissemination.

Governments have also recognized the link between a strong, technologically advanced industrial sector and the ability to wage modern war. Thus support for industries that might be militarily useful has sometimes gone beyond the level justifiable by the current level of military orders. This has been especially important since World War II. To a certain extent, the postwar support by certain European governments of their commercial aircraft and civilian electronics industries can be viewed as defense related in this sense (though the support thus given is not always funded out of the defense budget).

Especially after World War II, the idea that commercial strength in high technology industries might be created and nurtured *for its own sake* by governmental support programs began to gain prominence. Specific policies aimed at this objective were developed by several European countries. These were the topic of our 1971 paper. One of us has recently completed a monograph in which the history of this idea is traced and the policies described and considered in some detail (Nelson 1984).

Analysis of the Japanese policies must be different from analysis of the European ones, mainly because of the breadth of policies that are alleged to constitute important elements in Japan's high tech support strategy. Certain authors (such as Chalmers Johnson, who in his book *MITI and the Japanese Miracle* refers to Japan as a "developmental state") appear to argue that virtually *all* Japanese policies are aimed directly and consciously at creating competitive advantage for Japanese industry. Since the locus of Japanese competitive strategy is increasingly in the high technology industries, presumably all Japanese government policies would therefore qualify as "support of high technology industry." Other authors, such as Trezise (Trezise 1983), appear to be content to adopt the European model of high tech support and confine their attention to the conventional kinds of R&D support provided by the Japanese government to its industry.

At the very least, this dispute presents problems of where to draw the line in an essay like this. By defining the issue one way, one scholar is able to see vast influence; by changing the definition, another concludes quite reasonably that the extent of influence is substantially less. But even more worrisome, it suggests how scholars debating the question of what the Japanese government does in the way of support for its high technology industries could appear to be talking past each other.

In this essay we walk a narrow line between the pragmatic limitations imposed by space and the desire to explore the boundaries of this definitional issue. Although we go beyond the boundaries implied by the European model, we confine our attention to something quite a bit narrower than the whole of Japanese economic, cultural, and political life.

In the next section we examine the levels of Japanese spending on research and development and the nature of scientific and technical training provided within the country. The third section focuses specifically on targeted R&D subsidies, especially those given in support of joint industry research activities; we also move outside the realm of direct financial measures and explore Japanese policies on other forms of joint competitive activity and their impact. In the fourth section we turn to the contentious issue of favoritism in government procurement and mention briefly the sort of trade protection that Japan has in the past often provided its industry. Following this, we discuss the highly significant role that investment climate and both tax and financial policies play in establishing an environment highly favorable to rapid innovation and diffusion. We close the paper with a listing of lessons we believe can usefully be learned from Japan.

To preview our conclusions, these lessons are: (1) Pay careful attention to getting the basics right. Getting the investment climate, support for R&D, and support for education right may not be enough to ensure success for high tech industries, but not doing this can guarantee their failure, *whatever* else is done. (2) Be willing to move downstream from support for basic and applied research to support for the development of generic technologies. But in doing this, be careful to avoid making the commercialization decisions. (3) Be willing to permit a greater degree of joint R&D than the United States has historically felt comfortable allowing. But let industry take the lead in identifying where a joint endeavor is likely to be fruitful.

The Basic Inputs to High Technology

R&D Spending and Technical Training

In the United States, total R&D spending declined as a fraction of the GNP from the mid-1960s to the mid-1970s. In Japan, just the opposite occurred: total R&D spending as a share of GNP rose steadily throughout the 1960s and 1970s—from 1.39 percent in 1961 to 2.36 in 1981. Moreover, since real GNP grew so much faster in Japan than in the United States (about twice as fast on average over the 1961-81 period as a whole), the level of resources devoted to R&D in Japan increased enormously— twenty-two fold in nominal currency units.

The composition as well as the level of Japanese R&D is also worth noting. Much of the R&D in the United States—in 1980, about 30 percent of the total and about 50 percent of federally funded R&D—is defense or space related. While this R&D clearly has important civilian spin-offs, the large share of U.S. R&D that is defense related is a mixed blessing. On one hand, it helps to push out the frontiers in certain technologies to points far beyond where they otherwise might be. On the other, it may push the frontiers into inappropriate areas—or even counterproductive ones—from the standpoint of civilian commercial applications. There has been a lively and long-standing debate about the distortions that the "technology at any price" orientation of much of U.S. defense-related R&D may have introduced into the civilian economy.

Japan, of course, spends an extremely small share of its national income on defense. Its R&D spending also reflects this lack of defense emphasis. According to *Science Indicators 1982*, in 1980, only 4.9 percent of Japanese government R&D support was for defense purposes (see table 16). In 1980, fully 98 percent of total Japanese R&D (government and private) was classified by the U.S. National Science Foundation as civilian (nondefense and nonspace).

With much smaller defense and space expenditures, it is not surprising to find the Japanese government playing a considerably smaller role in total national R&D spending than the U.S. government does. Figures on

TABLE 16

Japanese Government Expenditures
on Large-scale Technology Projects and
General R&D Expenditures, 1980*

Project	Share (percent)	
Defense and Aerospace	16.8	
Defense		4.9
Space		12.0
Agriculture and Industrial	37.6	
Agriculture		25.4
Industrial growth		12.2
Energy and Infrastructure	34.4	
Production of energy		26.2
Transport, telecommunications		2.9
Urban planning		2.3
Earth and atmosphere		2.9
Health and Welfare	11.2	
Environmental protection		3.4
Health		6.1
Social development and services		1.7
Advancement of Knowledge	4.1	
Total specified R&D funding	100.0	

*Government intramural expenditures only (excludes general university funds).

Source: *Science Indicators 1982*, appendix table 1-7, p. 199. The *Science Indicators* numbers exclude general university funds and include government intramural expenditures only. But, as noted in the text, Japanese industry receives very little of its R&D funds from the Japanese government.

the share of total Japanese R&D funded by government vary by source, but they tell a consistent story. A recent report of the U.S. International Trade Commission cites MITI data indicating that in fiscal 1980 only 27 percent of Japanese nonmilitary R&D was government financed. The comparable figure for the United States is given as 33 percent (USITC 1983, p. 100). In 1979, 41 percent of Japanese gross expenditures on R&D was from government sources. The comparable figure for the United States in 1979 was 54 percent (*Science Indicators 1982*, table 1-1).

The Japanese government funds very little of the research undertaken by Japanese private industry—less than 2 percent. The comparable 1981 figure for the United States was 32 percent. This difference in the importance of government as a source of industrial R&D funding is largely another reflection of the relatively heavy expenditures by the U.S. government on defense and space R&D. Fully 76 percent of all federal R&D dollars spent by U.S. industry in 1981 was concentrated in just two industries—aircraft and missiles and electrical machinery. Excluding these two industries, U.S. government funds comprised only 7.7 percent of all R&D funds spent by industry—a figure much closer to that of Japan.

Where *does* the Japanese government spend its R&D dollars? As table 16 shows, most is spent in quite conventional ways. The highest proportion, about 51 percent in 1980, was concentrated in agriculture and the production of energy—the latter an understandable national priority for Japan in that particular year. About 12 percent of funding identified by objective was used for "industrial growth." The comparable U.S. figure in this category was 0.3 percent.

This difference in the proportion of government R&D funds devoted to "industrial growth" reflects an important philosophical difference between the United States and Japan concerning the legitimate role of government. In the United States, the bulk of government R&D spending serves three basic objectives: (1) In its role as a purchaser of high technology products, primarily in the defense and space area, the government pays for the R&D for these products. As we have seen, this accounts for at least half of all U.S. R&D funding. (2) The government funds a substantial amount of basic research, largely at universities. These two roles together account for about 45 percent of all federal R&D funding. (3) In its role as promoter of the general welfare, the federal government funds (and, in some cases, conducts) a considerable amount of research in such areas as environmental protection, automobile safety, and food and drug testing.

When the federal dollars attributable to these functions are added up, there is not all that much left. (Adding up these functions and eliminating double counting—such as basic research funded by DOD and NASA—accounts for about 80 percent of all federal research dollars. This figure was derived by the authors from *Science Indicators 1982*, appendix tables 2-12 and 2-13.) Indeed, whenever federal R&D funding objectives begin to approach closely the direct support of commercially relevant technologies, they have great difficulty in securing continuing political acceptability. This is because they raise, sometimes quite appropriately, the question of what business it is of the government's to be funding research in such areas.

The demise of three Carter administration-sponsored programs—generic technology centers, research on the commercialization of new energy technologies, and the Cooperative Automobile Research Program—illustrates this tendency. When Claude Barfield asked a budget official to comment on the Reagan administration's decision to terminate such programs, the reply was: "What was happening under Carter was what I would call a kind of creeping planned economy, where under the guise of 'reindustrialization' and 'overriding national needs' the federal government was intervening further and further upstream with product development and commercialization. Though defended as filling supposed 'voids' in the market, it was really anticompetitive, replete with bureaucratic and political prejudices and the desire to manipulate the outcome of the struggles of competing technologies in a capitalist economy" (Barfield 1982, p. 62). This statement may represent an extreme view. But it reflects the general suspicion that has existed in the United States of programs that too directly appear to be promoting industry—even high tech industry.

Unlike Americans, the Japanese have no difficulty with their government going beyond these purposes and into the direct support of commercial competitiveness. What sort of "industrial growth" projects does the Japanese government fund? According to Trezise, much of MITI's R&D budget is for projects that would appear to us properly classified under other objectives—environmental protection or the development of energy production, for example (as cited in USITC 1983, p. 102).

The picture that emerges of the total Japanese R&D effort is of a large and rapidly increasing flow of research funding, channeled primarily to the applied end of the R&D spectrum, and especially to commercial applications. Overall, this effort is less dependent on government spending than that of the United States, although this difference is largely due to the different levels of the defense and space efforts in the two countries. Moreover, the Japanese government is much more willing than the U.S. government to help ensure the development and dissemination of generic commercial technologies. This latter function comprises a relatively small share of Japanese governmental R&D spending, but it seems to us that it is an extremely important source of Japanese commercial strength.

Scientists and Engineers

An adequate flow of R&D funding is one important factor in ensuring vigorous high technology industries. Another is an assured supply of technically-trained personnel able to make use of the fruits of this funding (and, not unimportantly in Japan's case, also make use of imported technological know-how). Japan's emphasis on scientific and technical literacy starts early. According to *Science Indicators 1982* (p. 5): "Japan developed a science-based curriculum after World War II and has very high standards of accomplishment. In an international science test administered to 14-year olds from 19 countries, Japanese students ranked first in physics, chemistry, and practical science, and first overall. American students ranked fifteenth."

In 1980, with a population only about one-half that of the United States, Japan graduated more engineers than the United States: 73,500 in Japan and 69,300 in the United States. Of course, not all Japanese engineering graduates become practicing engineers. *Science Indicators* (p. 6) states: "In Japan ... national policies promote the training of [scientists and engineers] in greater numbers than are expected to engage in scientific and engineering professions. ... [M]anagerial positions in government and industry are often filled by engineers. For instance, in Japan, about half of both the senior civil service and industrial directors hold degrees in engineering or related backgrounds."

Nevertheless, the number of scientists and engineers engaged in R&D in Japan relative to its labor force is both high compared with most other countries in the world and has been growing rapidly, particularly with respect to the United States. In 1965, Japan had about 25 scientists and engineers engaged in R&D per 10,000 workers, a figure roughly equal to that of the United Kingdom, France, and Germany and less than half that of the United States (where the number was approximately 65). As figure 1 shows, by 1980 the Japanese figure had reached about 55 while the U.S. figure, after declining from 1969 to 1976, had returned to roughly its 1965 level. This dip, of course, largely reflects the changes in the level of U.S. defense and space R&D spending we referred to earlier. But this only emphasizes the magnitude of the Japanese educational effort. Making a rough correction for the proportion of U.S. scientists and engineers engaged in defense and space research, it becomes clear that the intensity of Japanese use of scientific and engineering personnel in the "civilian" portion of their economy currently exceeds our own, and may have done so for some time.

Figure 1

Scientists and Engineers Engaged in R&D
per 10,000 Labor Force Population
in Japan and the United States

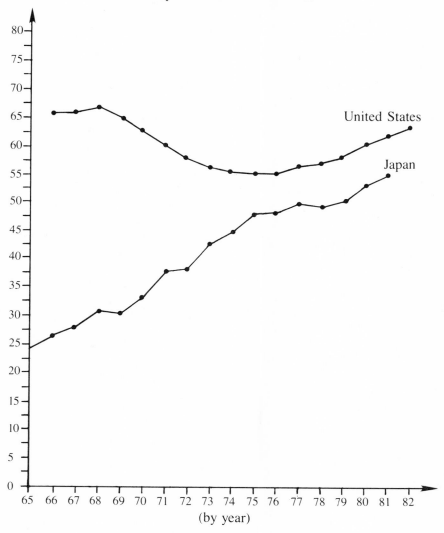

(by year)

*Includes all scientists and engineers on a full-time equivalent basis (except for Japan, whose data includes persons primarily employed in R&D).

Source: *Science Indicators* 1982.

Funding and Organization of Cooperative Industrial R&D

We noted earlier the much greater share of Japanese government R&D spending overtly devoted to "industrial growth" than is the case in the United States. A special feature of Japanese R&D spending in this area is its emphasis on cooperative R&D.

Perhaps the most famous of the cooperative projects funded by conditional loans was the VLSI project, undertaken between 1976 and 1979. This project cost $132 million and involved five of the largest Japanese electronics firms—Fujitsu, Hitachi, Mitsubishi Electric, NEC, and Toshiba. While MITI did not attempt to push the development of particular commercial products, the projects were carefully chosen for their likely commercial relevance. Companies whose personnel engaged in a successful project got a definite leg up toward a commercial design advantage.

The involved companies felt this very much. This led, on the one hand, to restrictions on the program to stay away from areas where particular companies already had a proprietary interest, and on the other, to jealousies among the companies regarding the projects they were assigned to work on. Apparently it took strong and subtle leadership to hold the program together.

Analysts disagree on how important the program was in achieving its goal of bringing Japanese semiconductor capacity up to the frontiers. Certainly the funds were small relative to those involved in the in-house efforts of the Japanese firms. But the program is regarded by some observers as having played an important catalytic role.

The Japanese government not only tolerates joint research; it sometimes uses its leverage actually to *force* it. This is what is alleged to have happened in the case of the VLSI project. Decisions whether to undertake joint research in Japan are thus not always purely private decisions.

The encouragement of joint research in Japan extends to the treatment of its competitive consequences. In general, joint research ventures of all types seem outside the reach of the Japanese antitrust laws, though according to USITC, no formal antitrust exemptions are given for such activities (USITC 1983, p. 106). In the United States, joint research activities are fully subject to the antitrust laws and significant cases exist where joint research activities had led to antitrust prosecution. (See the Yamamura essay in this volume.) Perhaps the best known of these is the case in which the major automobile manufacturers, having been given clearance to engage in joint research on pollution control devices, were sued by the government for having used this arrangement to slow down the development of such devices. Antitrust concerns have been claimed by American business to constitute a significant barrier to the conduct of joint research in this country. In recent years, in order to quiet this fear, the Antitrust Division has attempted to define much more clearly what sorts of activity are permissible. It is the Division's position that in most cases they have seen either a joint research proposal has been legal as presented or can easily be made legal in ways that preserve the essential benefits of the proposal.

There is one problem that assurances by governmental authorities cannot solve—the threat of the private antitrust suit. The Antitrust Division can decide that a particular joint research arrangement causes no antitrust concern, but this does not bar the filing of private suits. In Japan things are much different. There apparently is no *legal* bar to the filing of a private antitrust suit, but according to the ITC (USITC 1983, p. 115), no private plaintiff has ever won such a suit. This means that once Japanese governmental authorities give their assent—tacit or otherwise—to a joint research venture, it is effectively immunized from antitrust prosecution.

What is the case for encouraging joint research? There are two arguments that are generally advanced. The first concerns the large scale of certain research and development activities. Lacking the ability to conduct research jointly, private firms will be unable (or unwilling) to devote the volume of resources necessary to undertake such projects. The second argument relates to the "waste" involved in duplicate research. The coordination of information, it is claimed, makes possible a more efficient use of a country's scarce research resources. To these two arguments the Japanese case seems to add a third. When a nation is especially concerned with trying to close a "technological gap," it may be that permitting—or even forcing—firms to conduct research jointly is an efficient way of getting everyone up to speed.

These arguments deserve to be taken seriously. Economic theory suggests that research and development is likely to be underfunded because of its inappropriability. Techniques to conserve scarce R&D resources ought not to be lightly dismissed. But coordination has its price. Experience has shown that research can be planned only to a limited degree. Often a route that at first (or even well into a project) seemed most promising turns out to be a dead end. It is important, therefore, to maintain a diversity of approaches.

Where the size of a project is so large that the number of potential optimal-scale efforts is very small (maybe only one), then it is a question of joint research or no research. Fortunately, in the development of commercial technologies, such extremely large-scale activities are few. Aircraft and nuclear reactors are perhaps the two best examples.

The Japanese approach to joint research seems to have been structured to take advantage of these lessons. By and large, Japan has avoided getting heavily involved in the massively expensive technologies where the number of firms that the potential market can support is one or at most two. It has supplied modest amounts of funding for research on commercial aircraft in order to keep its options open. But, except in one instance, it has avoided the expensive "launches" that drained European government treasuries and enervated the European aerospace industry. (There are some signs, however, that this may be changing. The Japanese government funded a surprisingly large share of the development work for the Boeing 767 commercial airliner.) Japan's nuclear technology development program has also been limited in scope. As noted below, Japanese research goals have generally been kept modest and incremental. The aim appears to have been as much to ensure that the firms involved all achieve a certain level of technological sophistication, even if this requires that some lose relative position. Finally, the joint research projects stay away from specific product development. Decisions about commercialization are left to the individual firms.

Given the speeding up in the rate of advance of commercially relevent technologies, an increased use of joint research activities may well be appropriate in the United States. Japan provides useful lessons in both the positive effects and the potential costs of such research. Leading Japanese firms, fearful of losing competitive advantage, sometimes have to be "persuaded" by their government to participate in such arrangements. It is not clear that their fears are groundless. The effect, especially in high technology industries, of encouraging a high degree of research cooperation may be that the level of "typical" practice in Japan is greater than it otherwise might have been. However, in certain cases, this may have been purchased at the expense of really important breakthroughs that certain firms, had they been permitted to pursue their own ends, might have attained.

Even though Japan has managed to encourage a diversity of research approaches when pursuing a general research objective, the very encouragement of joint research runs the risk of overly narrowing research sights. An entire industry can get caught out on a technological limb—a limb that is longer precisely because of the success of the joint research it has undertaken. Borrus, Millstein, and Zysman suggest that this is just the risk that the Japanese are now running with respect to their concentration on producing semiconductor memory with greater and greater capacity, the dRAMs. If dRAMs continue to be the technology of choice for the world's computer industry, then the Japanese gamble will have been a good one. But if other technologies emerge victorious, then Japanese firms may well have to go through another period of catch-up (Borrus, Millstein, and Zysman 1983, pp. 76-81).

During a period when Japan has been a heavy net borrower of technology from abroad, a policy that favors rapid assimilation and diffusion of technology may indeed be optimal, provided the result is that not too much of the competitive spur is lost. But as Japan becomes more of a technology generator, it will be interesting to see whether such a strategy—a strategy furthered by extensive reliance on joint research—is still desirable.

The relatively high degree of industrial coordination permitted in Japan has its parallels elsewhere in the world, particularly in Europe (though the precise techniques by which this coordination is achieved are somewhat different). The interesting question is how the Japanese are able to permit this degree of coordination and still maintain internationally competitive industries. Despite occasional charges to the contrary, American opposition to permitting firms to decide jointly such things as investment and pricing is not based primarily on ideological grounds. On the whole, the record of its operation elsewhere is not good. In other nations—notably Europe—where cartel or quasi-cartel arrangements are tolerated, the result has been stagnation and loss of industry's competitive edge. Japan–at least so far—seems to have been able to balance cooperation and competition. But it is possible to discern warning signs. As Japan must now deal with the problem of phasing down some of the industries whose growth it previously encouraged, the Japanese reputation for harmony and consensus is being severely tested. Some Japanese firms granted the authority to jointly plan capacity rationalization have reduced capacity in a more or less efficient manner. (However, as is true in other countries, the burden of adjustment does not fall entirely on the least-efficient firms.) Others have used the arrangement to *add* capacity—the opposite of what the Japanese government is presumed to have desired (Boyer 1983 and Yamamura 1982).

Favoritism in Government Procurement as a Means of Promoting Commercial Development

Governments, as purchasers of high technology products, pay for the research and development associated with these products. In areas such as defense and space where the government is the *only* purchaser, it is considered entirely appropriate that the government bear the total cost of product development, including all of R&D. This is true even though there might eventually be significant commercial spin-offs. In this role, the government is merely emulating private firms which, when purchasing specialized manufacturing equipment or components, expect to pay for a share, if not all, of the development costs associated with the equipment.

The proposal to use a government's procurement leverage to aid domestic firms in commercializing products for which the government is *not* the major purchaser goes beyond this point. Indeed, it involves a form of subsidy to the industry in question. This is the tactic that the Japanese government has been charged with. Again the semiconductor industry is a prime example. It illustrates the dilemma created for a nation that wants a significant, competitive high technology sector but lacks the instruments others have (or are believed to have) to encourage development.

Most of the early R&D that led to the development of the U.S. semiconductor industry was funded by government through the Defense Department or drawn from private sources because of a perception of a large governmental market. During the early years of the industry's development, government orders made up an overwhelming share of its total sales. Levin's data indicate that, though the government's share was dropping rapidly by the end of the 1960s, for the period 1962-68 orders from the DOD, NASA, and the FAA constituted 49 percent of semiconductor industry sales (Levin 1982, p. 63). Although under normal governmental "buy American" policy, the bulk of these orders were reserved for American firms, there is no sign that the aim of the orders was in any sense to help develop a commercially viable semiconductor industry. The U.S. government needed semiconductors; it provided the market and the funds that ensured their development.

As the industry moved away from reliance on the federal government as a customer, the nature of its products changed—so much so that when in the late 1970s the government began to talk with the industry about funding a joint research project to advance very high speed, large scale integration devices (the VHSLIC project), concern was expressed by some in the industry that the technology developed might not be commercially applicable. U.S. government procurement thus can be credited with giving the American semiconductor industry an important "leg up," but only as a by-product of its normal procurement efforts.

The Japanese government, on the other hand, believing that it needed to provide a source of demand for Japanese semiconductor manufacturers, is said to have pressured the state-owned telecommunications monopoly, NTT, to "buy Japanese." In this case, since the American semiconductor industry already existed and was producing competitive products, this policy meant the exclusion of American firms from the Japanese market.

It is possible to debate the extent to which NTT's "buy Japanese" policy has been due to conscious policy versus corporate inertia. Certainly AT&T prior to its recent dismemberment was not known for favoring outside suppliers, preferring instead its Western Electric subsidiary. For whatever reason, American semiconductor firms failed to hold their share in the rapidly growing Japanese market: between 1975 and 1980, their share of Japanese domestic integrated circuit consumption fell from 20.3 percent to 14.9 percent, although the total volume did increase slightly (Borrus, Millstein, and Zysman 1982, p. 85).

In certain industries, favoring domestic firms in the matter of government procurement can be a powerful and effective tool of subsidization. If the products that governments buy are close enough to their civilian counterparts, this sort of subsidization can be an especially helpful aid to domestic firms in their struggle in international markets. But such subsidies can be a siren's lure, leading an industry away from rather than toward competitiveness. The U.S. electronics industry's concern about the VHSLIC project and about government orders that might eventually come from it is a healthy sign.

The Japanese government has used its procurement leverage to favor its domestic firms. But it has not attempted to use such leverage where its influence would be counterproductive to the goal of promoting competitiveness. For example, it has not sought to develop a commercial aircraft industry by reserving orders from the state-owned airline for Japanese firms. It is fortunate for Japanese industry that, unlike governments whose procurement needs are especially tilted toward weapons and other tools of defense, the products the Japanese government has granted favorable procurement status to have been especially well situated to benefit from procurement leverage.

The Japanese are under greater pressure today to end such favoritism. They seem to be responding to this pressure, albeit slowly and with great reluctance. However, with the growing success of pressures to liberalize Japan's formal trade barriers and to internationalize their financial markets, the Japanese government's ability to provide a sheltered domestic market (at least initially) through government procurement policies favoring Japanese firms has become perhaps the most important remaining form of direct governmental support for high technology industries. (This is certainly the view of Borrus, Millstein, and Zysman 1983, pp. 81-94.) For this reason, meaningful liberalization is likely to face continuing resistance on the part of the Japanese.

Financial Climate for Investment and Innovation

The general climate for savings and investment that exists in a country is not usually considered explicitly an aid to high technology industry. But the link between it and the ability of firms in a country to develop and efficiently produce high technology products and to incorporate high technology processes into their production is so close that to omit it from our discussion, especially in the case of Japan, would be to leave a major void.

Economists who study the importance of technological change to a nation's productivity performance have long recognized that the speed with which new innovations are incorporated into general practice within an economy is critical. A nation's industry can be highly inventive, but if the products of this inventiveness are never widely utilized, productivity is aided little. A climate highly favorable to rapid investment helps industry keep relatively close to the technological frontier by enabling it to invest in equipment embodying the most advanced technologies. Efficiently designed targeted investment incentives can, in principle, help to speed even further the diffusion of productivity–enhancing technologies.

Japan's extremely high rate of private savings and private investment is well known. Government policies have combined with demographic and social factors to produce a climate extremely conducive to the rapid diffusion of technology and to permit the rapid buildup of production capacity for high technology products.

Japanese tax policy is also highly favorable to investment and innovation. To start with, Japan's depreciation rates are extremely generous. On top of this, there are special depreciation measures that favor high technology industries. Firms can accelerate depreciation on R&D facilities and hardware. This can mean as much as a 60 percent first year write-off. Firms belonging to government-authorized research associations can take a 100 percent depreciation deduction for all fixed assets used in connection with association activities. Japan has for many years had the sort of incremental R&D tax credit that the United States adopted only recently (USITC 1983, p. 109).

This highly favorable investment climate combines well with the Japanese strategy of making continuous, small improvements in manufacturing technology and incorporating them rapidly into widespread use. This strategy has been documented most completely in the case of steel—an industry not usually considered a high technology industry. A study published by Barnett and Schorsch (1983) is a useful reminder of the extent to which the embodiment of new technology through investment was critical to the Japanese achievement in steel. Table 17, taken from this book, compares Japanese and American steelmaking costs for one important product, cold-rolled sheet (the steel used in automobile bodies, appliances, cans, etc.), in 1958 and 1980. Over this twenty-two-year period, Japan turned a U.S. cost advantage of $14 per ton (12 percent) into a Japanese cost advantage of $88 per ton (31 percent). This was done despite a substantial narrowing in wage differentials (Japanese wages in steelmaking were only 15 percent of those in the United States in 1958; by 1980 they were 59 percent) and despite higher coking coal and scrap costs. The Japanese secret? In part, it was shrewd purchasing of raw materials, especially iron ore. But mainly it was their massive reduction in inputs, especially labor. In 1958, Japanese steelmakers used 36.65 man-hours of labor to

TABLE 17

Estimated Operating Costs for Production of
Cold-rolled Sheet in 1958 and 1980, United States and Japan

	Unit Price of Input in $*		Use/Net Ton		Unit Cost ($/ton)	
	U.S.	Japan	U.S.	Japan	U.S.	Japan
1958						
Labor (hours)	3.75	0.58	11.58	36.65	43	21
Iron ore (tons)	10.64	14.73	1.44	1.47	15	22
Purchased scrap	34.07	43.25	0.20	0.20	7	9
Coking coal	10.50	19.35	1.04	0.98	11	19
Other energy					14	20
Other†					24	37
			Total materials (+ other)		71	107
			Total operating costs		114	128
			U.S. as percent of Japan		89%	
1980						
Labor (hours)	18.80	11.00	7.20	5.84	135	64
Iron ore (tons)	36.00	25.50	1.59	1.81	58	46
Purchased scrap	89.50	100.00	0.16	—	14	—
Coking coal	52.50	65.00	0.85	0.89	45	58
Other energy					46	42
Other (2)					76	76
			Total materials (+ other)		239	222
			Total operating costs		374	286
			U.S. as percent of Japan		131%	

*Dollars per hour for labor; dollars per ton for iron ore, scrap, and coking coal.
†Refractories, rolls, fluxes, alloying agents, etc.
Source: Barnett and Schorsch 1983, pp. 20 and 64.

make a ton of cold-rolled steel. By 1980 this had been reduced by 84 percent to 5.84 man-hours. U.S. labor requirements were also reduced, but not nearly so much.

In their detailed analysis of the sources of this amazing productivity improvement, Barnett and Schorsch make it clear that it stemmed not from any single technological breakthrough, but from attention across the board to ways in which steelmaking labor requirements could be reduced. Japan simply improved on steelmaking technology and incorporated these improvements into their plants.

Detailed studies of the Japanese success in high technology industries—
its remarkable success in large-scale semiconductor memory devices such
as the 64K dRAM, for example—reveal a strategy similar to that used for
steel. As Borrus, Millstein, and Zysman note:

> The early Japanese lead in the 64K dRAM . . . was not based on a
> strategy of innovation. Rather, the strategy that was used illustrates the
> characteristic production-refinement approach and manufacturing
> systems strengths of the Japanese. Japanese firms chose, essentially,
> a straightforward scale-up to 64K of their 16K dRAMs, which were based
> on . . . Mostek's [a U.S. merchant semiconductor firm] standard 16K
> design. They accomplished this through incremental improvement of
> older photolithographic techniques. . . . Pushing their historical strengths
> in innovation, U.S. producers adopted a range of novel approaches to
> the 64K device (such as redundancy, self-refresh) which made their
> development times longer and their production problems greater than
> those experienced in the straightforward Japanese effort. Thus, although
> Motorola and TI [Texas Instruments] managed through major invest-
> ment efforts to approximate the pace of Japanese introduction and scale-
> up, other U.S. merchants ran into difficulties. Intel withdrew its initial
> 64K entry in August 1981; Mostek was forced to redesign its first device;
> and National encountered manufacturing problems with its three-layer
> polysilicon approach and eventually licensed the part [*sic*] and manufac-
> turingtechniques from Japan's Oki [which, incidentally, was a firm that
> was left out of the VLSI project, though it had wanted to participate].
> As demand for the device grew, the market gap created by the delays
> in production by U.S. firms was filled by the aggressive and rapid Jap-
> anese production strategy. While the second-tier U.S. firms (behind
> Motorola and TI) concentrated on product innovations and new proc-
> ess development, their Japanese counterparts spent heavily to bring down
> production costs by *automating* their 64K dRAM production. They con-
> tinued to invest in highly automated capacity expansion for 64K dRAMs
> during the 1981-82 U.S. recession, while U.S. firms delayed or cut back
> their expansion plans. . . . *The ability to spend heavily during rough
> economic times, and the move to automation, illustrate again the
> characteristic domestic-based strengths of Japanese industry. The ability
> to spend was based on the stable access to cheap capital . . . afforded by
> the Japanese financial structure.* [Borrus, Millstein, and Zysman 1983,
> pp. 71-72; emphasis added.]

The payoff to this incremental-innovation and high-investment strategy
is shown in table 18, taken from Finan and LaMond (1984). Despite 25
percent higher wafer costs, Japanese firms have been able to price their
64K dRAMs 13 percent below U.S. producers, an important price margin
in a "merchant" semiconductor device. Finan and LaMond also present
data showing how much faster Japanese semiconductor investment grew
in the late 1970s and early 1980s than investment of U.S. firms. In 1976,

TABLE 18
Cost Comparison for U.S. and Japanese 64K dRAM

	U.S.	Japan
Components of Whole Wafer Cost ($ per wafer)		
1. Materials	$32	$ 49
2. Capital (depreciation)	29	37
3. Labor	24	20
Total	$85	$106
Determination of Factory Cost		
1. Wafer process cost	$ 85	$106
2. Wafer process yield	80%	95%
3. Yielded whole wafer cost	$106	$112
4. Die size (mil^2)	35,100	38,600
Total die/wafer	313	280
5. Wafer probe cost	$ 14	$ 12
Tested wafer cost	$120	$124
6. Probe yield	40%	52%
Tested wafer cost		
7. Good die	125	146
8. Cost per good die	$0.96	$0.85
9. Assembly cost	$0.20	$0.40
10. Assembly yield	90%	95%
11. Yielded assembly cost	$1.40	$1.32
12. Final test cost	$0.20	$0.20
13. Final test yield	80%	80%
14. Factory cost per good die	$2.00	$1.90
15. Cumulative yield	23%	38%
Number of good die	72	106
16. Gross margin	45%	40%
17. Final selling price	$3.64	$3.17
18. Total revenue	$262	$336

Source: Finan and La Mond 1985, p. 153.

Japanese investment was only one-eighth of the U.S. total. (Total in this case means the combined investment of both the merchant and the captive U.S. producers.) By 1983, Japanese semiconductor investment was nearly equal to U.S. investment (Finan and LaMond 1984, p. 6).

There is evidence in a study by Norsworthy and Malmquist (1983) of the importance of this favorable investment climate to the Japanese postwar success in both "high tech" and "low tech" industries. To uncover the sources of U.S. and Japanese productivity growth, they employ measures of gross output rather than using the traditional value-added measures. In addition to permitting the relaxation of some important aggregation assumptions—-assumptions the authors find are unfulfilled—the use of these gross output measures allows one to focus on the importance that improvements in the efficiency of use of materials handling and other manufacturing technology may have played in the Japanese productivity story. They appear to have been crucial.

Norsworthy and Malmquist conclude that the growth in Japanese productivity can be largely explained by increases in capital and materials per worker—that is, by improvements in the ability of Japanese labor to process increasing volumes of material. But this is exactly the result that Barnett and Schorsch found for steel. It is also what Borrus, Millstein, and Zysman found for semiconductors. It is what Abernathy, Clark, and Kantrow (1983) report for automobiles. Indeed, for all the stories that exist about the payoff to specific "targeted" Japanese policies, there are few if any industrial success stories in Japan that can be shown to have been possible in the *absence* of such a favorable investment environment. Such an environment may not have been a sufficient condition to explain the Japanese technological miracle. But it apparently was a necessary one.

Lessons for U.S. Government
Support of High Technology Industry

Having looked at the Japanese model of support for high technology industry and added its insights to those of the European model we analyzed in our 1971 paper, what conclusions do we reach for U.S. government policies? We admit to being prejudiced, but we find our earlier conclusions also applicable to the lessons from Japan. Indeed, we find that the Japanese experience vindicates our earlier analysis of what is likely to work and what is likely to fail as far as government support of high technology industry is concerned.

The first thing that the Japanese experience confirms is the importance of getting the fundamentals right. There has been much talk in recent years of Japan's success with high technology industries proving that it is possible to create comparative advantage. If that term means that Japan has been able to write on a completely clean slate with respect to its industries that would be successful, then it is surely *not* true.

It is important to recall that Japan was a pretty sophisticated industrial power before World War II, and during the war demonstrated impressive technological capabilities. Japan came out of the war destitute, but since 1950 has been able to achieve investment rates significantly higher than

Germany and France, and far higher than the United States and Great Britain. The educational attainments of the Japanese work force prior to World War II were close to European standards. Since World War II, the Japanese educational mill has ground at a furious rate and by the middle 1970s was turning out significantly more engineers per capita than the United States or the major European countries. Research and development spending by industry and by the Japanese government, at least in areas having clear-cut commercial potential, has been quite high and growing. From this point of view, the Japanese miracle translates into very high rates of investment in physical and human capital, with the former embodying significant advances in technology and the latter capable of using this technology and contributing to its improvement in incremental, though significant, ways.

The most important lesson here is that nations that aspire to strength in high technology industries had better attend to their general strength in technical education and establish and maintain policies and institutions that support economic growth generally. A possible danger of the recent rhetoric about the importance of high technology industries is that it may take attention away from these broader, less specifically focused policy areas.

Next to emphasizing the importance of getting the fundamentals right, we believe the Japanese experience confirms the value of government support for generic technology. In our view, this is where MITI R&D support has been most effective. However, into the 1980s, the Department of Defense and NASA have been virtually the only governmental supporters of such work in the United States. There are strong reasons for establishing a basis of support that is independent of DOD.

American companies now are giving strong indications that they would like to band together to fund cooperative generic research, even industries where DOD substantially finances such work, and even where no public funds are provided to catalyze the effort. In particular, a number of semiconductor and computer manufacturers have already banded together to do such research through the newly formed Microelectronics and Computer Technology Corporation. The Justice Department, in a preliminary ruling, has indicated it does not see any antitrust issues at stake, so long as the supported research stays generic in nature. The proprietary interests of the involved companies probably will ensure that this cooperative endeavor will not venture too close to what individual companies consider to be matters of great potential proprietary interest to them.

Given American traditions, it would appear that industry should lead in initiating such programs, with government encouragement, and with no attempt by government to force the program or to direct it in any detail. The Cooperative Automotive Research Program, initiated under the Carter administration and aborted under the Reagan administration, was for support of generic research of the kind discussed here. But the automobile companies had little to do with the initiation or design of the program and felt it was being rammed down their throats. The program might have gone quite differently had the automobile companies been urged to design it for themselves. On the other hand, since there are few domestic producers and an unfortunate past history of cooperative research efforts in the pollution control area, such an arrangement may have been problematical.

As the Microelectronics and Computer Technology Corporation indicates, the private firms themselves may be willing to invest heavily in such cooperative generic research programs. However, we would endorse the idea of having government funds sweeten the kitty. Such public funds might be provided on a formula basis, as through the provision of matching funds. Alternatively, the decision about whether to provide public support might be made on a case-by-case basis, though we are uncomfortable with the political and organizational problems that such a policy would engender.

One important policy issue regarding generic research cooperatives that is sure to arise involves the terms of exclusion from such groups. This is a delicate issue. A generic research cooperative that involves, say, the three largest firms in an industry and excluded others ought to be ruled in violation of the antitrust laws. In cases that do not involve public funding, we would argue a liberal rule of reason.

For programs employing public funding, however, we take a different stand. We believe it is in the interest of the United States, and of all countries taken together, that participation in publicly subsidized programs be open to all companies with a research and development presence in the sponsoring nation. We, the authors, would propose that U.S. government funded programs of this sort be open to foreign firms, *provided* genuine reciprocity is shown by a firm's home government on comparable programs. This, of course, is another argument for sponsoring these programs in the United States through a vehicle other than the Department of Defense. It will not always be easy to get other countries to abide by the ground rules we propose, but the pursuit of meaningful reciprocity provides one useful guide star for American diplomacy. A significant program of government-funded cooperative generic research, backed by a reciprocity policy, might give us leverage on the programs of other countries, most notably Japan, that we do not have at present.

American business has argued that our antitrust laws represent a formidable barrier to their conducting the sort of joint generic research we are advocating. They take some comfort from the permissive attitude currently being shown by U.S. antitrust authorities, but worry that this attitude could change. They also fear private antitrust suits. (Indeed, some firms that were considering participating in the MCC consortium claim to have been deterred from doing so by the receipt of a letter from a noted private antitrust lawyer threatening suit.)

Some American business organizations, looking fondly at the sort of antitrust "blank check" that exists in Japan with respect to joint research ventures, have asked for legislation that would provide similar protection from prosecution here. Congress has responded, under the National Productivity and Innovation Act of 1984. That act by no means provides a blank check for cooperative R&D activities, but was intended to quiet fears about the legality of R&D joint ventures if these are not anticompetitive. There are three operative provisions: (1) a definition of a "joint research and development venture" that describes activities included under this heading and also those that are excluded (such as certain joint marketing or production activities), (2) a statement that no activity undertaken by an R&D joint venture will be deemed illegal by a court without consideration of such a venture's procompetitive effects, and (3) a voluntary disclosure system that, if utilized by the participants, would limit private antitrust damage exposure to actual, rather than triple damages.

The United States and Japan certainly have different attitudes on the proper level of government involvement in promoting high technology industry. But where the United States has achieved high tech success, how different have its approaches been from those of Japan? Consider again the case of electronics. The policies that resulted in American dominance in electronics after World War II were associated with our national security programs. In Japan, the policies that facilitated fast catch-up have been associated with MITI economic direction in general. Virtually all analysts agree that these programs have had a lot to do with the success of the two countries in these industries. Without trying to make these obviously different policies appear the same, it nonetheless is worthwhile searching for common elements, for perhaps these can provide clues as to what kinds of policies are effective. In fact there are several elements in common.

Both programs involved a large protected home market. In the United States, this was basically a government procurement market. In Japan, the government procurement market was far less consequential, but the domestic civilian market was preserved for Japanese high technology firms. Both the American military and Japanese civilian markets were large enough so that a number of domestic firms could compete. In both cases, the relevant government agencies were unwilling to set up a particular national champion. While the industry has been sheltered from foreign competition, there was and is vigorous domestic competition and this has been the intent of those who have guided the policies.

This meant several things. Maintenance of a domestic presence at the forefront of an industry was not dependent on the performance of any particular firm. In the industries where forward or backward linkages were important, such as computers and semiconductors, a firm was not locked into one supplier, or one purchaser (except the Defense Department). And the strong demand for innovative products manifest in both markets motivated intense competition among domestic firms.

In both the United States and Japan, publicly funded R&D programs significantly enhanced the capabilities of the firms involved to produce advanced design products for commercial markets. In Japan the principal programs involved support of generic research, done by company-employed scientists and engineers, with the express purpose of enhancing the company's technological strength in commercial markets. In the United States the dominant programs were oriented to defense and space exploration and involved both support of generic work and massive expenditures on hardware development. While not specifically intended to augment a company's commercial capabilities, this was often the result.

Put another way, while the two programs differed significantly in purpose and structure, each provided both a strong competitive market for domestic firms wherein technological progress was rewarded and significant R&D support for firms in that market. In Japan, stimulus of commercial competence was direct and intended; in the United States, commercial competence was created because military technology pulled civilian technology in its wake.

Much of the current discussion of policies in support of high technology industries involves the term "picking winners." To what extent can the successful programs in the two countries be characterized in that way? If by that term one means relatively sharply focused attention on achieving certain practical results, the proposition is apt.

Within particular industries and technologies, both DOD and MITI picked particular areas for intensive attention, because of military potential in the former case and perceived potential commercial importance in the latter. In both cases particular companies or groups of companies were single out for support in these areas. The big dollars in the U.S. program have gone to particular companies on R&D and procurement contracts. DOD, of course, has not gotten into the business of supporting particular commercial ventures. And, contrary to some popular impressions, MITI has not in general tried to dictate to companies what kinds of products to design for sale on commercial markets. In both countries the enhancement of commercial competitive prowess has been through the strengthening of the design, development, and production capabilities of involved national firms which in turn they used for what they judged to be commercial advantage.

It is interesting to compare the U.S. and Japanese experiences with those of France and Britain (see Nelson 1984). While France (and to a lesser extent Britain) tried, neither of these countries established the same technology pull in their defense and space programs as the United States did. The total funds involved were much smaller. The efforts were less ambitious and generally aimed at catching up with the Americans, not establishing new grounds. While France has tried to protect its civilian market, membership in the European market has forced France to be more open than Japan. In addition, branches of foreign-owned firms established within France's borders greatly complicated the business of even *defining* a domestic industry.

The generic research support programs of these countries have been much less coherently oriented than those of the United States and Japan. In the French case, the commercially oriented aspects of the R&D support program got tangled with the objective of establishing or preserving a French capability to design and produce military equipment. As a result, clear commercial targets were not pursued, but industry was given shelter and subsidy simply to keep it operating. As noted, the French military program aimed only to stay close to the Americans, not break radically new ground, hence little innovation has come out of it. Support of generic research in the British electronics industry, even aside from that associated with defense procurement, has not been specifically focused on areas judged commercially promising in the same way as the Japanese programs. At the same time, the British and French programs have been prone to sink public funds into particular commercial designs. This has not been very fruitful in electronics.

Yes, the United States has something to learn from Japan concerning how to support high technology industries—much more than we have to learn from countries like Great Britain and France. But it is important for us to recognize that in designing its policies, Japan seems to have learned a lot from us.

Many years ago, in *Capitalism, Socialism, and Democracy* (1950), Schumpeter took the position that modern man was close to routinizing the innovation process, that the uncertainties and divergencies of judgment were being eliminated from it by rational calculation and discussion, and that the hurly-burly of capitalist competition, which he acceded had been a font of creativity and energy, would not be missed if lost. This seems a false forecast. The United States may be handicapped relative to other countries in the extent to which efforts at innovation can be coordinated. This may hurt us in some areas, particularly those in which the costs of the endeavors drive out much chance for sustaining many different approaches. But the sheer size of our corporations and our internal market may help us avoid being closed down in these areas, if we adopt sensible policies. And in most areas, economies of scale are not that overwhelming. The U.S. economy continues to have an openness of entry to new firms and new ideas and a degree of rivalry that other countries do not, and which they increasingly seem to be discouraging in the name of industrial policy. Japan's economy does not possess all of these attributes. But it is remarkable that, even while adopting a formidable set of industrial policies, Japan has managed to maintain, and even encourage, a high degree of internal competition and maintain flexibility. This puts it apart from its European rivals and accounts, we believe, for much of its industrial policy success.

As Imai suggests in his essay in this volume, having a MITI is not an unmixed blessing. The flexible industrial structure of the United States should not be discounted as a formidable engine of progress. We may be lucky that it so stubbornly resists being targeted, coordinated, or planned.

REFERENCES

Abernathy, William J., Kim Clark, and Alan Kantrow. 1983. *Industrial Renaissance: Producing a Competitive Future for America*. New York: Basic Books.
Barfield, Claude E. 1982. *Science Policy from Ford to Reagan: Change and Continuity*. Washington and London: American Enterprise Institute for Public Research.
Barnett, Donald F., and Lewis Schorsch. 1983. *Steel: Upheaval in a Basic Industry*. Cambridge, Mass.: Ballinger.
Borrus, Michael, James Millstein, and John Zysman. 1982. *U.S.-Japanese Competition in the Semiconductor Industry*. Berkeley: Institute of International Studies, University of California.
Borrus, Michael, James Millstein, and John Zysman. 1983. *Responses to the Japanese Challenge in High Technology: Innovation, Maturity, and the U.S.-Japanese Competition in Microelectronics*. Berkeley: Roundtable on International Economy.
Boyer, Edward. 1983. "How Japan Manages Declining Industries." *Fortune*, January 10, 1983, pp. 58-68.
Eads, George C., and Richard R. Nelson. 1971. "Government Support of Advanced Civilian Technology: Power Reactors and the Supersonic Transport." *Public Policy* 3:405-27.
Finan, William F., and Annette M. LaMond. 1985. "Sustaining U.S. Competitiveness in Microelectronics: The Challenge to U.S. Policy." In Bruce Scott and George C. Lodge, eds., *U.S. Competitiveness in the World Economy*, pp. 144-75. Boston: Harvard Business School Press.

Johnson, Chalmers. 1982. *MITI and the Japanese Miracle: The Growth of Industrial Policy, 1925–1975*. Stanford: Stanford University Press.

Levin, Richard. 1982. "The Semiconductor Industry." In Richard R. Nelson, ed., *Government and Technical Progress: A Cross Industry Analysis*, pp. 9–101. New York: Pergamon Press.

Nelson, R. R. 1984. "Policies in Support of High Technology Industries." ISPS Working Paper 1011, Yale University.

Norsworthy, J. R., and D. H. Malmquist. 1983. "Input Measurement and Productivity Growth in Japanese and U.S. Manufacturing." *American Economic Review*, 73:947–66.

Schumpeter, Joseph. 1950. *Capitalism, Socialism, and Democracy*. New York: Harper.

Science Indicators 1982.

Trezise, Philip H. 1983. "Industrial Policy Is Not the Major Reason for Japan's Success." *Brookings Review* 1(3):13–18.

U.S. International Trade Commission. 1983. *Foreign Industrial Targeting and Its Effects on U.S. Industries, Phase I: Japan*. USITC Publication 1437. Washington, D.C.: U.S. Government Printing Office.

Yamamura, Kozo. 1982. "Success that Soured: Administrative Guidance and Cartels in Japan." In Kozo Yamamura, ed., *Policy and Trade Issues of the Japanese Economy*, pp. 77–112. Seattle: University of Washington Press.

Contributors

GEORGE EADS, Dean, School of Public Affairs, University of Maryland

KEN-ICHI IMAI, Professor, Institute of Business Research, Hitotsubashi University, and Chairman of the MITI New Media Advisory Committee

YASUSUKE MURAKAMI, Professor, Department of Social Sciences, School of Liberal Arts, University of Tokyo

RICHARD R. NELSON, Elizabeth S. and A. Varick Stout Professor of Social Science, Departmment of Economics, Yale University

DANIEL I. OKIMOTO, Associate Professor, Department of Political Science, and Co-Director of the Northeast Asia–U.S. Forum on International Policy, Stanford University

HUGH PATRICK, R. D. Calkins Professor of International Business, Graduate School of Business, Columbia University, and a member of the Committee on Japanese Economic Studies

GARY R. SAXONHOUSE, Professor, Department of Economics, University of Michigan, and Chairman of the Committee on Japanese Economic Studies

KOZO YAMAMURA, Professor, Jackson School of International Studies, University of Washington, and a member of the Committee on Japanese Economic Studies

Index